Our comm

Our common wealth

The return of public ownership in the United States

Thomas M. Hanna

With a foreword by Gar Alperovitz and a preface by Andrew Cumbers

Manchester University Press

Copyright © Thomas M. Hanna 2018

The right of Thomas M. Hanna to be identified as the author
of this work has been asserted by him in accordance with the
Copyright, Designs and Patents Act 1988.

Published by Manchester University Press
Altrincham Street, Manchester M1 7JA

www.manchesteruniversitypress.co.uk

British Library Cataloguing-in-Publication Data
A catalogue record for this book is available from the British Library

ISBN 978 1 5261 3379 3 paperback

First published 2018

The publisher has no responsibility for the persistence or accuracy
of URLs for any external or third-party internet websites referred to
in this book, and does not guarantee that any content on such
websites is, or will remain, accurate or appropriate.

Typeset by Deanta Global Publishing Services
Printed and bound in Great Britain by TJ International Ltd, Padstow

Contents

Foreword: On the importance of democratic public ownership
   By Gar Alperovitz   vi
Preface: The return of public ownership
   By Andrew Cumbers   xi
Author's preface and acknowledgments   xix

Introduction: Public ownership in urgent political perspective   1

1 Public ownership in the United States and around the world   10

2 The efficiency debate   36

3 Why public ownership?   51

4 Public ownership and alternative system models   72

5 Toward a framework of public ownership for the twenty-first century   83

Conclusion: Systemic crisis and democratic public ownership   132

Notes   150

Index   214

Foreword: On the importance of democratic public ownership

Gar Alperovitz[*]

A little under 10 years ago, the United States government essentially nationalized several major American corporations, including General Motors, Chrysler, and AIG (one of the largest insurance companies in the world and hence the manager of extraordinarily large pools of capital). It also established indirect authority over several other large Wall Street banks as part of its wide-ranging bailout program. The 2008 financial crisis was a historical turning point of a kind that rarely comes about. The fundamental question of political economy – of *what, if you don't like corporate capitalism and you don't like state socialism, you actually want* – has come rushing back into circulation. In diverse quarters, ongoing economic pain in everyday life has also given rise to new possibilities. The seeds of a new economic paradigm have begun to sprout. Innovative new complexes of community-cooperative ownership have begun to spring up. Social movements have started to engage with novel, participatory forms of economic development. Worker ownership, neighborhood ownership, municipal ownership, and even large-scale enterprise are back on the table in a serious way for the first time in many decades.

What makes current experimentation with democratic ownership different from historic efforts is that the mix of public and quasi-public economic institutions now being discussed follow lines of what the late E. F. Schumacher termed 'appropriate scale.' Instead of ideological debates, the discussion is largely about different structures designed to meet the requirements of different functions (local farmers' markets on the one hand; nationalized rail systems on the other) – and all open to demanding (researchable) questions: Does this approach actually meet community and public needs? Is

---

[*] Co-Founder of The Democracy Collaborative and Co-Chair of the Next System Project; former Fellow of King's College, Cambridge; and former Lionel R. Bauman Professor of Political Economy at the University of Maryland.

it efficient? Effective? Responsive to community and national concerns? Ecologically sustainable? Supportive of democracy, equality, liberty – even, perhaps, community?

Thomas Hanna's tight, deeply researched study on public ownership could not have been published at a more opportune moment: It is a time when such questions are fast becoming matters of public and political concern. In the 1960s, I was a Legislative Director in both the US Senate and the House of Representatives as well as a Special Assistant policy advisor in the State Department until my departure during the Vietnam War. Thereafter, I also worked on projects with Dr. Martin Luther King, Jr. and the Mississippi Freedom Democratic Party, and I was active in organizing opposition to the war. As transformative as that era was in many very important ways, I can say without a shadow of doubt that now, today, this era, is of equal and perhaps even greater importance in American history. We are well and truly at a crossroads; we cannot go forward following the traditional twentieth-century path. Economic stagnation, political stalemate, community instability, and climate change won't allow it. In 2005, in the preface to my book *America Beyond Capitalism*, I stated that I was no utopian, and that confronted with these obstacles the country could well turn down a dark path before things got better. With the far right now ascendant in much of the world, including the United States, and a dangerous and erratic right-wing populist holding the reins of power (and the nuclear codes) in the White House, I fear that this projection is coming true – and sooner than I thought. Yet, as in 2005, I remain hopeful; history amply demonstrates that the seeds of transformative change are commonly sown when the night is darkest.

And, indeed, we are also now seeing the emergence and growing sophistication of two interconnected discussions. First are new political and economic movements committed to democratic forms at all levels (especially in the economy), which have been steadily developing in recent years, accelerated greatly by the financial crisis and Great Recession. Often termed the 'New Economy Movement' or the 'Solidarity Economy Movement' (or some variant of both), people across the world are beginning to connect with each other to share experiments, models, and best practices as they build bottom-up alternatives to corporate capitalism and neoliberalism. From reclaimed workplaces in Argentina and Greece, to solidarity cooperatives in Quebec, to local currencies in the United States, to new open-source software that knows no borders, the breadth and energy of the movement is encouraging. Moreover, every year such efforts grow in sophistication, linking to public policy and large institutions to offer pathways once considered impossible.

Second, as the economic problems of traditional political-economic systems deepen – and as such modern threats like climate change converge with traditional problems of inequality, poverty, race, and community degradation – an increasingly informed and sophisticated debate about 'the system' (or rather, about the 'next system') has also taken on new power, and urgency, in many countries. Here the question is posed in the very largest terms: If both traditional state socialism along Soviet and Eastern bloc lines and modern forms of corporate capitalism offer little hope of showing the way toward a democratic, egalitarian, liberty-supporting and ecologically sustainable system, *what specifically might be a viable systemic answer for the future? One that both achieves and nurtures such values and, we must add, more peaceful and more equal relationships between peoples and nations?*

The 'system question' – or 'what makes sense if neither traditional capitalism nor traditional socialism meets critical criteria?' – is clearly on the table now, both politically and intellectually, in ways that it has never been, at least in my lifetime. And to the degree that none of the traditional systems offer hopeful solutions to deepening problems at various levels, the question of what has sometimes been termed 'systemic architecture' comes increasingly to the fore. At the heart of that question is: What specific forms of economic institutions offer greatest hope – taken together – of helping develop pathways forward to the evolution of new systems beyond the decaying twentieth-century models? How, really, might we achieve a more participatory, equal, peaceful, and ecologically sustainable democratic system that values both community and liberty?

The 'how' in this case focuses not only on attitude, but on the underlying architectures of different systems that lead in certain directions (or restrain others). At the very heart of this overarching question are the issues Hanna takes up in this book: What, really, do we know about different forms of democratic ownership? And how might different forms, taken together, help us structure 'the next system' beyond the traditional decaying twentieth-century models? Guided by an intense concern with what is actually known and can be backed up by research, Hanna ventures only very carefully into this terrain. First things first: What do we know and what can we demonstrate? After we have gotten that clear, what can we begin to explore experimentally? And beyond that, what can we theorize about?

Foreword: On the importance of democratic public ownership

By and large, this book demonstrates that publicly owned enterprises can be – and often are – as efficient or even more efficient than privately owned firms. The 'bottom line,' as the saying goes among economists and political economists, is that a number of traditional myths are shattered. There is also evidence that public ownership can be far more responsive to social and ecological concerns than private ownership in certain sectors. The picture that emerges is of an ownership form at different levels that is flexible enough to address the large-order economic, social, and ecological challenges in front of us, but which also allows for increased participation, liberty, and equality – values that are essential to stemming the rising tide of what threatens to become populist forms of fascism. The book also reports on many particularly interesting and innovative local developments that point in the direction of stabilizing and rebuilding communities from the ground up.

One example that Hanna and I have frequently discussed elsewhere is the Evergreen network of worker cooperatives in Cleveland, Ohio. Here not only does the linkage (via a community-wide neighborhood corporation) build a 'community' interest into the very structure of the approach, it also thereby opens the way to public and other support that no single private enterprise (cooperative or capitalist) could enjoy on its own. One result is that major public and non-profit enterprises – universities and hospitals (termed 'anchor institutions' by virtue of their inability to move without great cost) – have begun to support such linked community-building cooperatives through purchases of goods and services (since public health and educational institutions enjoy major public financial support, the result of such targeted and stabilizing purchases is a form of local economic planning – in this case, planning for community stability). A related and equally impressive model based on similar principles has emerged in Preston in the United Kingdom, where there are plans to add a publicly owned bank and energy company into the design.

The kind of research detailed in the following pages is certain to help us gain leverage on a number of important further questions: 1) What advantages and disadvantages might publicly owned enterprises offer in terms of democratic politics? Can public disclosure requirements beyond those that can easily be imposed on private firms, for instance, make it more difficult for large enterprises to have undue political impact? 2) Might public forms of enterprise be more easily regulated, especially in connection with such pressing issues as climate change? 3) Might public firms ultimately be more easily adapted to reduced growth or no-growth economics as limits are reached in certain areas? 4) Most important in many ways, I believe: In an era when local economic changes and dislocation undermine individual lives (and where regulation and incentive systems regularly fail), might public forms of enterprise be brought into planning systems that help stabilize local economies, and thereby increase the possibility of building renewed democracy, and perhaps even a deeper sense of community, from the bottom up?

These are some of the questions, beyond those taken up in this work, which Hanna's research brings us to. Put another way, the book offers a point of departure for asking some of the most important, and yet very traditional, questions in quite new ways. It uses empirical reporting to establish a foundation for the ongoing inquiry of how, specifically, to build a more equitable and sustainable world. These are questions that cannot be answered in a serious way without the kind of informed research concerning alternative economic forms that this work addresses. I suspect they are the kinds of questions Hanna himself will make increasing contributions to as time goes on.

It is only fair, I think, to mention that Hanna is a colleague and friend who has worked closely with me in support of various research projects. So, my appreciation for this work is both personal and also longstanding. His book is the product of many years of intense study. It is a gift to us all as we look for new ways forward at this difficult time in the increasingly painful economic and political world in which we live.

Preface: The return of public ownership

Andrew Cumbers[*]

Public ownership is coming back into the center of mainstream public policy debates. Indeed, as this excellent book by Thomas Hanna rigorously and systematically documents, it never really went away and continued to thrive in the most unlikely places. Its resurgence, taking a number of forms since the bank nationalizations of 2007–2009, should be welcomed, but with a few caveats for progressives concerned with its potential to advance economic democracy. For approximately two decades – the period of neoliberal globalization from the collapse of the Soviet bloc to the financial crisis – public ownership had few friends or advocates. The UK Labour Party, which had been one of the strongest and continuing advocates of public ownership since 1945 – 'common ownership of the means of production, distribution, and exchange' in its celebrated Clause IV phraseology – finally ditched its commitment in the Blairite New Labour modernizing 'Third Way' project in 1995.

In the 1990s, the center left tried to outdo the right throughout the world in demonstrating its commitment to privatization, attempting to burnish its business-friendly credentials in creating the right market conditions for foreign investment. Offering up public assets to foreign investors through privatization was a way of demonstrating that a country was 'open to business.' Privatization and market deregulation policies were pursued with as much ardor under French socialism, Italian or, for that matter, Indian variants of communism in places like Kerala and West Bengal, or German social democracy as they were under British conservatism. Such was the mood of the times. All world regions had their particular experiences of neoliberal-inspired privatization programs – at the behest of the EU, World Bank, IMF, OECD and other cheerleaders – and subsequent

---

[*] Professor of Regional Political Economy at the University of Glasgow and author of *Reclaiming Public Ownership: Making Space for Economic Democracy* (2012).

experiences of deteriorating services, decaying infrastructure and profit appropriation by corporate and financial elites.

The return of public ownership and the continuing battles against privatization and vested interests

The new millennium has seen a decisive shift in mood. Beginning in Latin America with an open revolt against the consequences of water privatization by the very poorest in Bolivia and Argentina, but spreading out to the European and North American heartland of capitalism, cities, regions and national governments have rediscovered the merits of public ownership amidst the failings of privatization to deliver effective public services and modernization of infrastructure. What is remarkable is the sectoral, geographical and political diversity of this trend. It involves a range of sectors, most predominantly water and energy but also including transport, education, waste, local government and social services.

As a phenomenon, it has covered all continents and a vast range of cities: from Paris to Houston, from Dar-es-Salaam to Jakarta, from Buenos Aires to Berlin. France, the United States and Germany have become the unexpected epicenters of remunicipalization campaigns. The political diversity is also striking, involving Republican heartlands in the United States, Gaullist strongholds in France and relatively conservative regions and cities in southern Germany. In many cases, remunicipalization is the result of effective grassroots campaigns driven by a combination of citizens aggrieved at the effects of poor service delivery and rising costs (which cuts across traditional political fault lines), green groups motivated by tackling climate change and movements for more radical democratic control of public services.

Hamburg has been an inspirational example. The city established its own public energy company in 2009 and now has 130,000 customers – enough to produce a profit, which is now being reinvested back into producing renewable energy from solar and wind power. But Hamburg shows the political tensions and problems of trying to implement new democratic forms of ownership in the face of well-entrenched vested interests and political cross-currents. There, local social democratic politicians and energy-sector trade unions, wedded to coal and nuclear power and with close links to the Swedish corporation, Vattenfall (which has been running the privatized local energy system), have been a powerful coalition against remunicipalization. Despite a successful 2013 referendum, fought by a citizens' campaign, to take the privatized electricity grid and heating system back into public ownership, the ruling social democrats have so far blocked moves for a fully integrated municipal energy company. This has stymied efforts to make a serious advance toward the complete eradication of fossil fuels, or tackling fuel poverty in a more robust manner.

Equally significant to the big city trend in Germany have been remunicipalization campaigns in smaller towns and cities. Many rural towns in otherwise conservative regions such as Bavaria and Baden Wurttemberg have seen impressive grassroots campaigns led by local residents that push local governments into taking action. An oft-quoted example is the town of Wolfhagen (population approximately 14,000) in the state of Hessen, which has won a federal government award as 'an energy efficient town.' The local town council bought back the grid from EON Mitte in 2006, following a six-year campaign against privatization. Like many other parts of Germany, Wolfhagen still retained a small energy-producing public company, which gave it the technical expertise both to strike a tough bargain with EON but also to devise a new strategy to promote renewables with the goal of being self-sufficient in renewables by the end of 2015 (achieved), realized through the construction of five wind turbines and a 42,000-panel solar park. Wolfhagen also shows how a new hybrid approach to public ownership can combine citizen involvement with state support; the municipal company that was created involved the setting up of a community cooperative that gives local residents a 25 percent stake, sharing revenue but also fostering greater civic engagement. This kind of 'public–public partnership' is becoming common in many other cities, from Copenhagen to Buenos Aires, and points the way toward more democratic and citizen–engaged models of public ownership.

Despite these hopeful signs, it would be premature to herald the demise of neoliberalism. Powerful organizations such as the EU, World Bank, IMF and OECD continue to advocate privatization and public-sector cutbacks as policy solutions to economic crises, rather than viewing them as part of the problem. In some cases, there is a geopolitically selective amnesia to all this. In the wake of the Eurozone crisis, centrist politicians in countries such as Germany and Denmark, belonging to parties that are rediscovering the merits of public ownership at home, happily continue to insist on privatization and the selling off of valuable state assets to rentier foreign corporate interests in countries such as Greece and Italy. Ironically, the EU's forced austerity and privatization in Greece has opened a pathway for the Chinese state to invest in the cash-strapped country, one of the unintended consequences being that a Chinese state owned entity, Cosco, now owns the main Greek port of Piraeus after a half-billion-dollar investment.

Faltering neoliberalism, the return of the state and the need for radical democratic alternatives

Despite its continuing advocacy at the highest levels, privatization is failing everywhere to deliver the effective modernization and efficiencies promised back in the 1980s. It continues because it serves elite interests – particularly rapacious financial institutions, which recognize that there is considerable value to be extracted from essential services such as energy and water, for which 'market demand' is a constant. One of the most sobering examples comes from London, the heartland of global privatization, where the local water utility, Thames Water, was until recently owned by a consortium led by the Australian bank, the Macquarie Group. The latter recognized the opportunities to be made from leveraging future revenue streams from water charges to London's populace for financial innovation. This involved developing securitized debt schemes, which could be packaged up and sold against expected future revenues, which could then feed into high dividends and returns for shareholders. Over a 10-year period, this meant that the local company became saddled with £8 billion of debt, finding itself unable to pay for much-needed renewal of the sewerage system involving a new £4 billion tunnel. Not surprisingly, when it tried to persuade consumers to pay an increase of 10 percent on their water charges to fund the tunnel, there was a considerable outcry. Yet Macquarie was able to escape censure or legal action because of the poorly regulated privatized system.

Despite many similar examples, privatization continues to be in vogue with global elites. A recent OECD country report on Slovenia is typical in this respect. Like many EU countries, Slovenia is currently 'under instruction' from the Eurozone troika to pursue austerity and balanced-budget objectives into the 2020s. The country is urged to 'pursue faster, well thought out privatisation so as to further reduce public debt and the high level of contingent liabilities.' Little is said here of the country's tradition of varied forms of public ownership and strong economic democracy, which have helped keep inequalities down and made it one of Eastern Europe's few success stories in the transition to capitalism.

Despite the continuing grip of basic neoliberal tenets, the state is coming back into economic governance because of the failings of privatization and austerity policies and the increasingly angry public mood in the face of more elite-driven globalization. As Karl

Polanyi long ago reminded us, left to its own devices, a deregulated economy eventually unravels, which at some point results in a social and political response. Important questions for progressives in these circumstances are what kind of state emerges and whose interests are served? Can we link state action to the renewal of a democratic public sphere? As the recent presidential elections in the United States and France demonstrated, though in slightly different ways, if progressives fail to advocate their own more democratic and radical alternatives to the status quo, they risk being marginalized by a xenophobic economic nationalism, represented by Le Pen, Trump, Brexit and the far right on the one hand and the stubborn, obdurate, but ultimately doomed neoliberal project, as represented by the new Elysee incumbent, Emmanuel Macron, on the other. The center-left 'modernizers' of the 1990s and centrist throwbacks (operating as if it were still 1999) such as Macron and the UK former finance minister George Osborne and indeed the Wall Street-dominated Obama regime, through their continuing adherence to the doomed market utopia of neoliberalism, continue to sow the seeds of the far-right populist harvest against globalization and expose the hollow shell of liberal democracy.

Rethinking public ownership for the twenty-first century

In the face of such challenges, progressives need to be far more vocal in both revealing the creeping corporate autocracy of economic life while renewing a project for a more radical democratic vision. This should of course include public ownership and, as Thomas Hanna shows, there is no shortage of ideas and alternative models for how this could work. And, as Hanna and others argue, there is no one-size-fits-all approach. We should be alert to and tolerant of, diverse forms of collective ownership, recognizing the need to align our models with the variegated economic practices that make up the contemporary capitalist landscape, if we are to transition to the next system.

But, as I have argued elsewhere, we also need to engage with and expose some of the myths on the right about failures of past nationalization programs. A questioning of the rationale behind private ownership should not take us back to the monolithic state enterprises characteristic of the Soviet Union or even western democracies from the 1940s through to the 1990s. Instead, we should be open to the possibilities that new and diverse forms of public ownership offer. To do this effectively, the left needs also to wrestle back its older concerns with freedom, democracy and individual dignity from their capture by the Hayekian right.

Critically, we need new forms of collective ownership that draw upon a diverse and pluralistic set of institutional arrangements as the best means for stimulating economic democracy, innovation and social justice. In my recent book, I set out five guiding principles for a renewal of public ownership:

- A commitment to social justice as class justice in the sense advocated by Marx, where individuals have decision-making power with respect to their own labor and how they use it;
- A renewed engagement with older forms of mutualism and collectivism to build alliances beyond the left's traditional social base;
- A commitment to the promotion of knowledge creation, innovation and diversity in economic practice;
- The importance of dialogue and pluralism in economic decision-making;
- A regime of decentered and distributed decision-making.

The last point is particularly important to countering the neoliberal hold on the public realm. Following Friedrich Hayek's devastating critique of public ownership as centralized planning, it is unrealistic to imagine that all economic decisions can be subject to collective democratic planning. Nevertheless, this does not detract from the need to try to find solutions that open up the economy to more collective and participatory decision-making processes as a general philosophy.

While an alternative political economy will also require the need for planning and ownership at higher geographical scales in some strategic sectors, these need not necessarily be concentrated within particular places, organizations or social groups. What it does require is a commitment to the decentering of knowledge and decision-making power wherever possible to a plurality and diversity of organizations (e.g. mutual bodies, trade union research networks, small business associations, government and autonomously funded think tanks) to offer alternative and competing interpretations of economic problems that contribute to public debate. Of course, there are no guarantees in any economic system that elite or special interests will not capture policy agendas to the detriment of the social body as a whole, but dispersing functions, knowledge and institutional capacity does at least provide important countervailing tendencies, as I show in my book with the different examples of relatively successful public ownership in Norway's state owned oil industry and Denmark's decentralized and collectively owned renewable energy complex.

Beyond twentieth-century dystopias and pathways out of the current crisis

The twentieth century was marked by two competing visions. On the one hand was a vision of socialism as centralized state ownership (or nationalization) that could deliver equality and happiness to the masses and on the other was Margaret Thatcher's (and perhaps Hayek's) dream of a property-owning democracy. Both proved to be hopelessly abstract and undeliverable chimeras when confronted with the realities of economy and society and the political and institutional mechanisms, practices and variegated geographical traditions and trajectories that underpin them.

As the twenty-first century unfolds, we have a series of developing and related political-economic crises which need radical alternative solutions. First and foremost is the looming ecological crisis of global warming, at root caused by an unsustainable economic growth model which suits certain vested private interests at the expense of the rest of the planet. Despite the overwhelming scientific evidence of climate change, these vested interests are doing a good job at preventing effective collective action. Trump's decision to withdraw the United States from the Paris climate agreement is a symbolic moment in an elite counter-revolution, which creates its own populist narrative, thus signifying a deeper malaise.

This in turn signifies a second crisis brought about by the growing division between the elite decision-makers and opinion formers and the citizens whose lives are adversely affected by top-down economic-policy prescription on everything from trade to labor-market security to welfare reform. The distrust of scientific evidence, even that which is firmly established by a vast majority of academic studies, is grist to the mill of post-truth populists like Trump and others on the far right. In the UK, the success of the Brexiteers was similarly based on the pillorying of 'experts.' But, for our purposes here, this growing disconnect between the broad mass of citizens and a 'post-political,' technocratic and 'sensible' class – which, in the words of Jacques Ranciere, 'polices' the rest of us – serves to remind us of the dangers and superficiality of a liberal-democratic project in a globalizing world of deep and accelerating inequalities. We are in a world that looks increasingly like a global Weimar Republic, with the danger of revisiting the twentieth century's tragedies with an added element of farce.

Related to this is a third, unresolved crisis: one of neoliberal economic governance. Despite its many failings, the holy trinity of privatization, market deregulation and unfettered competition rolls on. While we can report on the growing resistance through new forms of public ownership at the local and regional levels in particular, national and global economic governance is still in thrall to the small-state austerians, with devastating consequences for many of the most disadvantaged citizens and communities worldwide. Finding a way out of the current impasse requires that we develop new thinking with regards to the best paths to embark on in delivering the French Revolution's still relevant triumvirate of *liberté*, *égalité* and *fraternité* (or solidarity). As I have argued, Karl Marx's nineteenth-century critique of capitalism and the appropriation of common wealth for private interests remains the central failing of global capitalism today as it did when he wrote it.

A reinvigorated demand for greater public ownership is an important element in a next system-alternative project. As Hanna rightly notes, this involves both learning from past mistakes and accepting that there is no 'off the shelf' nationalization model of public ownership that can be applied everywhere to retake the economy from elite interests. Rather, there is a need to work with existing and diverse collective and mutualist traditions in civil society to push forward an alternative economic project. Books such as this, which take stock of the incredible richness and diversity of already-existing forms of public ownership and illuminate their roles in addressing vital collective policy goals and problems, are an important part of that.

A final and critically important point is that in developing new forms of public ownership for the twenty-first century, we nurture and sustain respectful, but critical, forms of public discourse and collective learning. At the root of many of today's problems of economic marginalization and political alienation, which threaten the very fabric of democracy, is both the colonization of economic decision-making by an elite, but also its consequences for public participation and engagement in the economy. As we organize, campaign for and write about a transition to a more progressive economic system of diverse and democratic forms of public and collective ownership, it is important that the public itself is involved and has rights of control and ownership of decision-making. This would mean developing institutional arrangements – such as, for example, new hybrid multi-stakeholder models – that help spread participation and knowledge about the economy and its functioning.

Author's preface and acknowledgments

As long as I can remember, I have had a keen interest in history. Yet, growing up it wasn't the stories of antiquity or the Middle Ages that particularly excited me. Rather, it was modern history – the events and people that I could see as having directly shaped my world. In hindsight, I feel that in a sense I was trying to understand both my own family history (which was greatly impacted by the upheavals of the twentieth century) and another period of change happening all around me that I could not yet contextualize. I vividly remember being glued to the television, watching people a world away take hammers to the Berlin Wall, knowing that something big was happening but unsure yet of the significance. I watched bodies and oil wells burning in the Kuwaiti and Iraqi deserts and Boris Yeltsin standing atop a tank before the Russian Parliament. And then, closer to home, came Ruby Ridge, Waco, the Oklahoma City bombing, the capture of the Unabomber, and the Columbine school massacre.

I was also becoming acutely aware of the stark contrast between my relatively privileged, leafy, middle-class suburban neighborhood and the deep poverty mere miles away in the capital of the supposedly most powerful nation on earth. By the time I entered high school, this had developed into the start of an understanding that there was something fundamentally broken with an economic system that even during its boom years was marked by tremendous inequality and suffering. This led me first to the burgeoning anti-globalization movement, and then to the Green Party campaign of Ralph Nader in 2000. The former opened my eyes to the immense power of multinational corporations, while the latter shook my faith in mainstream politics as a vehicle to effect real, substantive change. I saw how in the American political system the deck was firmly stacked against outsider candidates, and I was castigated by the liberals with whom I had previously identified for having encouraged people to 'throw their vote away' and let George W. Bush into the White House.

Less than one month into my first semester at university, the 9/11 terrorist attacks occurred – followed by a sickening anti-Muslim backlash at home and the invasion of Afghanistan abroad. At the time, I was studying another period of intense domestic and international turmoil in United States history: the 1960s and 1970s. This not only gave me an important alternative perspective on the momentous events unfolding around me, but also embedded in me a deep appreciation of 'history from the bottom up' and the forgotten (or deliberately erased) stories of everyday radicals, subversives, and activists. It also introduced me to the likes of Howard Zinn, E. P. Thompson, C. L. R. James, Staughton Lynd, Harold Cruse, Gabriel Kolko, Stuart Hall, and C. Wright Mills, to say nothing of the legendary activists of the time, such as Malcolm X, Dennis Banks, Angela Davis, Bayard Rustin, Tom Hayden, Assata Shakur, and Fred Hampton, among many others. Furthermore, my studies of this historical period – along with activism against the disastrous invasion and occupation of Iraq – reinforced in me the need to participate actively in various ways, both in the street and in the library, in the struggle for a better world.

Another historian I came across during my studies was Gar Alperovitz. While he is a well-known political activist in his own right, I became acquainted with Gar through his groundbreaking historical work challenging the dominant narrative around the dropping of the atomic bombs on Hiroshima and Nagasaki at the end of the Second World War. This was part of my own efforts to really begin to understand the development and implications of the projection of American military and economic power around the world. Years later, while searching for a job during the worst economic crisis in 80 years, I came across Gar again and applied for a job as his research assistant. It was working with Gar that really sparked my interest in political economy and economic history, and the role institutions play in both. It was at Gar's suggestion that I began to focus on public ownership when, at the time, this seemed to be no more than a provincial backwater of political economy, a curious relic of a particular historical conjuncture in a modern, globalized world. I am profoundly thankful to Gar for all of his wisdom, training, support, and encouragement these past seven years. Without him, this book would not have been possible.

I am relating this personal story at the outset because if studying history has taught me one thing above all, it is that objectivity is largely a myth – and a dangerous one at that. Every writer comes to their topic with their own conscious and subconscious biases.

Being as forthright as possible about these is, in my opinion, important. Lest there be any doubt, I happily confess up front that I am a broadly sympathetic proponent of public ownership. I believe it is a powerful institutional strategy with deep historical roots, one with the potential to address some of the pressing political-economic problems facing our world in the early part of the twenty-first century. When deployed to support the development of broad-based and prosperous economies from the ground up, it stands in marked contrast to the increasing dominance of giant, increasingly unaccountable, and monopolistic for-profit multinational corporations. For me, however, public ownership is a means and not the end goal, and I do not believe it is the only strategy to get there (wherever *there* may be). Nor am I uncritical. In my view, public ownership cannot simply be expanded in its most common contemporary forms. It must, I feel, be democratized and embedded within a broader movement toward some vision of an alternative system based around principles of economic democracy. This book, in other words, argues that public ownership – by virtue of being tried, resilient, popular, and scalable – has the potential not only to be deployed more widely to deliver real, tangible socio-economic benefits, but also to be reimagined and reinvented in such a way that it can serve as the institutional basis for a more far-reaching transformation of our failing contemporary political-economic system.

What is probably apparent by now, or will be soon, is that I am no straight economist. I don't profess to be fully immersed in the minutiae of economic theory or an expert in statistical analysis. If you are looking for a book loaded with tables, graphs, and calculations, you are going to be disappointed. I also do not identify with any particular school of economic thought, although I would say that my orientation falls within a broad conception of heterodox economics, and that the approach taken in this book reflects that, often incorporating elements from a number of different theoretical schools. Yet, I believe, and hope, that what is presented in the following pages is broadly accessible both to people operating from a more orthodox perspective and those who have never been exposed to these distinctions. Lastly, this book has an explicit focus on the United States (and, to a much lesser extent, Great Britain). This is due in part to my personal experience of emigrating to the former from the latter as a child. However, it is also because I have found that the United States is grossly underexplored in the modern literature and politics around public ownership. In no way do I intend to discount the rich history and experience of other countries, particularly in the developing world. In many ways, political movements in some of these countries are already blazing a trail for the scaling up of public ownership and its reimagination along more democratic lines that many supposedly more economically advanced countries like the United States and the United Kingdom can only hope to follow.

I had been researching and writing about public ownership for a few years when, in 2015, I stumbled upon the fact that the entire electric system in the fairly politically conservative state of Nebraska was publicly or cooperatively owned, with a very interesting history as to why that was the case. I realized at that point that public ownership in the United States was far more widespread and extensive than even I had recognized, and that this was something about which other people might be interested to learn. I therefore decided to consolidate several years of research and writing on the topic of public ownership into a short report. That short report became a long report – which then became this book.

Throughout this process, I have been extremely fortunate to have had the support and assistance of a great number of people to whom I owe a debt of gratitude. First and foremost, to my best friend and wife Caroline Lalonde-Hanna and our two children, for whose unconditional love and encouragement I am eternally grateful. Also, to my family who, although not agreeing with everything I espouse, read and share it all anyway. I want to specifically recognize my grandfather, Romano Borzoni, a survivor of the Blitz and a veteran of the Second World War who passed away in the spring of 2017 while I was writing this book. Much of my interest in history and politics is due to his influence (and classic movie collection); To all my friends and colleagues at The Democracy Collaborative, past and present, many of whom played key roles in helping shape and produce this book – specifically, Ted Howard, who, as President of the organization, has been both a mentor and a guiding light, and Steve Dubb, the former Research Director, who always had the time to thoroughly review my material and provide both constructive criticism and encouragement;

To my close friend, collaborator, and comrade Joe Guinan. Many of the ideas contained in this book we hashed out together over after-work drinks and in jointly authored articles (all errors are, of course, mine alone); To the research team at The Democracy Collaborative – Emily Sladek, Will Flagle, Kaylee Thornley, and Jarrid Green – who did a phenomenal job of reviewing the text and slogging through the hundreds of citations; To Adam Simpson and Johanna Bozuwa, who helped me think through the issues of automation and energy democracy respectively; To the far-sighted philanthropic individuals and foundations whose generous support made all the work that has gone into this book possible through their support of either The Democracy Collaborative or its Next System Project, including the Kendeda Fund, the Nathan Cummings Foundation, the NoVo Foundation, Richard and Marilyn Mazess, the Surdna Foundation, and the V. Kann Rasmussen Foundation.

To the team at Manchester University Press, who have been positive and supportive throughout the publication process and incredible to work with; To Andrew Cumbers, whose trailblazing book on public ownership inspired my own, and whose insights continue to shape and advance my thinking on the subject; To my close friends and confidants Justin Adly, Mateo Gasparotto, Guillermo Zamora, Alex Cena, Will Pattie, Hilary Berwick, Marcelo Nina Valencia, Robin Slusser, Jimmy Fox, Benyam and Yoseph Teklemariam, Adam Sledd, Martin O'Neill, Andrew Small, Coy McKinney, Ashby Scott, Ryan Schell, Ariel Sedeno, Jesse Wagner, Nick Zamora, Kyle Dudley, and Ryan Scarano; and to all those I have neglected to mention by name but who have played a crucial role in shaping my life and work.

Thomas M. Hanna
October 2017

Introduction
Public ownership in urgent political perspective

In late September 2017, in Brighton on the south coast of England, Jeremy Corbyn, the veteran left-winger who had become the unlikely leader of the British Labour Party, took to the stage in front of a packed convention hall at the annual party conference. To a standing ovation he declared that the center of political gravity had shifted and that a new popular consensus was forming in favor of 'something different and better.'[1] The breathtaking pace of political events in recent years makes it hard to disagree. One of a small band of Labour leftists isolated by but surviving the long decades of neoliberalism under both Thatcher and New Labour, Corbyn improbably won the election as leader of his party in 2015, survived a coup attempt and forced leadership contest, and went on to pull off a remarkable comeback in the snap general election of June 2017, in which his 'unelectable' party was supposed to have been annihilated. But Corbyn simply would not keep to the script, producing a vote-share increase for Labour greater than any achieved since 1945.[2] At the time of writing, he leads a government-in-waiting that is being courted by British industry – an incredible turnaround in just two years.[3] A new world of political possibility is opening up right before our eyes.

At the same time, whether through Brexit or the election of Donald Trump or the broader re-emergence of fascism and hard-right nationalism around the world – all smeared with an ugly veneer of xenophobia, racism, anti-Semitism, and white supremacy – the political status quo is clearly coming apart at the seams. Add to this a global refugee crisis, a seemingly endless cycle of war and terrorism (both state and non-state), the existential threat of climate change (along with a host of other deteriorating ecological trends), austerity, the lingering effects of the financial crisis, and exploding income inequality, where wealth exists side by side with deep, endemic poverty, and it is becoming evident to growing numbers of people that the dominant political-economic narratives of recent decades are fundamentally flawed. The unwavering faith in deregulated markets, profit maximization, large corporations, financialization, globalization, and privatization is increasingly discredited and must be urgently re-appraised. However, the response from defenders of the established order, many of whom profess to be liberals or 'centrists,' has been both disheartening and wholly predictable. Faced with the prospect of losing control, many have soured on democracy in favor of rule by an international technocratic elite. Right-wing extremism masquerading as populism simply cannot be defeated in this way. Instead, the answer must include a process of genuine and increased democratic engagement and participation, especially in the economic sphere. What we need, in short, is more democracy, not less – and this includes *economic democracy*.

Like Corbyn, more and more thinkers and activists around the world are beginning to articulate the need for a reclamation of long-standing democratic economic forms, not least among them public ownership, as a vitally important component of this process. Public ownership has existed in one form or another for as long as humans have organized themselves together into formal societies. And, contrary to the recently prevailing economic orthodoxy, it continues to thrive. As the following pages will show, even in the United States – hardly considered the most hospitable environment for public ownership – it not only persists (albeit largely below the level of everyday political consciousness) but is expanding, including in important new sectors of the economy, such as broadband internet provision. Perhaps even more surprisingly, public ownership is also relatively popular at the local level, including in many politically conservative areas of the country. This popularity has allowed public ownership to remain somewhat insulated from, and resilient in the face of, national political changes, including the resurgence of the Republican Party at the state and national level in recent years. Public ownership in the United States has therefore proven much more able to withstand periodic cycles of privatization than might have been expected given experience elsewhere – especially in the United Kingdom (the UK, in fact, is an extreme outlier when it comes to privatization, accounting for fully 40 percent of the total value of assets privatized across the OECD between 1980 and 1996).[4]

Meanwhile, all around the world public ownership has also begun to re-emerge as a viable strategic option for communities and political leaders in the wake of the 2007–2008 financial crisis and Great Recession of the late 2000s – events that continue to have ongoing political repercussions, challenging in fundamental ways the supposed supremacy of the private over the public in the minds of ordinary people. This profound ideological shift is reflected in two documents put out by Corbyn's Labour in the run-up to their stunning electoral performance in June 2017. The first is the party's widely praised manifesto, *For the Many Not the Few*. Among other policies, it unapologetically calls for re-nationalization of the railways, the energy system, the water system, and Royal Mail, as well as the establishment of a publicly owned National Investment Bank, a network of regional public development banks, and new local publicly owned banks (perhaps through the breakup of the Royal Bank of Scotland, which was nationalized following the financial crisis and is still in state hands).[5] The second is a report commissioned by Shadow Chancellor of the Exchequer John McDonnell and Shadow Secretary of State for Business, Energy and Industrial Strategy Rebecca Long-Bailey, entitled *Alternative Models of Ownership* – a remarkable document coming from a major political party that lays out the case for increasing public and worker ownership as a way to combat inequality, political disenfranchisement, and underinvestment.[6]

Polling suggests that in Britain, as in other countries, such policies are broadly popular. An October 2017 poll released by the Legatum Institute, a free-enterprise think tank, found to their horror that 83 percent of respondents favored nationalizing the water sector, followed by 77 percent for gas and electricity, 76 percent for trains, 66 percent for defense and aerospace, and 50 percent for banks. Nearly a quarter were even in favor of nationalizing travel agents.[7] Reflecting on these poll results in the *New Statesman*, George Eaton declared that 'the voters back Labour's interventionism,' and 'few expected public ownership to return in any significant capacity. But after the beginning of the global financial crisis, the state was roused from its slumber.'[8] Given current economic conditions, and the likelihood of continuing deep social, ecological, and other challenges, it is reasonable to expect that public ownership will only continue to grow in importance, both as a vital element in our existing political economy and as a pathway to something very different. 'The state,' as Joshua Kurlantzick recently put it, 'is back in business.'[9]

Moreover, the empirical and theoretical literature on the subject (which, contrary to the conventional wisdom, never spoke with one voice) is beginning to be unearthed and put to good use by scholars, politicians, and activists seeking to challenge the foundations of the under-examined and unsupported belief that private ownership is inherently economically superior to public ownership. For today's emboldened political left, newly emergent from decades-long hibernation beneath the permafrost of neoliberalism, public ownership is assuming renewed importance as an explicit strategy for tackling the iniquities of the present system and building a coherent alternative. As Robin Blackburn has argued, public ownership is 'the vital missing ingredient' in the menu of options for promoting a new political economy.[10]

What follows is an examination of the contemporary experience of public ownership, with a specific focus on the United States, as well as some of the economic debates surrounding it, all with an eye to informing those interested in generating and developing ideas about what a new system (or any future system) of political economy might look like. Alongside a survey of how public ownership is envisioned in a variety of alternative political-economic systemic designs and theories, this provides the groundwork for a sectoral analysis of the possibilities of, and rationale for, its further institution, evolution, and development. The goal, therefore, is not only to call into question some of the flawed and limited assumptions underpinning mainstream discourse around how economies should be organized, but to also to provide the foundation for a realistic, and viable, transitional pathway to a new political economy built on democratic economic forms that can achieve broad popular support.

Public ownership in historical context

Political-economic systems can to a large extent be defined by their dominant property relations.[11] Karl Marx famously viewed human history through the lens of the differing forms of ownership of the means of production. In tribal societies, for example, communal ownership and cooperative labor was widespread. Ancient societies, by contrast, were characterized by patrician ownership, with slave labor – while not necessarily numerically predominant – serving as the critical source from which the propertied classes extracted their surplus.[12] In the feudal societies of the Middle Ages, agriculture owned by landed elites served as the primary economic driver, with labor provided by a peasant class tied to the land. Under industrial (and financial) capitalism, on the other hand, the means of production has largely been in the hands of capitalists, to whom the working class sell their labor for wages.[13] Due in part to Marx's intervention, and to the resulting titanic twentieth-century ideological, political, and military struggle between capitalism and communism, much popular understanding of ownership in the economy has been reduced to a simplistic dichotomy – complete private ownership, on the one hand, and full public ownership, on the other.[14]

This binary understanding, however, can obscure as much as it uncovers. Modern political economies are much more complex than such a dualism allows, and many encompass a variety of ownership forms and arrangements. In 1962, for instance, British economist Peter Wiles identified 10 different ownership models that ranged from 'primitive capitalism' to 'full communism.'[15] Similarly, in their classic work *Politics, Economics, and Welfare*, Robert Dahl and Charles Lindblom described an economic system as a continuum that 'displays something of the variety of techniques possible between an unregulated private enterprise, on the one hand, and a business like the post office run as an ordinary government department, on the other hand.'[16]

This book also suggests, however, that for a new political-economic system to be more equitable, democratic, just, and sustainable, simply shifting ownership forms alone will be insufficient. Both contemporary and historical experience with public ownership – especially in the centralized, undemocratic Soviet-state socialist model, which exhibited many obvious flaws – demonstrates the necessity of re-conceptualizing and embedding public ownership in active democratic practice. In other words, public ownership needs also to be re-imagined. It must be reconciled with the rights of the individual to fully and freely participate in the economy (both at the micro- and macro-level) as well as with notions of appropriative justice (in addition to productive and distributive justice, to use George DeMartino's framework) – that is, 'fairness in the processes by which some individuals and/or groups in society receive the social surplus produced by themselves or by others.'[17] As Cat Hobbs, founder of UK pressure group We Own It!, puts it: 'Let's build public ownership with the right culture, management and incentives. Let's create accountable, transparent institutions that give us, the public, a real say.'[18]

Some terminology

To begin moving beyond the constricted ideological horizons that limit both theoretical debate and objective analysis on the topic, it is important to offer clear, concrete definitions of public ownership. In modern discourse, the term *public enterprise* most often refers to economically productive entities or business organizations owned by the state – such as mines, factories, banks, and railroads. These are sometimes also called state owned enterprises (SOEs) or government owned corporations (GOCs). However, this definition tends to exclude other entities or services owned and operated by the state, such as schools, universities, hospitals, roads, parks, and land. As such, the more inclusive term *public ownership* is preferable, as it captures trillions of dollars in economic value that would otherwise be excluded from the analysis.

To complicate matters, the ownership structure of companies, especially large national or multinational corporations, can often be quite convoluted. In many cases, for instance, public or quasi-public entities, such as government development agencies, public pension funds, and sovereign wealth funds, own shares in companies alongside other private and institutional investors. Moreover, as economists Aldo Musacchio and Sergio Lazzarini describe, new models of public ownership are emerging – especially in rapidly developing nations – in which the state 'works hand in hand with private investors in novel governance arrangements.'[19] While precise delineations and structures differ from country to country, a company is often considered to be wholly publicly owned if more than 50 percent of shares are held by public institutions and bodies.[20] In companies where a singular public institution or body owns less than 50 percent of shares, but enough that it can prevail in any stockholder votes, it is sometimes said that the public owns a controlling stake or interest. The Swedish government, for instance, owns 37.3 percent of the shares of Telia Company, the predominant telecommunications provider in Sweden and Finland, making it the single largest shareholder (out of around 500,000 nominal owners).[21] Additionally, governments have also sometimes retained or acquired 'golden shares' – essentially a minority shareholding that includes important designated rights not given to other shareholders – in certain companies, especially those that were formerly wholly owned public enterprises, as a way to ensure continuing control over decisions of vital public interest, such as appointments to the board or responses to foreign takeover attempts.[22]

In what follows, *public ownership* will most often refer to companies in which public institutions and bodies have at least a controlling stake, but this framework may not always be applicable, especially when outside studies are referenced. Similarly, the terms *private corporations*, *private companies*, or *private businesses* (or *privately owned* corporations, companies, or businesses) will be used to describe any for-profit ownership form whereby non-state actors (apart from workers or cooperative members) own all or a substantial share of the enterprise. This includes both closely held 'private' companies, which do not trade shares on public stock exchanges, and 'public' companies that do. It also includes companies whose shareholders may include certain public institutions (like pension and sovereign wealth funds), but where those institutions do not hold a majority or controlling stake.

Theoretical perspectives

Many discussions of public ownership historically, especially on the left, have followed the distinction laid down by the Dutch astronomer and Marxist theorist Anton Pannekoek – namely, that public ownership refers to 'the right of disposal, by a public body representing society, by government, state power or some other political body,' while common ownership is 'the right of disposal by the workers themselves; the working class itself – taken in the widest sense.'[23] In modern discussions, however, this distinction is sometimes absent, and the term public ownership can include forms of common or worker ownership. For instance, Andrew Cumbers, author of the award-winning book *Reclaiming Public Ownership*, prefers to 'use the term "public ownership" in its broadest sense as encapsulating all those attempts, both outside and through the state, to create forms of collective ownership in opposition to, or perhaps more accurately to reclaim economic space from, capitalist social relations.'[24]

For those following Cumbers' approach, public ownership could also include so-called 'social ownership' – a hybrid form that is positioned in between private and government ownership, and which is sometimes envisioned as a substitute for direct 'common ownership' by workers.[25] Saul Estrin explains that during Yugoslavia's experiments with worker self-managed socialism – one of the few real-world experiments with social ownership – 'workers in each enterprise [were] permitted to appropriate the surplus normally allocated to owners and to make accumulation decisions, but retain[ed] no individual or marketable rights over the assets.'[26] What this actually entailed in practice, however, changed over time, and the state continued to play an important role in management, allocation, and distribution decisions. While there are certainly many merits to expanding the conception of public ownership in these ways, in what follows, *public ownership* is used almost exclusively to refer to ownership by the state or entities within the state at various levels of governance.

The relative ubiquity and unobtrusiveness of public ownership in people's everyday lives makes it easy to forget how important it is to the functioning of most modern political economies. Furthermore, the long-term resilience of public ownership, and its ability to withstand momentous shifts in political and ideological paradigms, sometimes obscures the reasons why public ownership forms were adopted in the first place. Few today, for instance, remember the momentous debates around economic development, rural electrification, and the role of the state that led to the formation of the Tennessee Valley Authority (TVA) in 1933. For these and other reasons, the very concept of public ownership – as well as arguments for and against it in various circumstances and contexts – must be re-introduced to new public audiences for new purposes in new political eras. The following material is also intended as a resource guide for those now seeking an entry point into the developing debates and questions around public ownership – including economic efficiency, environmental sustainability, scale, and economic democracy.

Organization of the book

This reintroduction starts in an obvious place – a brief exploration of actual, existing experience with public ownership. Chapter 1 takes a bird's-eye view and attempts to demonstrate how widespread public ownership actually is in the United States and around the world. This helps put the economic debates around efficiency reviewed in Chapter 2 into perspective. Contrary to conventional wisdom – and despite the best efforts of free market ideologues – public ownership is decidedly *not* inherently less efficient than private ownership, and this partly explains why the former remains vibrant (and expanding in certain areas) despite more than four decades of neoliberal pressure for privatization. Additional possible reasons for its resilience and continued popularity are covered in Chapter 3, including its role in correcting market failures, generating revenue to support social services, enhancing local economic stability, reducing inequality, managing technological change, bolstering democracy, enhancing public participation and transparency, and addressing growing ecological concerns. These reasons, and others, are why public ownership, in one form or another, plays an important role in most alternative political-economic system models and approaches – especially those originating from the political left. In Chapter 4, a number of these are quickly analyzed in order to gain some initial insights into the role public ownership might play in future systemic arrangements superior to and beyond contemporary corporate capitalism. These, as well as the lessons of the preceding discussions on efficiency and real-world experience with public enterprise, are then combined in Chapter 5 as part of attempts to begin thinking through how, and in what form, public ownership might be deployed, scaled, and utilized across a variety of existing economic sectors. The question of form is then taken up in the Conclusion, as part of a discussion on the need to re-imagine, re-structure, and democratize public ownership. This is critical in light of the deep systemic challenges the United States and other countries around the world are facing, and will increasingly face, as the twenty-first century unfolds.

For those well versed in the political-economic discussions of the 1920s and 1930s, the 1960s and 1970s, or the late 1980s and early 1990s, much of this may be well-trodden ground. However, the political balance of forces in the United States and much of Europe is once again shifting importantly, throwing up new challenges to which public ownership may in part be a solution. In a turbulent new era marked by wars, mass migrations, fiscal retrenchment, decaying social protection, terrorism, financial instability, rampant inequality, and looming ecological calamity, once again understanding the possibilities, pitfalls, and potential applications of public ownership will be critical to making sense of – and coming to grips with – a world in kaleidoscopic motion. Written off for so long as a relic of the past by ideological warriors for the status quo, public ownership may once again be taking its rightful place in the panoply of institutions and strategies for creating a better future. If this book contributes to that in any small way, then it will have served its purpose.

Chapter 1

Public ownership in the United States and around the world

Despite more than four decades of pressure for privatization, public ownership in practice remains incredibly common – and popular – on the ground throughout the developed and developing world. A 2014 report by the OECD, for instance, found that in just 34 countries there were 2,111 state owned enterprises with around 6 million employees and a total value of over $2 trillion (this was only at the central or federal level of government. Local and regional publicly owned enterprises were not included in the survey).[1] Counting companies in which the government owned a controlling stake added $860 billion in value and another 2.8 million employees to the total.[2] 'Although varied in size and sectoral scope,' the report stated, 'all countries in the sample maintain some level of state ownership in commercial enterprises.'[3] The most important sectors for public ownership include electricity and gas (24 percent of all SOEs by value), finance (24 percent), transportation (14.3 percent), and primary sectors such as mineral extraction (14.3 percent).[4]

Similarly, a 2013 report by researchers associated with the OECD found that state owned companies – defined as those with more than 50.01 percent public ownership – *globally* accounted for 43 percent of the mining support sector, 41 percent of the civil engineering sector, 40 percent of the land transport and transport via pipelines sector, 35 percent of the coal and lignite mining sector, 34 percent of the crude petroleum and natural gas extraction sector, 27 percent of the electricity, gas, and steam sector, 20 percent of the telecommunications sector, 20 percent of the financial mediation sector, 17 percent of the warehousing sector, 15 percent of the tobacco manufacturing sector, 14 percent of the architectural and engineering sector, 13 percent of the air transport sector, and 13 percent of the fabricated metals manufacturing sector.[5]

Many of the companies involved are well known. Publicly owned companies control roughly 75 percent of all oil worldwide.[6] Most of the biggest oil and gas companies are state owned, including

Saudi Aramco, Gazprom, National Iranian Oil Company, Rosneft, PetroChina, and Statoil.[7] Similarly, public ownership of significant or controlling shares in many highly visible international airlines is also common.[8] For instance, the rapidly expanding Middle East luxury airlines Emirates, Etihad, and Qatar Airlines are publicly owned by the governments of Dubai, Abu Dhabi, and Qatar respectively. Airbus Group – producer of Airbus planes and helicopters and a defense and aeronautics provider – is partly owned by government entities in France, Spain, and Germany.[9]

In many countries people interact with a variety of publicly owned enterprises on a daily basis, often without realizing it. Such entities operate advanced, high-speed rail systems in France, Spain, Belgium, Germany, Italy, the Netherlands, China, and South Korea.[10] Brazil, now an economic powerhouse, has more than 100 state owned or controlled enterprises, including major banks and utilities.[11] Fast and widely available internet access is provided in many countries where public corporations exist side by side with private companies. Public ownership of telecommunications companies is common around the world, including in Austria, Belgium, Japan, Sweden, France, Germany, Italy, Switzerland, Sweden, Turkey, and Norway.[12]

In the European Union, more than 200 public and semi-public banks, along with another 80 plus funding agencies, account for around a fifth of all bank assets.[13] In Germany, there are 413 publicly owned municipal savings banks (Sparkassen) with more than €1.1 trillion in assets and 233,742 employees.[14] (Unlike some of the larger banks, these banks have, according to *The Economist*, 'come through the crisis with barely a scratch.')[15] The Savings Banks Financial Group – an umbrella organization comprised of a number of publicly owned entities, including the savings banks, regional Landesbank groupings, regional building societies, public insurance groups, real-estate companies, equity-investing companies, and municipal-advising companies – employs around 332,000 people and has business volume of some €2.8 trillion.[16] Japan Post Bank is the world's largest public bank and one of that nation's largest employers.[17] In Costa Rica, Banco Popular is combining public and cooperative ownership with major advances in democratic governance and public participation – resulting in a large, economically successful bank that is on the cutting edge of ecological sustainability and the green transition.[18]

Country-specific data in the aforementioned 2014 OECD report details how pervasive and varied public ownership is in some advanced economies. For instance, France had three majority owned companies listed on the stock market, 11 minority owned companies listed on the stock market, and 54 non-listed majority owned companies, statutory corporations, and quasi-corporations.[19] Norway had three majority owned companies and five minority owned companies listed on the stock market, as well as 42 non-listed majority owned companies, statutory corporations, and quasi-corporations.[20] These companies were found in a wide variety of sectors, ranging from manufacturing to banking to media to communications.

In many countries, such enterprises – often owned and/or controlled by the central state – are just the tip of the iceberg on public ownership, which extends down through the regional, state, or provincial level to local communities. A 2015 report from the global professional services firm PricewaterhouseCoopers, for instance, stated that 'regionally and locally-owned SOEs also form an important part of the SOE landscape. And these tend to outnumber centrally-owned SOEs, while being smaller in size.'[21] According to this analysis, there are around 2,563 publicly owned enterprises in Sweden alone, with local, municipally owned enterprises comprising 69 percent of the total, and regionally (county) owned enterprises comprising 5 percent. In Germany, there are around 15,186 publicly owned enterprises, with 89 percent owned at the municipal level and 9 percent at the regional (state) level.

In recent years, the re-municipalization of public services has been gaining support throughout the world, often as a way to address pressing economic and ecological concerns while establishing local democratic control over the economy. In a 2017 study, the Transnational Institute (TNI) identified 835 municipalizations and re-municipalizations involving some 1,600 cities in 45 countries.[22] While re-municipalizations were most prevalent in the energy and water sectors, they have also occurred in transportation, education, housing, and healthcare, among others. 'These (re)municipalizations generally succeeded in bringing down costs and tariffs, improving conditions for workers and boosting service quality, while ensuring greater transparency and accountability,' the report found.[23] Since 2007 in Germany, for instance, more than 70 new municipal-level publicly owned electric utilities have been established and hundreds of service concessions have been acquired by public entities from private operators – reversing the privatization wave that swept the sector in the 1990s.[24] This process of *rekommunalisierung* ('re-communalization') is part of a larger effort to comprehensively transition the country's energy sources from coal and nuclear to renewable sources called *energiewende* ('energy transition').[25] In September 2013, voters in Hamburg (Germany's second largest city, with 1.8

million residents) voted in favor of re-municipalization in a referendum backed by a coalition of more than 50 consumer, religious, and environmental groups – and despite the opposition of the business community, the city mayor, and various major political parties.[26]

In Spain, both Madrid and Barcelona, the two largest cities in the country, are exploring public ownership options under the leadership of new political groupings sympathetic to the idea, namely en Comú, which controls the Barcelona City Council, and Ahora Madrid, which controls the Madrid City Council. Following the lead of 14 other Catalan towns that have re-municipalized their water systems, Barcelona has decided to establish a publicly owned water utility to replace the for-profit company Aguas de Barcelona, which has operated for a century without a formal contract.[27] However, even before the long-simmering political crisis between Catalonia and Spain exploded in late 2017 (with the former declaring independence and the latter imposing direct rule), the central government in Madrid had been attempting to block the re-municipalization effort.[28] Other cities in Spain that have re-municipalized services in recent years (or are considering it) include the Catalan district of Castelldefels, which saved around €3 million a year by taking refuse collection back into public ownership, Valladolid, which found that private street sweeping cost 71 percent more than the city doing it directly, and Terrassa, which is aiming to bring its water system back into public ownership after the private operator's 70-year contract expired in 2016.[29]

The United Kingdom has long been at the forefront of privatization, but one of the great ironies of the privatization wave that swept the country in the 1980s is that in several high-profile cases, newly privatized industries didn't remain in private hands for very long. They were subsequently bought up by large international state owned enterprises from other countries that were entering the world market as globalization took hold. A classic example relates to Britain's electricity system – a strong, centralized, publicly owned system for most of the twentieth century. In 1990, the 12 local electricity providers (the regional electricity boards) were sold off as private companies, followed by three new generation companies (taking over coal and nuclear plants that were previously publicly owned), and finally, by 1996, the transmission network that held the system together (the National Grid). As James Meek describes in the *London Review of Books*, the newly privatized system was rife with abuses, attracting foreign takeovers. In addition to private companies from America and elsewhere, the major player that entered the British electricity market was the French state owned energy giant EDF. 'Beginning with the takeover of London Electricity in 1998, exploiting the Thatcherites' open-door market structures and their decision to split the electricity industry into small, easy-to-swallow chunks,' Meek writes, 'France in effect renationalised the industry its neighbour had so painstakingly privatised. Renationalised it, that is, for France.'[30]

Even more surprising to many observers has been the recent willingness of the Conservative government in Britain to allow Chinese state owned enterprises to participate in the construction and management of new nuclear reactors, alongside EDF. In June 2015, a leading advisor to the government (and free-market proponent) attacked the plan, stating: 'add in the military and security issues of letting Chinese state owned companies into the heart of the British nuclear industry, and it seems positively perverse to prefer Chinese government money to British government money in so sensitive a national project.'[31] In September 2016, however, the government approved a proposal to allow EDF and CGN (China's state owned nuclear company) to begin designing and constructing new nuclear reactors – starting with Hinkley Point C. The agreement provides the companies with up to £30 billion in subsidies over 35 years and gives the British government a 'golden share' which will allow it to veto any future changes in ownership if it wishes.[32]

The United Kingdom, by virtue of its geography, is particularly suited to dramatically expanding its renewable energy generation through wind power. Here too, however, foreign publicly owned enterprises are dominating development. A September 2017 report published by the Labour Energy Forum revealed that more than half (51.16 percent) of all offshore wind capacity in the UK was owned by foreign, publicly owned companies. Under 8 percent was owned by British companies as a whole, and just 0.07 percent by British publicly owned companies – a single 7 MW turbine owned by the Offshore Renewable Energy Catapult as a demonstration project.[33] One such foreign state owned company is Vattenfall, which is aggressively pursuing wind-power generation in order to satisfy EU requirements that 20 percent of the region's energy consumption come from renewable sources by 2020.[34] One of the world's largest wind-power operators, running more than 1,000 wind turbines in several European countries, Vattenfall owns large British windfarms including Kentish Flats, the Kentish Flats Extension, Ormonde (51 percent ownership), and Thanet.[35] In essence, much of what privatization achieved in the case of Britain's electricity system (other than enriching a small handful of politically connected elites) was to shift the benefits of public ownership, especially revenues, from the local communities where those assets are produced or consumed to communities in other countries. While this need not be a negative in and of itself (especially in the context of movement toward greater genuine international cooperation), this has serious implications for local economic stability, democratic control, participation, and transparency – especially when those international institutions and frameworks are built around economic models that are financially extractive.

There are, however, signs that the British electricity sector may be ripe for fundamental change. Under Jeremy Corbyn and John McDonnell, the Labour Party has vowed to take utilities back into public ownership and 'transition to a publicly owned, decentralised energy system.'[36] And on the ground, some local municipalities are taking the lead by forming publicly owned electric companies to compete with the traditional, large, for-profit suppliers. According to recent reports, such companies now exist (or are close to existing) in Islington (the first such publicly owned company in London in more than 100 years), Doncaster, Portsmouth, Nottingham, Bristol, Liverpool, Derby, Leeds, and Sussex (where several municipalities are joining together).[37] In London, Labour Mayor Sadiq Khan has committed to a publicly owned company called Energy for Londoners, but it is still unclear what form this might take.[38] The movement is being driven by a desire to lower costs for consumers (with millions struggling to pay their utility bills in what is often referred to as 'fuel poverty'), generate new revenues in a time of crippling austerity at the local council level, and provide a way to interface with local constituents.

However, unlike in some countries (especially the United States) these municipal electric companies by and large do not, as of yet, own much in the way of transmission infrastructure or generation facilities. In many cases, they purchase much of their energy from wholesalers and sell it on to customers regardless of geography (although usually local residents receive lower rates). This structure has the advantage that start-up costs are relatively modest, especially when compared to the cost of municipalizing a vertically integrated monopoly electric utility in the United States. However, by having to compete in a market and not having complete control over either transmission or generation, the margin for both economic viability and social benefit is low. Much of the discussion in the UK is now moving on to questions of competition (and whether there should even be a market and competition in the energy sector) and bringing the grid and generation facilities back into public ownership as well.

The surprising prevalence of public ownership in the United States

The United States, often considered the beating heart of free-wheeling, no-holds-barred market capitalism, is frequently assumed to have little contemporary experience with, or interest in, public ownership. However, public ownership in the United States is much more common than most people understand, with the relative decentralization of the US political system allowing for local control in ways that don't exist in other countries where public ownership is often centralized at the highest, national level of the state – the traditional state owned enterprise. A prime example is the electric utility sector where around 2,000 publicly owned utilities – along with consumer owned cooperatives – provide around 25 percent of the nation's electricity.[39] In one state – conservative Nebraska – every single resident and business receives electricity from a community owned institution rather than a for-profit corporation. There, 121 publicly owned utilities, 10 cooperatives, and 30 public power districts provide electricity to a population of around 1.8 million people.[40] As we shall see, a common concern with public ownership, especially in larger-scale systems, is that it can lead to inefficiency, unaccountability, and bureaucracy. But Nebraska's nearly century-old experience with a completely public and community owned electricity system demonstrates that this does not necessarily have to be the case. The principles of subsidiarity – generally, that matters of decision-making should be devolved to the lowest level possible – and local control can, in fact, be preserved through a networked mix of publicly owned institutions at various scales without sacrificing efficiency or service quality.

Most publicly owned electric utilities are conventional in their operations, and a number under current management approaches have poor ecological records. On the other hand, some are at the forefront of city and state attempts to implement climate action plans and reduce greenhouse gas emissions. A particularly instructive effort is the ongoing campaign in Boulder, Colorado to municipalize the local electric utility to confront climate change. Concerned that the existing private corporation, Xcel Energy, derived around 60 percent of its energy from coal, local community groups and policymakers united around a plan to assert public control through public ownership.[41] Despite the fact that Xcel outspent supporters of the effort by roughly 10-to-one, the initiative was approved by a small margin in a 2011 referendum.[42] Two years later, a new effort backed by Xcel that would have crippled the municipalization effort was overwhelmingly defeated – again despite huge imbalances in campaign spending.[43]

It currently appears that the city of Boulder is pursuing a twin-track strategy consisting of moving forward with the municipalization effort on the one hand (including the complex legal maneuvering it takes to acquire and transfer Xcel's assets to the city), and negotiating with Xcel in the hopes of coming to a compromise which would leave Xcel as Boulder's electric provider but greatly enhance the city's control over its sources of energy on the other.[44] In April 2017, just days before a Public Utilities Commission (PUC) hearing, Xcel presented the Boulder City Council with two proposals aimed at ending the municipalization fight. The first was an offer to remain the city's electric provider, but allow for more renewable energy projects (critically, however, the company would not endorse the city's commitment to 100 percent renewable energy by 2030) and the second was an offer to sell the company's local assets to the city up front (rather than go through the PUC process) at a premium.[45] After a hearing in front of an overflow crowd (where the comments were overwhelmingly in favor of rejecting Xcel's offers), the city council voted six-to-three to continue with the PUC process.[46] In September 2017, the PUC released a ruling that, the city feels, 'creates a path forward for the city to proceed with municipalization,' and in November 2017 residents voted to renew a special tax that funds the effort.[47] A related campaign in Minneapolis, Minnesota also scored a major victory in late 2014 when the threat of municipalization forced Xcel and another energy corporation, CenterPoint, to sign a landmark 'clean energy partnership' with the city. Although the agreement did not include municipalization, it required the company to implement the city's comprehensive climate action plan, shortened its franchise agreement to 10 years (down from 20), established a community advisory committee, and gave the city an option to cancel the franchise after the fifth year.[48]

An interesting variant on public ownership tied to renewable energy development is Community Choice Aggregation (CCA). Now legally available in seven states, CCA allows local governments to pool consumer demand in order to secure new, clean sources of energy, offer electricity at lower rates than for-profit utilities, create local jobs and development, and regain local democratic control over energy-related decision-making. In the CCA model, a publicly owned agency is responsible for purchasing or generating electricity, which is then transmitted to the end user through the incumbent utility. 'Like [publicly owned] utilities,' the Local Energy

Aggregation Network explains, 'CCAs offer cost efficiencies, flexibility, and local control. But unlike munis, they do not face the capital-intensive and open-ended challenge of valuing, purchasing, and maintaining expensive utility infrastructure. CCA offers a "hybrid" approach that exists between the investor owned (often monopoly) utility and a municipal (or member coop) utility.'[49] In California, four CCAs – Marin Clean Energy, Sonoma Clean Power, Lancaster Choice Energy, and CleanPowerSF – are currently serving hundreds of thousands of people, and dozens of others are in development in most major jurisdictions.[50]

Around 87 percent of the US population is served by publicly owned water systems at the local, municipal level – significantly higher than in some other advanced economies.[51] Attempts at water privatization in the United States over the past few decades have generally been disastrous, and many have been reversed amidst public outcry. Between 2007 and 2014, the number of privately owned systems fell by 7 percent (and people served fell by 18 percent).[52] In Florida, for instance, a group called Friends of Locally Owned Water (FLOW) organized a highly successful campaign against the private water company, Aqua America, due to its repeated rate increases and poor service. In 2013, the company bowed to this pressure and sold off most of its water systems to the Florida Governmental Utility Authority as well as other local governments.[53] New efforts to privatize water systems are often met with concerted resident opposition. For instance, in 2013, residents in Bethel, Connecticut quickly mobilized against a proposal to sell the town's water utility to Aquarion, a company controlled by an Australian bank. In the resulting referendum, townspeople voted overwhelmingly against the sale.[54] More recently, in 2017, a coalition of activists in Atlantic City, New Jersey (including local and state chapters of the NAACP and ACLU) came together to protect the city's publicly owned water system from being sold off as part of the state's emergency takeover of city operations.[55]

One area experiencing tremendous public expansion is local, municipal ownership of high-speed internet systems. In recent years, more than 750 communities have established publicly owned full or partial networks, including 130 (in 27 states) with super-fast networks.[56] These publicly owned systems commonly provide higher speeds, better service, lower costs, and updated infrastructure in communities often neglected by large for-profit companies. In Chattanooga, Tennessee, the city's publicly owned utility (EPB – Electric Power Board), for instance, has been operating a fiber network since 2009, and was the first location in the United States to offer 1gb service.

The emergence of a municipal broadband network in the city has also forced the corporate provider, Comcast, to reluctantly invest in upgrading its service – even as EPB provides faster speeds and lower costs. In Wilson, North Carolina, the municipal broadband network became profitable nearly a year ahead of schedule. Market pressures have forced Time Warner to keep its prices down to compete (between 2007 and 2009 Time Warner raised its rates in non-competitive neighboring jurisdictions – where it exists as a monopoly – by as much as 52 percent, but kept prices stable in Wilson).[57]

Because of their increasing popularity, publicly owned internet networks have become a target for corporate lobbying. As a result, 20 states have enacted laws banning or restricting local municipalities from engaging in this type of wealth democratizing initiative, although some communities have begun to push back against these laws.[58] For instance, in the 2014 mid-term election, seven Colorado municipalities voted, via referendum, to opt out of state law in order to pursue publicly owned broadband networks (this was followed by another 19 during the 2017 election).[59] In an early 2015 decision, the Federal Communications Commission (FCC) backed such efforts by declaring its intent to pre-empt such state laws restricting local municipalization efforts with federal regulation. As expected, state governments – led by Tennessee and North Carolina – sued the FCC to overturn the pre-emption ruling. In August 2016, the Sixth Court of Appeals overturned the FCC ruling, stating that only a direct act of Congress could pre-empt state-level bans on local publicly owned broadband networks. However, the Court also affirmed the FCC's conclusion that municipal broadband had a variety of public benefits, including increasing competition. Speaking after the decision, Christopher Mitchell of the Institute for Local Self Reliance's (ILSR) community broadband initiative stated that 'this case is disappointing. [But] if the FCC had been affirmed, there would've been an appeal. We would've had another 18 months of uncertainty ... The FCC brought a lot of attention to the need for more [broadband] investment, and a lot of communities around the country have heard that. Even though the FCC had a setback, I think we're much better off since the FCC stepped in.'[60]

Another area seeing intense organizing is local, publicly owned banking. For instance, in late 2014 Santa Fe, New Mexico Mayor Javier Gonzales announced that his city was moving forward with a study on how to create a public bank. The city's existing provider of financial services, Wells Fargo, he explained, 'take[s] city revenues, taxpayer dollars, and [uses] those dollars as part of a loan portfolio for folks outside of Santa Fe and New Mexico.'[61] In late January 2015, the Santa Fe City Council approved a $50,000 contract with a local firm to investigate setting up such a bank, and a year later that firm released its findings, indicating that a public bank is indeed feasible and could provide an economic benefit to the city of more than $24 million in just its first year of operations[62] (the report also laid out a series of recommendations and incremental measures that could be introduced in lieu of or in preparation for the creation of a public bank).[63] In April 2017, the Santa Fe City Council voted unanimously to set up a Public Bank Task Force to study and establish the steps necessary for the creation of a city public bank.[64]

In early 2016, a month after the Santa Fe report was released, a hearing was held in Philadelphia, Pennsylvania on a public bank proposal after it was authorized unanimously by the city council.[65] In Oakland, California, city council members – with the backing of activist groups, including Friends of the Public Bank of Oakland (FPBO) – are moving forward on a public bank feasibility study.[66] And in July 2017, Los Angeles city council president Herb Wesson introduced a motion to begin investigating the possibility of a public bank in the nation's second largest city.[67] In addition to its potential to help Angelenos with affordable housing, one of the main motivations for setting up a public bank in the city is to support the state's booming legal marijuana sector, which is largely prevented from using traditional banking services due to federal drug laws.[68]

Several *states* are also moving in the direction of public banks. In early 2014, for instance, residents in more than 20 Vermont town meetings voted in favor of a proposal to turn the Vermont Economic Development Authority into a state bank.[69] Ultimately, the effort accepted a compromise in the state legislature, with the authorization of up to 10 percent of the state's cash balance (currently totaling around $350 million) being made available for investment in local enterprise – more or less fulfilling what would have been one of the proposed state bank's most important functions.[70] In New Jersey, Democrat Phil Murphy, recently elected to replace outgoing Republican Governor Chris Christie, has promised to pursue a public bank.[71] 'A public bank will allow New Jersey to invest in New Jersey, period,' Murphy has stated. 'It's the type of big thinking we need to get back on track.'[72] Similarly, in California, Lieutenant Governor (and 2018 Gubernatorial candidate) Gavin Newsom has expressed his support for a state-level public bank, echoing comments at the city level in Los Angeles and Oakland that such an institution is needed to support the state's marijuana industry.[73]

In the wake of the financial crisis of the late 2000s, much has been written about the nearly 100-year-old publicly owned Bank of North Dakota (BND), which has around $7.4 billion in assets and a loan portfolio of $4.3 billion.[74] Formed by an offshoot of the Socialist Party (the Nonpartisan League) in the aftermath of the First World War, the bank survived an early concerted assault by opponents (including a Wall Street boycott), eventually thriving and becoming institutionalized in the state's financial landscape. It directly helped North Dakota weather the financial crisis and recession by continuing to contribute revenues to the state's budget, backstopping local banks with liquidity (thereby ensuring that the state had the lowest foreclosure rate and lowest credit card default rate in the country, as well as no bank failures for more than a decade), and making loans to consumers while private banks were freezing credit.[75]

In praising the record of the Bank of North Dakota, it is important not to lose perspective. Operating in a politically conservative state, it has hardly been an engine for social justice and the development of alternative economic institutions. Recently, the BND was widely – and rightly – criticized for lending the state as much as $10 million to cover the costs of policing the American Indian-led Standing Rock protests against the Dakota Access Pipeline (although it is unclear whether or not the bank could have legally refused the state's order even if it had wanted to).[76] But its operating record as an instrument of state economic development is impressive nonetheless. In addition to the bank, North Dakota has another state-level public enterprise, formed around the same time, but that is far less well known. The North Dakota Mill operates eight milling units, an elevator, and a packing facility. It receives no subsidies from the state, has a payroll of $14 million, and contributes around 50 percent of its yearly profits back to the state's general fund.[77] Together, these institutions demonstrate that public enterprise can continue to flourish even in seemingly unfriendly political soil.

In neighboring Wisconsin, similar political and economic winds in the early twentieth century led to the creation of a publicly owned life insurance company in 1911. The State Life Fund is a non-profit business that offers basic coverage to any state resident at low costs. It receives no state subsidies and keeps its costs down by not advertising or using commissioned agents (also by being exempt from federal income tax and not extracting a profit).[78] As of 2013, the State Life Fund had 26,558 life insurance policies in effect amounting to around $204 million.[79] While enrollment has always remained relatively low (due to the low cap on coverage), the Fund has nevertheless withstood numerous privatization and repeal attempts over the course of its more than hundred-year history.[80]

Historians often refer to the US economy of the late nineteenth and early twentieth centuries as the 'Gilded Age,' a time of robber barons and monopolies when the wealth and opulence of the few stood in stark contrast to the poverty and squalor of the many. Aligned against this system was an interacting and evolving set of mass movements, political parties, and radical agitators representing different constituencies, ideologies, and strategies, including the Knights of Labor, the National Grange Movement, the Farmers' Alliance, the People's Party (the 'Populists'), the Progressive movement, the Socialist Party, and the New Dealers.

While most of these groups supported public ownership in one form or another, it was within the burgeoning socialist movement that it was most comprehensively articulated as part of a fully fledged systemic alternative. 'The whole of industry will represent a giant corporation in which all citizens are stockholders, and the state will represent a board of directors acting for the whole people,' the famous Socialist Party leader and five-time presidential candidate Eugene Debs declared in 1908.[81] The party's 1912 platform called for public ownership of, among other things, railroads, communication infrastructure, transportation, grain elevators, stock yards, warehouses, mines, oil wells, forests, water utilities, banks, and land.[82] In 1912, Debs received nearly a million votes in the presidential election, roughly 6 percent of the total popular vote.[83]

Reformist elements within the socialist movement saw local municipal politics as a vehicle toward socialism through gradual, rather than revolutionary, means. One of the most prominent municipal socialists was Victor L. Berger – co-founder, with Debs, of the Social Democratic Party (a forerunner to the Socialist Party), newspaper editor, and United States Congressman from Milwaukee, Wisconsin. 'Municipal Socialism is very important,' Berger wrote in 1906. 'There can be no doubt that Social-Democrats will carry cities and towns before they carry states, or before they carry a national election. Like everything else that is growing, Socialism must grow from the bottom up.'[84] Local public ownership was specifically conceived as one of the first steps in a political-economic program that would eventually provide the structural basis for the extension of socialist power to the state and national level. Through the takeover of utilities and other enterprises by the municipal government, wages and service would be increased while work hours and costs reduced. 'Little by little the conditions of the people are to be improved,' Carl Thompson, a socialist member of the Wisconsin State Legislature claimed in 1907, 'and thus, in every way, society will be gradually prepared for and led into the experience of Social-Democracy.'[85] For his part, Debs supported municipal socialist efforts but warned that they were, by themselves, not sufficient to build a socialist system.[86]

The question of how specific communities involved in building 'municipal socialism' related to larger socialist efforts and systemic theory was widely discussed at the time. 'The party,' historian Richard William Judd recalls, 'in fact, formulated a sophisticated justification for municipal politics ... In essence, this rationale was neither hopelessly idealistic nor grossly reformist. City politics was, above all, an educational exercise ... Municipal campaigns provided ideal forums for exploring class issues that touched workers' lives in very immediate and personal ways, and yet could be generalized into a Socialist critique of capitalism.'[87]

In practice, however, the 'socialist' component of municipal socialism was something of a misnomer. Despite political affiliation with the Socialist Party and ideological justification of the approach, the local policy agenda has been described by many historians as 'reform within the existing framework of government and economy.'[88] Upon seizing the reigns of municipal government, socialists often found themselves constrained by legal authority, opposed by hostile business and political interests, and limited by political ambition and a desire to remain in office. In some cases, this resulted in municipal socialists embracing progressive reform principles that were popular with both the socialist rank-and-file and the middle class and business interests. In others, it led to factionalism, infighting, and the fall of socialist administrations. Nevertheless, institutionally and rhetorically, public ownership was without doubt one of the lynchpins of the municipal socialist approach and a key component of its popularity. 'American socialism,' historian Bruce Stave writes, 'was most successful in winning power when it was most progressive; as "gas and water socialism," it espoused democracy rather than revolution.'[89]

Under socialist direction, many municipalities took direct control of public transport (including subways, trolleys, and buses), power systems (including power plants), telephone systems, sanitation systems, railroads, ice plants, transportation facilities (bus and train stations, as well as freight shipping facilities), grocery stores, coal distribution companies, and lodging houses. In Minneapolis, Minnesota, union machinist Thomas Van Lear was elected mayor in 1916 as a representative of the Public Ownership Party, a local offshoot of the Socialist Party that advocated for municipal ownership of utilities (among other things).⁹⁰ In Milwaukee, Wisconsin – one of the most long-lasting and also most reformist socialist strongholds – the 24-year administration of Socialist Party Mayor Daniel Hoan (1916–1940) established several publicly owned enterprises, including a stone quarry, a sewage disposal plant, a water purification plant, and a street lighting system.⁹¹ Starting in 1926, Milwaukee began producing and selling Milorganite, an organic fertilizer derived from the city's water reclamation process. This publicly owned enterprise continues to this day under the auspices of the Milwaukee Metropolitan Sewerage District.⁹²

In Schenectady, New York, the Socialist Party came to power in 1911 with the election of Pastor George Lunn (the young Walter Lippmann was his personal secretary). Two of the local government's first actions were to establish municipal ice and coal distribution businesses that would sell to customers at cost (court injunctions against the plans forced Lunn and his associates to skirt, or outright subvert, both the law and the businesses' 'public' nature in order to keep them running). Other public ownership initiatives established in the city with varying degrees of success included a municipal grocery store, a municipal employment bureau within the Department of Public Works, a municipal lodging house and farm, and a 'school of social science.'⁹³ For decades, the Public Ownership League of America (officially non-partisan, but led by municipal socialists, including long-time Secretary Carl Thompson) documented thousands of similar efforts across the country. In February 1922, for instance, it reported that 'over 700 cities have established municipal [electric] plants in the last five years,' and other publications that year included stories about the long struggle to municipalize railways in Detroit, attempts to municipalize sewer systems in Texas, and the success of publicly owned waterworks in almost all of America's largest cities.⁹⁴

Municipal socialism, and early twentieth century support for public ownership more generally, continues to have a lasting influence on ownership patterns in local economies decades after the last socialist strongholds fell. For instance, nearly all public transportation systems around the United States are publicly owned. These vital economic drivers directly and indirectly employ tens of thousands of local residents and move millions of people to and from jobs and other activities. Moreover, municipal ownership and development of land around public transport stops is becoming increasingly common. In Washington, D.C., for instance, the District government purchased land around the Minnesota Avenue Metro stop from the publicly owned transit authority and then built a municipal office building, a garage, and a residential building with ground-level retail.[95] This variant of 'transit-oriented development' allows the public at large to benefit from the rising property values around transit stations that occur due to substantial public investment, rather than seeing these benefits syphoned off by private developers. Moreover, to the extent that public ownership and development of such land is done with an eye to preserving affordability for lower-income residents, this can also ease growing gentrification and displacement pressures currently being experienced in many cities.

Similarly, many cities own public markets where space is rented out to individual vendors. Faneuil Hall in Boston and Pike Place Market in Seattle, both favorites of visiting tourists, are two of the most famous examples. Another kindred municipal land- and property-ownership strategy relates to hotels. Taking advantage of tax law changes in 1996 that allowed the use of tax-exempt municipal bonds to finance hotels (with certain criteria attached), publicly owned hotels can now be found in communities as different as Chicago; Omaha, Nebraska; Myrtle Beach, South Carolina; and Vancouver, Washington (near Portland, Oregon).[96] Moreover, according to Robert R. Nelson, many of these publicly owned hotels are constructed in support of another prominent element of local public ownership – convention centers.[97] The Vancouver Hilton Hotel & Convention Center, despite its name, is actually owned by the Vancouver Public Facilities District and leased by the Downtown Redevelopment Authority. In 2015, more than 126,500 people attended nearly 1,500 events at the convention center and the hotel generated $16.1 million in city revenue. Together, the hotel and convention center employ nearly 200 people (80 percent of whom live in the surrounding area) and spend $1.63 million with vendors in the state (45 percent in the surrounding area).[98]

Airports are perhaps the most obvious economically important areas of public ownership. These commonly operate like large real-estate businesses, in which airlines and shipping companies, together with restaurants, car rental companies, clothing stores, newspaper and magazine outlets, and many other businesses, all rent space. There are nearly 500 publicly owned commercial airports operating in the country (all told, there are more than 4,000 publicly owned airports).[99] In 2010, these airports were estimated to support directly and indirectly some 10.5 million jobs with total payrolls of $365 billion while producing $1.2 trillion in annual output.[100]

Alongside the post office and Amtrak (discussed below), airports have for many years been high up on the privatization wish list for conservatives and libertarians. In 1996, Congress authorized the Federal Aviation Administration (FAA) to begin a pilot program on airport privatization. Despite being re-authorized in 2012 (and the number of open slots in the program increased to 10), no major commercial airports have been privatized during the program's more than 20-year existence.[101] Midway Airport in Chicago was close to going through, but the deal stalled and then finally collapsed in 2013 amidst blowback from other failed privatizations in the city.[102] Currently, there are only three airports in the privatization program – two small, non-commercial airports, in White Plains, New York and Clewiston, Florida, and the medium-sized Luís Muñoz Marín International Airport in San Juan, Puerto Rico, which remains owned by the Puerto Rico Ports Authority but is operated on a 40-year lease by a private company.[103] Despite this thin record, President Trump has recently revived the idea of privatizing airports as part of an effort to jumpstart his infrastructure plans.[104]

There are also hundreds of publicly owned commercial ports in the United States that directly and indirectly support millions of jobs and trillions of dollars in economic activity.[105] Major port authorities include the Port Authority of New York and New Jersey, the Port of Los Angeles, Port Miami, the Port of Houston Authority, and the Port of South Louisiana. The Port Authority of New York and New Jersey, for instance, owns and operates five major airports, six bridges and tunnels, three bus terminals, five marine terminals, the PATH transit system, industrial parks, waterfront development projects, and the World Trade Center.[106] Though commonly dominated by special interest groups, and prone to political interference – as evidenced by the Port Authority, which is mired in political scandals, intra-agency feuds, and project mismanagement – a future, democratized model could deploy this precedent of large-scale public ownership for broader, more far-reaching purposes.

Around 20 percent of community hospitals in the United States are publicly owned (and another 58 percent are non-profit).[107] One of the more interesting models is Denver Health, a highly successful community-benefiting institution structured as an innovative blend of state-level public ownership and direct municipal accountability. As a subdivision of the state of Colorado, the Denver Health and Hospital Authority now has relative autonomy over decision-making, yet is subject to the state's open-meetings law (allowing for public involvement) and has a board that is appointed by the city's mayor.[108] In response to increasing healthcare costs, some states are also beginning to experiment with publicly owned health clinics for state employees. In 2012, the state of Montana opened a publicly owned health clinic that provides free checkups, blood tests, and shots to state employees and their dependents (the Montana Health Center now has six locations and is open to some local municipal workers as well).[109] While the facilities are run by a private company, the state purchases supplies, covers the total cost of patient visits, and pays all the employees' wages. Because of its ownership structure, the facilities are actually saving the state money because the lack of markup on services, the ability to buy supplies at lower prices, and the paying of doctors by the hour (rather than by the number of procedures they order) results in a lower cost per visit for patients. The vast expansion of preventative care associated with the clinic is also leading to a reduction of the costly hospital visits and major medical procedures that become necessary when diseases are left untreated.[110] In 2015, New Mexico opened a similar publicly owned clinic for state employees in Santa Fe. Launching the clinic, Republican Governor Susana Martinez stated that it would provide high-quality preventive care and save the state millions of dollars per year.[111]

There are roughly 98,300 public schools (kindergarten through 12th grade) in the United States. These schools educate around 50.4 million students and employ nearly 3.1 million teachers.[112] While not commonly thought of as such, public schools are large economic drivers in many communities. In *Public Schools and Economic Development: What the Research Shows*, former White House adviser Jonathan Weiss describes how public schools enhance productivity (at the local and national level), help localities attract and retain businesses, increase property values, stabilize the local tax base, and generate an economic multiplier effect (through payrolls, purchasing, construction, etc.).[113] Similarly, more than two million people are employed at the nation's nearly 2,000 public two- and four-year universities and colleges.[114] These institutions have annual expenditures of around $335 billion and tens of billions of dollars in endowments, making them major economic players in local communities.[115]

In many states, public ownership of alcohol distribution facilities is the norm. In Virginia, for instance, the Department of Alcoholic Beverage Control (ABC) operates 359 stores across the state, as well as wholesale and distribution facilities. It employs around 3,278 people and is a leading revenue producer for the Commonwealth. Since 1934 it has transferred $9.5 billion to Virginia's general fund (used to pay for education, public works, police and fire, etc.). In 2016, this public enterprise generated a record $165 million in profits and returned $433 million (another record) to the general fund in profits and taxes collected.[116] Similarly, most states own and operate lotteries which generate funds that are usually allocated to local public schools. Of course, public ownership of alcohol distribution and lotteries can be controversial. On the one hand, they are often criticized as amounting to an extra tax, of sorts, on poorer and more vulnerable residents.[117] On the other hand, they are sometimes attacked for their restrictive rules and regulations that are frequently rooted in religious objections to alcohol and in the so-called 'blue laws' (ABC stores in Virginia, for instance, operate restricted hours most days while further restricting hours on Sundays).

However, public ownership in this sector is both logical and rooted in historical experience. On the one extreme, such 'vices' could be banned outright. But this does not, and never will, prevent demand. When such bans are enacted and enforced, organized crime, together with the violence and corruption that accompanies it, can be counted upon to step into the void (this happened with both alcohol prohibition in the 1920s and Mafia control of gambling into the 1970s). At the other extreme, were these 'services' to be completely privately owned and operated, the ability to regulate consumption and abuse is usually diminished while wealth is funneled upwards from the mostly poor and middle classes to the rich (this is the pattern with for-profit casinos). For many localities, therefore, public ownership is a middle ground, by which gambling and alcohol are legal but regulated, with proceeds being returned to public purposes in the form of investments in services such as education and public safety.

For these reasons, public ownership is increasingly being considered as states across the country begin legalizing the sale of recreational marijuana. In addition to the growing calls for public banks to support the new industry, there are experiments with other more direct forms. In North Bonneville, Washington, for instance, the North Bonneville Public Development Authority has opened the nation's first publicly owned marijuana shop.[118] Championed by Mayor (and ex-Marine) Don Stevens, Cannabis Corner's mission is to 'revitalize the local economy and promote economic growth' and focus on 'public health and safety.'[119] Across the border, in the Canadian province of Ontario, the government has announced that publicly owned businesses will have the exclusive preserve on selling marijuana when it becomes legal on July 1, 2018. The 150 new stores (by 2020) will be run by the Liquor Control Board of Ontario. The government sees this as a way of generating substantial revenue and maintaining oversight and control of the industry (as well as shutting down existing illegal marijuana storefronts, some of which are operated by organized crime).[120]

Several US states also operate large publicly owned investment funds, sometimes called 'sovereign wealth funds.' The state of Alaska famously collects and invests proceeds from the extraction of oil and minerals in the state, and dividends from this fund – the Alaska Permanent Fund, administered by the publicly owned Alaska Permanent Fund Corporation – are paid out annually to all state residents.[121] In Texas, the publicly owned and operated Texas Permanent School Fund was formed in 1854 and subsequently endowed with large tracts of land and associated mineral rights. In 1953, coastal 'submerged lands' were added after being relinquished by the federal government.[122] Each year distributions from the earnings of this almost $40 billion fund support education in every county in the state, amounting to $1.05 billion in FY2016 alone.[123] Another $17.8 billion fund, the Permanent University Fund, owns more than two million acres of land and helps underwrite the state's public university system.[124] In other words, public ownership of land and investments in a variety of assets supports public education and other social services in ways that significantly reduce the state tax burden on local residents and businesses. State funds similar to those in Alaska and Texas exist in Alabama, Louisiana, Utah, New Mexico, Wyoming, and North Dakota.[125] Like other sovereign wealth funds around the world, these publicly owned funds are hardly paragons of participation, accountability, and transparency. However, given their structure and vast resources, they form the basis for numerous proposals to move, over time, in the direction of democratized community funds or public trusts, and provide a real-world precedent for advocates of a citizen dividend.[126]

On the federal level, one of the most cost-effective healthcare enterprises in the United States is a public entity – the Veteran's Administration (which is generally supported by veterans and their advocacy groups despite concerns over inadequate resources).[127] So, too, is the Social Security Administration, one of the largest pension providers in the world with more than 1,400 offices across the country and around 60,000 employees.[128] Around one-third of all the land in America is publicly owned and managed by federal, state, and local governments.[129] The federal government alone makes around $2 billion a year from oil, gas, and timber royalties, and $40 billion in tax revenue from tourism and recreation.[130] The federal government also operates around 140 banks and quasi-banks that provide loans and loan guarantees for a wide range of economic activities.[131] In 2009, then Secretary of Agriculture Tom Vilsack commented that if all of the US Department of Agriculture's lending activities were accounted for, it would be 'the seventh-largest bank in the country.'[132] One of the best known of these quasi-banks is the US Export–Import Bank, which provides trade financing options to American businesses when the private sector is unable or unwilling to do so.[133] In 2015, this previously obscure 80-year-old publicly owned enterprise came to public attention when Republicans in Congress, under pressure from their base to crack down on corporate welfare, let its authorization lapse. However, several companies, including GE and Boeing, threatened to move jobs overseas or lay off workers unless the bank was reconstituted, and powerful lobbying groups like the US Chamber of Commerce and the National Association of Manufacturers began pressuring legislators in both parties.[134] In late October 2015, the House of Representatives voted to re-authorize the bank as part of an unrelated highway funding proposal that was subsequently signed by President Obama.[135]

One of the most important public enterprises in the United States is the TVA. Established during the New Deal, this large publicly owned energy corporation currently serves nine million people in seven states around the Tennessee River Basin.[136] While it takes no taxpayer funds, its board of directors is appointed by the President and confirmed by the Senate.[137] At one point in the 1930s, President Franklin Delano Roosevelt supported legislation that would have created seven 'little TVAs' as a step toward a much more expansive economic development plan. 'If we are successful here,' he stated, 'we can march on, step by step; in a like development of other great natural territorial units within our borders.'[138] In part due to the centralizing thrust of the New Deal and then the Second World War, the TVA largely succumbed to bureaucratic and other corrosive pressures and has been rightly criticized on a number of issues, including a lack of democratic participation and a poor ecological record. Nevertheless, the TVA has endured as a publicly owned enterprise for the best part of a century despite the occasional proposal to privatize it. This is, in part, because it has built a local constituency of support in the region that crosses party and ideological lines. When President Obama proposed privatizing the TVA in 2013 as part of his annual budget, local Republican legislators, concerned with higher prices for consumers and less money for their states, vigorously – and successfully – opposed the idea.[139]

A similar situation exists with the United States Postal Service (USPS), a massive public enterprise that employs around half a million Americans (493,381 'career employees,' plus another 131,732 'non-career employees,' as of January 2016), operates a fleet of 214,933 vehicles and has operating revenue of $68.8 billion.[140] Interested both in eliminating a low-cost public competitor to private corporations such as FedEx and UPS and facilitating a mass transfer of valuable real-estate assets to private hands, the post office has been in the cross-hairs of US corporate interests and their political allies for years. As part of this lobbying campaign, Congress has repeatedly crippled the post office's ability to remain economically viable. In 2006, the Postal Accountability and Enhancement Act forced the USPS to pre-fund 75 years of its possible future retiree benefits in just 10 years – a whopping $103 billion a year. 'This is something that *no other government or private corporation is required to do and is an incredibly unreasonable burden,*' renowned consumer advocate Ralph Nader wrote in opposing the move.[141] According to Nader's calculations, if the pre-payment obligation had not been imposed, the USPS would likely be a profitable entity. Moreover, Congress has repeatedly stymied any and all attempts by the post office to rectify their financial situation by ending Saturday deliveries or closing sparsely used locations. However, so far, despite at least a decade of intense, concerted effort by the forces of capital and their political allies, the post office remains in public hands, a fact that looks unlikely to change in the near future. According to Richard Geddes of Cornell University, 'the U.S. Postal Service is nowhere close to being ready to be privatized. I wouldn't say it's impossible, but it would be well into the future at a minimum.'[142] Much of the reason for this is related to the widely anticipated negative reaction of the American public toward the consequences of privatization – namely, higher costs and reduced access, which has been the case with other postal privatizations such as the sell-off of the UK's Royal Mail.

The post office aside, perhaps the most well-known federal level public enterprise in the United States is Amtrak, the National Railroad Passenger Corporation. Amtrak currently carries around 30 million passengers a year, employs more than 20,000 people, and serves 500 destinations in 46 states, as well as the District of Columbia and three Canadian provinces.[143] Amtrak was created by Congress in 1970 after a series of privately owned railroads went bankrupt. The most spectacular of these was Penn Central Railroad, one of the top 10 largest corporations in the country at the time with over 100,000 employees. According to New America Foundation Senior Fellow Philip Longman:

> Penn Central's feuding top managers disagreed on just about everything except one point: they wanted in the worst way to get out of the railroad business. So they neglected maintenance of track and equipment, cooked the company's books, and used what capital they could raise trying to become a modish, 1970s-style conglomerate ... Penn Central's top executives also spent plenty of company dough securing the companionship of comely young women. Congressman Wright Patman fumed that this was 'one of the most sordid pictures of the American business Community that has ever been revealed in official documents.'[144]

Most of the remaining privately owned railroads voluntarily (and eagerly) transferred their passenger service routes and equipment to Amtrak, enabling them to focus on more profitable freight rail service.[145] Given the severely degraded state of the rail infrastructure Amtrak inherited – old locomotives and cars, crumbling stations – together with waning ridership numbers, most observers at the time, including politicians, saw the creation of Amtrak as a temporary experiment that would be quickly phased out along with passenger rail service altogether. However, as Amtrak upgraded infrastructure, addressed deferred maintenance issues, and centralized operations, ridership and popularity increased. It is now a critical part of the transportation system, especially in the well-travelled 'Northeast Corridor' between Washington, D.C. and Boston, Massachusetts.[146] Like the post office and the TVA, despite longstanding ideological opposition, Amtrak continues to survive as a publicly owned enterprise with support across ideological lines. In the Deep South, for instance, some state and local Republicans have recently endorsed and are promoting an effort by Amtrak to re-open the service between New Orleans, Louisiana and Orlando, Florida that was discontinued in the wake of Hurricane Katrina in 2005. 'I think we can make Amtrak work,' Republican Mississippi Sen. Roger Wicker told *Politico* in early 2017. 'We can make it more friendly to the taxpayer, and more efficient, but I think we need Amtrak, and I'll just say it.'[147] Interestingly, these local Republican politicians explicitly make the case for public ownership as a way to stabilize local economies. 'You're going to depopulate rural communities if you can't connect them to the larger economy,' John Robert Smith, a former Republican mayor of Meridian, Mississippi told the same reporter.[148]

In 1976, Congress created another publicly owned corporation – the Consolidated Rail Corporation (Conrail) – to begin operating the freight rail activities of Penn Central and five other bankrupt East Coast rail companies.[149] By the mid-1980s, Conrail had repaired the terrible state of the infrastructure and rolling stock it inherited from the private corporations, freed itself from price controls and other regulations, and streamlined its operations and management.[150] In 1986, the profitable and efficient company was privatized by the Reagan Administration. This pattern of nationalizing failing private corporations, returning them to profitability, and then selling them back to private owners in the name of the supposed superior efficiency of private ownership is an irony that has often been repeated throughout the modern era!

Another example of superior public operation of rail was the East Coast Mainline in Britain. Following the Thatcher-inspired, Major-implemented privatization of British Rail, extremely poor service and rising costs for consumers plagued the new privately owned railroads, despite sizable government subsidies.[151] In 2009, service on the East Coast Mainline route was re-nationalized (and subsequently run by a small publicly owned enterprise called Directly Operated Railways) after the private operator National Express simply walked away from the franchise.[152] Public ownership of the line improved service dramatically and began returning profits back to taxpayers – around £1 billion between 2009 and 2014. Despite this success (or perhaps because of it), the British government under Conservative Party Prime Minister David Cameron re-privatized the service in 2015. 'David Cameron's ideological selloff has ended a public sector service which has delivered over £1bn to the Treasury, kept fares down, had record passenger satisfaction and engaged the workforce with unparalleled success,' Labour Party Shadow Transport Secretary Michael Dugher lamented at the time.[153] A similar pattern, of course, was followed with the de-facto nationalizations and then quick re-privatizations of General Motors, Chrysler, AIG, and Citigroup during the financial crisis (discussed in further detail below).

Most publicly owned enterprises in the United States are structured traditionally in that the government, at various levels, exercises ownership rights directly – through an agency or department – or indirectly through a semi-autonomous authority. Workers, residents, neighboring jurisdictions, and others in the community usually have little opportunity to participate in decision-making when it comes to those rights (outside of the mostly advisory function served by public meetings). However, there are signs, albeit limited ones, that this may be beginning to change, at least in some areas. For instance, there are interesting new experiments and ideas around so-called 'public–public partnerships,' whereby publicly owned enterprises and services partner with other municipalities, workers, non-profit organizations, unions, public pension funds, or community groups. In the region around Baltimore, Maryland, for instance, small, local publicly owned water systems have begun to pool their purchasing with Baltimore City in order to lower costs and provide better service.[154] In Michigan, municipalities are contracting with other municipalities to upgrade infrastructure and provide services rather than with private companies, thus saving local taxpayers some money.[155] In Nashville, Tennessee and Miami-Dade County, Florida the local municipality has partnered with workers and their unions to cut costs and increase efficiency rather than resort to privatization. In the Miami-Dade case, the effort saved $35.5 million between 1998 and 2010 and led to increased service quality throughout the system.[156] And in Nebraska, publicly owned utilities have begun to engage and consult with residents around the construction of more renewable energy infrastructure, particularly wind.[157] There have also been some recent advances in harnessing the vast potential of public pension and union pension funds to partner with public entities for large-scale infrastructure projects. In 2011, for instance, the American Federation of Teachers and other unions pledged to invest $10 billion in American infrastructure over five years (in 2014, it was announced that they had met this goal two years ahead of schedule).[158]

While perhaps something of an outlier due to its progressive political orientation, Burlington, Vermont – where self-proclaimed Democratic Socialist and 2016 presidential candidate Bernie Sanders was once mayor – offers a look at how embedded public ownership is at the local level in the United States.

The city's waterfront – formerly a decaying industrial area – has been extensively redeveloped into a leisure and cultural center after residents voted in 1990 to pursue a public ownership and control strategy following the failure of previous private development proposals in the 1970s and 1980s.[159] The city's publicly owned electric utility – the Burlington Electric Department – is one of the greenest utilities in the United States, announcing in late 2014 that Burlington was the first city of substantial size in the nation to supply its residents with 100 percent renewable energy.[160] The municipally owned Burlington International Airport is a major economic driver in the region and has increased the number of passengers served in recent years. The city owns and operates the Church Street Marketplace, which operates 100 percent on self-generated revenues and has less than a 1 percent vacancy rate. It also runs the Fletcher Free Library, the largest and busiest public library in the state. The city owns and operates 700 apartments for senior citizens and people with disabilities, as well 340 apartments for low-income residents. The publicly owned Chittenden County Transportation Authority averages nearly 10,000 passengers a day. The Chittenden Solid Waste District owns and operates 10 solid waste and recycling facilities. The Winooski Valley Park District acquires natural land in and around Burlington for the purpose of conservation and permanent preservation. The Department of Public Works administers the city's publicly owned water and sewer systems, and the city also operates and maintains public schools, parks, infrastructure, cultural programs, a community and economic development office, a community justice center, community centers, and more.[161] Add to this the publicly owned University of Vermont and various federal public enterprises and funds (such as Amtrak, which stops at nearby Essex Junction, Medicare, Medicaid, Social Security, and the Veterans Administration), and it is highly likely that the typical Burlington resident encounters and interacts with public ownership many times each day.

For the most part, this local experience with public ownership in the Unites States, and in many places around the world, is uncontroversial – and a world away from the highly charged ideological debates and demands for wholesale privatization that have been part and parcel of the neoliberal consensus.

Chapter 2
The efficiency debate

The charge most commonly leveled against public ownership is that as a form of economic organization it is *inherently* less efficient than private enterprise. This belief became commonplace in the era of deregulation and privatization ushered in by Margaret Thatcher and Ronald Reagan and was greatly enhanced with the fall of the Soviet-style command economies.[1] 'The Thatcherites argued that wherever public enterprise played a major role, it suffered from bureaucratic inefficiency and waste,' radical economist Michael Hudson recalls.[2] The relentless public relations campaign waged against public ownership by the New Right in the postwar era was remarkably successful and continues to this day – as is evidenced in the still-common political refrain that 'government is the problem, not the solution.'

In reality, decades of studies have yielded no consensus as to the relative economic merits of public versus private ownership, and the issue remains hotly contested. 'The conviction that public production is inefficient has been sufficiently strong for empirical evidence to seem irrelevant,' economist Johan Willner wrote in 1996. 'Successful counterexamples do not make headlines ... The empirical research has been unsystematic, but there exists by now a fairly large number of industry studies which throw light on the relative efficiency of public ownership.'[3] 10 years on, revisiting the issue in 2007, Willner had not changed his mind.[4] In 2000, Tel Aviv University professor Yair Aharoni agreed, concluding that 'the assumption that ownership per se creates an environment that is conducive to high or low performance is not proven, and empirical research on this point has yielded conflicting results.'[5] More recently, Andrew Cumbers reviewed the experience of Korea, Taiwan, and Singapore and explained that 'contrary to the current received wisdom, the experience and performance of statist public ownership was highly varied.'[6] Moreover, Cumbers has concluded that the evidence does not support the widely held theory that privatized companies perform better than their previously nationalized counterparts.[7]

A plethora of other studies draw similar conclusions. In 1997, economists Stacey Kole and J. Harold Mulherin studied US government ownership of seized American subsidiaries of German and Japanese companies during and after the Second World War. They found no difference between these publicly owned firms and their private counterparts and stated that the 'results stand in contrast to the typical results regarding the inefficiency of government enterprise.'[8] Nor does experience from the developing world change the picture. In 2006, writing in the *World Bank Economic Review*, Colin Kirkpatrick, David Parker, and Yin-Fang Zhang found that, with regards to African water utilities, 'the results for cost efficiency and service quality fail to show that privatized water utilities perform better than state-run utilities' (these results supported similar prior research on the sector).[9] In a 2007 report for the United Nations Department for Economic and Social Affairs, Cambridge University economist Ha-Joon Chang found that, when it comes to performance, there is no clear case against state owned enterprises (and that, when such a case is made, it is often under 'stringent' and 'unrealistic' conditions).[10] In 2008, political economist Germá Bel and city and regional planning professor Mildred Warner analyzed 35 studies from the water and sewage sectors and found that in the majority there was 'no difference between public production and private production.'[11] Writing in the *Harvard International Journal* in 2009, Francisco Flores-Macias and Aldo Musacchio maintained that 'the world has changed' and certain modern public enterprises can be 'efficient, even in comparison to their private counterparts.'[12] And in 2014, the OECD summarized a number of studies of publicly owned German banks and wrote that 'savings banks appear to be at least as efficient as commercial banks.'[13]

Furthermore, recent studies of the British experience with public ownership offer a much more nuanced picture than the traditional view espoused by Thatcher and her supporters and successors. Productivity growth in nationalized British mining, utility, transportation, and communication firms, for instance, consistently outpaced similar privately owned industries in the United States.[14] 'Although it would not sit comfortably with the beliefs of new Conservatism,' observes economist Michael Oliver, 'economic historians have found that the long-term trend of productivity in Britain's nationalized industries was no lower than that for private firms.'[15] Similarly, the late economist and journalist Christopher Johnson – a supporter of privatization– found that 'many of the improvements in manning and productivity claimed for privatisation took place in nationalised industries before privatisation and in those not privatised.'[16] Michael Hudson argues that many of the problems that were emerging in British publicly owned enterprises by the time Thatcher came to power were due to a lack of capital investment and modernization resulting from Britain's unexpected embrace of monetarist money policy and IMF-led austerity in the 1970s. 'The problem,' Hudson writes:

> Could have been cured by letting government departments operate as independent public agencies off the balance sheet, like America's Tennessee Valley Authority (TVA) and other such entities. But the monetarist objective was not to make governments work better. Just the opposite: it was to claim that they could not work efficiently ... The last thing Mrs Thatcher and her advisors really wanted to see was a reform that would enable public enterprises to be run more efficiently.[17]

How efficiency is defined and conceptualized is rarely discussed, yet crucial to this debate. Most empirical studies focus purely on observable financial metrics, such as profits. For instance, in a 2001 survey of empirical studies – one of the most commonly cited pieces of evidence for the supposed superiority of private enterprise – privatization experts William Megginson and Jeffry Netter stated that 'to a large extent we ignore the arguments concerning the importance of equitable concerns such as income distribution ... The effects of privatization on productive efficiency, or at least observable variables that are proxies for productive efficiency, is the focus of most

Table 1 Productivity growth: UK and the US, 1950–1973 (annual average % growth in total factor productivity)

Sector	UK	US
Electricity	5.51	3.93
Gas	4.71	3.02
Coal mining	1.34	0.82
Railways	1.60	4.45
Air transport	11.53	9.55
Communications	2.13	1.73
Manufacturing	3.28	1.95

Table adapted from Robert Millward, *Private and Public Enterprise in Europe: Energy, Telecommunications and Transport, 1830–1990* (New York, NY: Cambridge University Press, 2005), p. 277.

of the empirical literature we review here.'[18] However, because publicly owned enterprises often exist to fulfill social, not just market, requirements, such traditional measures of efficiency are not always adequate as the basis on which to make comprehensive judgements. In their recent book, *Public Service Efficiency: Reframing the Debate*, Rhys Andrews and Tom Entwistle write:

> Our basic argument is that efficiency in the public sector is not just about maximizing the quantity of production outputs and minimizing the cost of production inputs; it also comprises the quality of production outputs, whether some citizens should receive more or better quality of outputs on the grounds of need, whether current output should be reduced to support investment in future service production, and the fit between the types of output produced and the outputs citizens want. In making the argument that there is more than one dimension (or face) of efficiency, we seek to establish that efficiency is a broader and more important concept than is often acknowledged ...[19]

Moreover, as Aharoni explains, in order to really measure efficiency accurately, it is necessary to measure the 'stimulus' public ownership provides to other social and economic activities.[20] In 2015, Holger Muhlenkamp conducted a comprehensive review of the efficiency comparison surveys to date and directly challenged Megginson and Netter, stating that:

> Counter to the argument of Megginson and Netters [sic] (2001) ... research does not support the conclusion that privately owned firms are more efficient than otherwise-comparable state-owned firms. This result might hold using profitability measures, but it does not hold if we use adequate performance indicators for public enterprises like productivity, cost, or welfare. When including the latter measures most of the recent studies find no support for the proposition that private firms perform economically better.[21]

Many other studies come to similar conclusions.[22] Even the World Bank summarizes the efficiency argument with an important warning about its focus on the profitability measure. 'An enterprise's profitability summarizes all the indicators of economic efficiency as seen from the viewpoint of its private owners,' it states:

> But from the point of view of national economic growth and development, social costs and benefits, which are not reflected in profitability, can

be no less important. For example, when a privatized enterprise achieves profitability by dismissing its excess workers, the economy as a whole does not necessarily become more efficient. If economic conditions prevent the fired workers from finding other employment or starting their own business, this downsizing might lead to an overall economic loss for the country because people were moved from low-productivity jobs to zero-productivity unemployment. Additional social costs may include increased child labor/lower educational achievement, a heavier load on the government budget for providing social services, higher crime, and greater social and political instability.[23]

A good example of how this focus on profits as the predominant metric of efficiency quickly becomes untenable can be seen in the case of 'remailing' in the postal industry. Remailing involves routing letters and packages through a third country that has lower postage rates.[24] For instance, a piece of mail being sent from the Netherlands to Germany (a neighboring country) could be sent first to India. 'The result is post being dragged all over the planet in order to increase profit!' Mark Rutgers and Hendriekje van der Meer explain. 'The number of actions and people involved, level of pollution, amount of time, etc. increase; remailing can only be judged efficient from the perspective of creating higher revenue (more profit) as the desired outcome. From every other conceivable perspective, it is inefficient.'[25]

Additionally, and again contrary to the dominant perspective, comparing the efficiency of public and private enterprises is actually quite difficult. 'In comparing SOEs to privately owned firms,' Megginson and Netter wrote, 'it is difficult, if not impossible, to determine the appropriate set of comparison firms or benchmarks.'[26] Furthermore, for a variety of reasons, including natural monopolies and suppression of competition, there are not usually directly comparable firms operating within the same sector of the same country at the same time. In one of the few studies to investigate roughly comparable firms – in this case public and private railways in Canada – Douglas Caves and Laurits Christensen found that competition improves efficiency and 'our principal conclusion is that public ownership is not inherently less efficient than private ownership'[27] (the issue of competition is analyzed further below). Another exception, often considered the best comparison, is the utility sector in the United States, in which public enterprises operate alongside private investor owned companies in roughly comparable markets (although they often don't compete directly). However, many studies, including those of Aharoni and Harvard professor John Donahue, have found that, in general, public ownership is no less efficient than private ownership in the sector.[28] In fact, a recent American Public Power Association (APPA) study found a median net transfer to municipalities of 5.5 percent of revenues for public utilities, 31 percent more than the median tax payment of investor owned utilities.[29]

Even when public ownership is deemed to be economically inefficient, there is often disagreement as to why this may be the case. Some argue that it is, in fact, due to ownership, while others contend that environment (such as competition, access to capital, political interference, etc.) plays a more important role. For instance, one study of the Indonesian privatization program of 1981–1995 by economist Ann Bartel and management professor Ann Harrison found that in fully privatized firms productivity rose by 1.6 percent, but that 'the same result, however, could be achieved by manipulating the environment.'[30] In other words, given certain changes to outside (not ownership) factors, publicly owned enterprises could have been as economically efficient as their privatized successors. 'Public ownership by itself,' they concluded, 'has no independent negative effect on either the level of productivity or on productivity growth.'[31]

Similarly, many analysts recognize that the theory of greater efficiency in privately owned firms depends on a number of factors and macro-economic conditions that often do not exist in real-world economic systems. For instance, a 2014 report for the International Monetary Fund (IMF) suggested that 'when certain conditions are met, competitive markets, with private firms supplying goods and services, do best at meeting consumer demands.' These 'conditions' include: 'a market for every good and service; perfect competition (i.e., no agents have market power); uniform information (everyone knows what anyone knows); costless contract negotiation and enforcement; uniform tastes and social welfare functions; [and] decreasing returns to scale production structures and no externalities.' When such conditions are violated, the report conceded, the public might be able to deliver the product or service more efficiently.[32] Needless to say, whether these 'conditions' have ever, or could ever, exist in practice is highly questionable, meaning that in most situations the theory of inherently superior efficiency of private enterprises does not hold.

None of this is to say that there are not inefficient public enterprises. There have been plenty – just as there have been a great number of extremely inefficient private enterprises. Nor is it to say that privatized firms have never produced better results than their publicly owned predecessors. Some of them, of course, have. The question is whether or not one type of ownership form (public) is less efficient than another (private). On this point, the empirical and theoretical literature is far from settled or unanimous. Understanding this is critical not only to demolishing the 'There Is No Alternative (TINA)' narrative that is used to justify privatization and the transfer of broadly held assets to a small elite, but also to enabling the development of a rigorous sectoral analysis, based on a broader array of economic, social, and environmental measures, to determine which different forms of ownership may deliver optimal results in which settings and circumstances. Lastly, removing the comparative inefficiency stigma can allow policymakers and others to more objectively analyze the structures, relationships, and support systems that can enable public ownership to be more successful.

Competition and autonomy

Diving deeper into the micro-economic efficiency discussion helps illuminate two issues that are important in attempting to understand how public ownership operates in contemporary economies and how it may fit into alternative political-economic models. First is the debate around the issue of competition and its effect on the efficiency of both public and private enterprise. On the one hand, many studies have shown that in certain circumstances competition improves efficiency in public enterprises. 'Empirical comparisons of public and private sector firms and studies of the effects of privatisation, measured in terms of costs of production, productivity, employment and various financial ratios, have tended to find that competition is more important than ownership in explaining efficiency differences,' Willner and his colleague David Parker wrote in 2007.[33] Similarly, World Bank researchers Mary M. Shirley and Patrick Walsh stated in 2000 that in theory the widely held view that competition increases efficiency could be extended to publicly owned companies.[34] They went on to discuss many of the studies for and against such an interpretation. Some of those that support the competition thesis include: John Vickers and George Yarrow (1989), who cited 'competition's information effect as an important influence on public-sector performance, but [did] not quantify the effect relative to ownership';[35] John Kay and D. J. Thompson (1986) who suggested that 'if competition is must be [sic] combined with a viable threat of exit such as a hostile takeover or bankruptcy, it will promote productive efficiency';[36] George Yarrow (1986), who, based on a study of firms in Britain before and after privatization, concluded that 'performance depended more on market structure than on ownership';[37] and Paul Cook and Colin Kirkpatrick (1988), who argued that in the developing world massive market failures would lead privatization to result in private monopolies and as such 'promotion of competition and continued state ownership produce the best results.'[38]

Additional studies published subsequently include those by: Scott Wallsten (2001), who studied telecommunications privatizations in Africa and Latin America and found that competition significantly impacted service quality and price, yet privatization by itself did not appear to have many benefits;[39] and Yin-Fang Zhang, David Parker, and Colin Kirkpatrick (2008), who studied privatization in 36 developing and transitional countries between 1985 and 2003 and concluded that while any economic performance gains from privatization and regulation were minimal, competition did seem to have a positive effect.[40]

However, on the other hand, some scholars are not as certain about the benefits of competition on public enterprise efficiency and even go so far as to suggest that in certain cases competition can reduce efficiency. In his classic work *Exit, Voice, and Loyalty*, the late economist Albert Hirschman relayed a story about the effect the building of roads and the introduction of trucking had on the publicly owned railroad in Nigeria. He theorized that one of the reasons the Nigerian railroad failed to improve efficiency in the face of competition was because 'the most aroused and therefore the potentially most vocal customers were the first ones to abandon the railroads for the trucks.'[41] In other words, a lack of competition may actually force customers (or members of society, in Hirschman's additional example of competition in public schools) to successfully agitate for greater public enterprise efficiency, service, or quality.

Another of the more commonly cited studies on the topic was published in 1989 by business professors Anthony Boardman and Aidan Vining. They began by confirming that existing empirical evidence 'provides weak support' for the theory that public enterprises perform less efficiently than private enterprises. However, they suggested, this was due to the fact that most studies focus on firms that enjoy either a natural monopoly (utilities, refuse collection, fire services, etc.) or a regulated duopoly (airlines, railroads, and financial institutions in certain places), or sectors (like healthcare) where 'output is not or cannot be priced by competitive forces.'[42] They went on to compare the 500 largest manufacturing and mining corporations in the world on the basis that they competed with one another, had a mix of ownership forms (private, public, and mixed), and were primarily concerned with profit maximization.[43] They concluded that 'there are performance differences between public and private companies in competitive environments,' and, more specifically, that publicly owned enterprises were less profitable than private enterprises, but more profitable than mixed enterprises.[44] In a 1992 follow-up study, Boardman and Vining stressed again that studies showing equivalent efficiencies in public enterprises and private were mostly based on firms that do not compete (monopolies) or have minimal competition in a regulated environment (duopolies). 'While these studies tell us something about the effect of ownership on performance in non-competitive, monopoly environments,' they wrote, 'by definition they cannot inform us about the effect of ownership in competitive environments.'[45]

In their 2007 paper, Willner and Parker added an important caveat, contending that competition may not increase efficiency in *all* circumstances. 'As for the impact of competition,' they stated, 'firms may in some situations become *less* efficient after entry … This may seem controversial, but the result applies to an oligopoly and does not mean that firms in an atomistic market would necessarily be less efficient than a monopolist.'[46] Thus, the evidence on the competition question is often varied, industry specific, and (at times) contradictory. Summarizing the debate, Muhlenkamp writes that 'the degree of competition seems to be meaningful. In a competitive environment the distinctions between public and private enterprise diminish or even disappear. This is the conclusion of several survey authors … Yet some authors reach the opposite conclusion. They state that private enterprise is preferable in markets with full competition.'[47]

Despite the conflicting results and conclusions of these studies, most scholars agree on one important component. Namely that in certain sectors and industries competition is *not* appropriate from an efficiency standpoint. 'There are, of course, some cases in which effective competition is neither possible nor desirable,' Shirley and Walsh wrote. 'These cases are usually natural monopolies, where indivisibility of networks or ever-increasing returns to scale dictate that the most efficient market structure is a single firm.'[48] Similarly, Megginson and Netter concluded that 'the justification for privatization is less compelling in markets for public goods and natural monopolies where competitive considerations are weaker.'[49] And Chang writes that 'SOEs are often in activities where there is a natural monopoly, and increasing competition is either impossible or socially unproductive.'[50]

From the perspective of developing a theory of how public ownership may fit into or become the basis for an alternative systemic model, the competition debate within the efficiency discussion suggests a mixed approach is likely optimal and offers some basic clues as to where public ownership may be desirable. To follow these clues, it is also instructive to review the so-called four conditions of perfect competition: homogenous products (each seller's products are essentially identical); many small buyers and sellers (so as to ensure that no individual seller or buyer, or group of sellers or buyers, can influence price); perfect information (all parties have the same high level of information about price, quality, supply, etc.); and low or no barriers to entry (new firms can enter the market at will and compete with existing firms).[51] Almost all economists agree that these conditions are likely never met in real life, leaving varying degrees of imperfect competition in different sectors.

In some sectors, it may be appropriate for publicly owned enterprises to compete with privately owned enterprises, cooperatively owned enterprises, or even other publicly owned enterprises. In others, it would be best if public enterprises existed without competition or with minimal competition in a highly regulated environment.[52] And in still others, public ownership may not be necessary, and cooperative/worker, private, and or community/social ownership is likely to yield better results. More specifically, the academic studies alongside real-world observations suggest that in sectors where natural monopolies exist, especially with regard to the provision of essential or basic goods and services, public ownership is a viable option and should likely exist with little to no competition from private enterprises, depending on the sector and the performance of the publicly owned enterprise. In instances where publicly owned enterprises are judged to be performing poorly economically, yet it is important that they be kept in public hands for social, economic, or environmental reasons, a limited amount of competition – with private or even other public enterprises – may serve to improve performance.

The second issue is that of autonomy (sometimes referred to as managerial or operational autonomy) and its effect on efficiency. The focus on the effects of autonomy has its roots in various management theories and schools of thought, including agency theory, property rights theory, and New Public Management (NPM). 'These theories,' Koen Verhoest and his colleagues write, 'emphasise the benefits of autonomy in the sense of specialisation and the consequent superior performance (economy, efficiency and effectiveness) but only if enough incentives for the public agency to perform well are present.'[53] However, whether or not there is a strong link between managerial autonomy and increased efficiency is debatable. Verhoest *et al.*, contend that the empirical evidence linking autonomy to better performance is 'inconclusive.'[54] However, economist Henry Tulkens suggests that if certain measures are taken to remove 'factors over which the firms' management has no control,' then some studies 'show that efficiency is indeed enhanced by increased managerial autonomy.'[55]

The traditional response in economics and public policy to concerns over the managerial autonomy of public enterprises – outside of advocating for privatization – has been to promote reforms that often maximize managerial autonomy and independence. The OECD, for instance, published a report in 2015 titled *Guidelines on Corporate Governance of State-Owned Enterprises*, itself an update to a similarly titled 2005 report, in which they provided suggestions 'for how governments should exercise the state ownership function to avoid the pitfalls of both passive ownership and excessive state intervention.'[56] First and foremost, the report is remarkable in that, despite protestations of support for privatization and private enterprise, it is essentially an acknowledgment by some of the world's most powerful champions of neoliberalism (the OECD and its member state representatives, as well as the World Bank and a host of other inter-governmental organizations which were observers to the group producing the report) that public enterprise serves a critical economic and social role throughout the world, one that is unlikely to disappear any time soon.[57]

Second, the report proposes many common sense reforms, such as: clearly defining what part of the state is responsible for exercising ownership rights; having that (preferably singular) entity held accountable to relevant representative political bodies; providing public enterprises with clear objectives and autonomy to achieve those objectives; ensuring that the ownership function is separated from other relevant state functions (such as regulation of the enterprise); actively exercising the state's ownership rights; implementing transparency, disclosure, and reporting standards; and establishing compensation strategies that attract and retain skilled professionals and also incentivize medium- to long-term positive performance.[58] Many of these suggestions have been seconded by scholars and other international organizations.[59] Ha-Joon Chang, for instance, explains how South Korea reformed its SOE sector in the 1980s by focusing on managerial autonomy – and, specifically, on streamlining government inspections and audits, banning the appointment of outsiders to managerial positions (to reduce political interference), and introducing a new evaluation and bonus system that took into account both traditional measures like profitability and productivity, and qualitative measures such as long-term planning, product quality, research and development, and organizational improvements.[60]

Some of the OECD guidelines, however, are more controversial from the perspective of how public enterprises might operate in an alternative future political-economic system. For instance, the report states that 'SOEs undertaking economic activities should not be exempt from the application of general laws, tax codes and regulations. Laws and regulations should not unduly discriminate between SOEs and their market competitors.'[61] Part of this would include mandating that 'SOEs' relations with all financial institutions, as well as non-financial SOEs, should be based on purely commercial grounds' and that 'economic activities should not benefit from any indirect financial support that confers an advantage over private competitors' – including not receiving 'inputs (such as energy, water or land) at prices or conditions more favourable than those available to private competitors.'[62] Another component would be to allow creditors to push public enterprises into bankruptcy if necessary.

Given what we know from the discussion of public ownership thus far, it is not difficult to anticipate ways in which this could be problematic if it were incorporated into an alternative systemic design. In most advanced capitalist economies, a 'level playing field' between competitors regardless of ownership doesn't exist anymore than does a 'free market.' Deliberately targeting some of the advantages public enterprises enjoy for the sake of competition seems counterproductive, especially given the empirical research suggesting conflicting results regarding the effect of competition on efficiency. For instance, publicly owned utilities in the United States have an advantage over private utilities in that they are able to access capital at lower interest rates through municipal bonds (which are generally exempt from federal taxes).[63] These advantages allow public utilities to return more money to their localities (in lieu of local taxes) as well as offer lower or comparable rates to consumers. Moreover, it is unclear how much of a financial advantage this amounts to vis-à-vis private utilities, given that the latter are often larger and can thus take advantage of economies of scale (to say nothing of public subsidies derived from their political power) in a way publicly owned utilities usually cannot. Either way, deliberately increasing the cost of capital by removing the municipal bond financing or tax-exempt advantages to create a 'level playing field' would serve only to weaken and harm publicly owned utilities, as well as, by extension, municipal finances and local economies and consumers. Similarly, one could envision a future systemic arrangement whereby for a variety of reasons related to local control, inequality, economic development, and the provision of basic services, a publicly owned bank would lend capital to a public enterprise at a preferential interest rate – or even at no interest.

Many of the reforms articulated by organizations like the OECD point generally in the direction of corporatizing public ownership and aligning its structure and incentives with traditional market-based economic approaches. However, structuring public ownership in this way risks replicating some of the detrimental social, environmental, and ecological outcomes found in private corporations – such as a constant pressure to suppress labor 'costs' (including wages), externalize environmental costs, undermine regulations, move production facilities, participate in risky (even fraudulent) business practices, and subvert or ignore democratic control. Therefore, while not ignoring short-term economic and financial measures, the question of managerial autonomy generally, and suggestions to reform the management and oversight of publicly owned enterprises specifically, must be analyzed carefully and through the lenses of democratization, participation, transparency, public accountability, sustainability, and long-term social benefit.

A more immediate problem arises when we consider how public enterprises are, and should be, operated during times of crisis. As we have seen, a dominant feature of the prevailing system of corporate capitalism is that large, 'systemically important' private companies are saved by the state (rather than allowed to fail) – often through outright or de facto nationalization. Moreover, it is relatively uncontroversial that there will be further economic crises – especially given the increasingly financialized banking system. As law professor Steven Davidoff revealed in an extensive paper on the ownership and governance structure of entities nationalized during the financial crisis of 2008–2009, the dominant pro-market, pro-private enterprise economic perspective led to the worst of both worlds when it came to the governance of enterprises bailed out or nationalized during the crisis.

First and foremost, the government was ideologically committed to making the interventions as temporary as possible.[64] Second, the government was loath to take appropriate equity stakes in the companies it was bailing out with public funds (as would have been the norm in any commercial investment), leaving 'money on the table' and diminishing returns. Last, and most important, the government explicitly and purposefully forfeited its ownership rights and direct control in order for the enterprises to retain their corporate and commercial orientation. For example, the US Treasury Department stated with regards to the GM nationalization that 'after any up-front conditions are in place, the government will protect the taxpayers' investment by managing its ownership stake in a hands-off, commercial manner. The government will not interfere with or exert control over day-to-day company operations.'[65] However, according to Davidoff, 'in practice ... the government, including the Treasury Department, surpassed these principles. In its AIG, Bank of America, Chrysler, Citigroup, GM, and GMAC investments, the government deliberately ceded even more control than this policy envisioned.'[66] This included refusing to vote the government's shares in all but the most critical decisions and a reliance on 'soft-control mechanisms.'[67]

This type of governance structure opens up the possibility for all sorts of opaque backroom dealings that are at the heart of the managerial autonomy critique. For instance, with regards to AIG, Davidoff writes that:

> Behind the scenes, though, the government still exerted real control ... News reports gave the impression that the Treasury Department still wielded great day-to-day authority ... The government thus operated AIG in a queasy vacuum. AIG was supposed to be a private company but the government's ownership brought political considerations into its operating decisions. Its quasi-public nature often left the public wondering about the measure of control the government asserted ... Meanwhile, it was an open question about how this ambiguity affected the day-to-day performance of the company and its ability to create value for its largest stakeholder, the federal government.[68]

Other problems identified by Davidoff include: an adversarial relationship between ownership (the government) and management (private businesspeople); the government's lack of ability to restrict executive compensation (seen as unfathomable by the general public); the sporadic or non-existent implementation of important government economic programs, such as lending and preserving home ownership; and the general re-allocation of wealth to private owners (rather than the general public). In Davidoff's view, the potential deficiencies of this approach to nationalization were never really tested due to a market upswing (as the result of other government policies, such as the stimulus) that restricted taxpayer losses, and the swift and determined transition back to private ownership. In essence, by going to such extreme lengths to avoid accusations of outright nationalization, the US response to the financial crisis was a disaster from a management perspective, invoking every standard criticism of state intervention into market economies. Yes, in most cases the government made its money back (and some), but the process was devoid of transparency and left the basic, flawed structure of the industry and its perverse incentives essentially intact. It is hard to believe that a pure capital for stock transaction with the government exercising full voting rights, establishing direct and delineated control, and setting specific goals (social, economic, or otherwise) in a fully transparent manner would not have been preferable to the messy, hybrid approach actually taken by the US government.

While the debate around efficiency is complex and at times highly technical, one conclusion is inescapable. When considering what role public ownership can and should play in contemporary and alternative systems, it is vital to carefully examine both the internal structure of the enterprise and its relationship to other political and economic institutions. Getting the structure and relationships wrong – for instance, establishing a publicly owned monopoly where some degree of competition would be appropriate, or tasking a public enterprise with potentially conflicting objectives (such as both maximizing employment and maximizing profits), or establishing so much managerial autonomy that public accountability is forfeited – risks undermining popular and political support for the enterprise (and the concept of public ownership more generally) and opens the door to criticism (and arguments in favor of privatization) on economic efficiency or other grounds.

Chapter 3
Why public ownership?

Public ownership need not be ruled out as a tool of economic policy and strategy on efficiency grounds, but why would we want to deploy it anyway? There are countless reasons why a local community, region, or nation–state might want to pursue public ownership – many based on local customs, culture, and priorities. The 2015 report by PricewaterhouseCoopers discussed above notes that 'the motivations for state ownership can wax and wane over time, but … SOEs are likely to remain an important instrument in any government toolbox for societal and public value creation given the right context.'[1] From a purely economic perspective, one of the most enduring and important reasons societies have repeatedly turned to public ownership over the years is *market failure* – broadly defined as the inability of markets (within a market-based economic system) to allocate goods or services efficiently, or at all.[2]

'Markets do not work well under strong economies of scale combined with large sunk costs leading to market power of incumbent firms,' economist Ingo Vogelsang wrote in 1990. 'The traditional public interest view of public enterprises then is that they were created to correct such market failure. It turns out that many public utilities and public transport have precisely these characteristics (natural monopoly, large and lumpy sunk cost, nonstorable output, nontradeable, strong linkages).'[3] Similarly, Shirley and Walsh found that in certain political systems with significant market failures, those running publicly owned companies could produce better results than their private sector counterparts.[4] More recently, University of Texas management professor Mike Peng and his colleagues have argued that 'despite SOEs' many imperfections, one of their often unacknowledged *benefits* is that they reduce transaction costs in economies infested with severe market failure.'[5] Market failure can manifest itself in a multitude of different ways, but common examples include the refusal of private enterprise to serve less profitable or unprofitable geographies and populations (like rural residents, the poor, or the sick) or the detrimental effects private enterprise can have on other people and businesses, also known as *negative externalities* and including, for instance, environmental pollution or even the destabilizing of the entire global financial system.

In addition to correcting market failures, public enterprises can also exist for a variety of other social and economic purposes including, as was noted in a 1979 World Bank report by Armeane Choksi, industrialization, planning, regional development, technology transfer, national security, employment maximization, and the reduction of inequality.[6] Other purposes suggested over the years include aiding macro-economic policy through setting and controlling prices and increasing the quality of products.[7] In his 2007 report, Ha-Joon Chang added two more: capital market failure and externalities. The first refers to a scenario in which private investors refuse to fund (or refuse to fund with reasonable conditions) a project or industry that has high short-term risk and/or high long-term rewards.[8] The second is when there are 'discrepancies between private and social returns' – or, in other words, when the long-term benefit to the overall economy of having a publicly owned enterprise outweighs 'the return to the company alone.'[9] Finally, there is also the reason of natural monopoly – when various technical and capital requirements tend to favor a single supplier and, for reasons of curbing or regulating the abuse such a position of political economic power incentivizes, a publicly owned enterprise is often preferable (this will be discussed further below as part of a sectoral analysis of public ownership options).[10]

For governments at the local or regional level, one of the principal motivations for pursuing public ownership is its capacity to generate revenues that can then be used to support social services or reduce taxes. This is the case with large public sovereign wealth funds such as those in Texas, which underwrite the education system, and Wyoming, where proceeds are used to fund state services in lieu of an income tax – a fact about which conservatives there are very proud.[11] In smaller communities, revenues from publicly owned utilities are often a crucial component of city budgets. In Edmond City, Oklahoma, for example, the local public utility, Edmond Electric, contributed more than $6 million to the city's general fund as well as $500,000 to the Economic Development authority in 2013–2014, amounting to around 13 percent of total city revenue. 'Such assistance,' the city manager Larry Stevens stated at the time, 'has allowed the City of Edmond to avoid any increases in the general sales tax rate in the General Fund for many years.'[12] Returns from profitable public enterprises are also used to underwrite high-quality public service provision. In Munich, Germany, for instance, the large publicly owned utility company Stadtwerke München uses revenues from its operation of electricity, transportation, gas, and water businesses to run 18 state-of-the-art public swimming facilities as well as various sports, culture, and education programs.[13]

Public ownership and inequality

Another important reason advanced in favor of public enterprise is that it serves as a public policy instrument that can be used to reduce income and wealth inequality. 'Public enterprise,' Vogelsang maintained, 'is a means to effect less visible income and wealth redistribution than could be obtained by direct transfer and more precise redistribution than by regulation.'[14] The most obvious way in which this operates is through the return of profits to the general public via public balance sheets, rather than allowing them to accrue to a small elite group of individual owners. Another means is through the deliberate reduction of differentials in remuneration rates by which executive compensation is kept in check. In his best-selling 2014 book *Capital in the Twenty-First Century*, Thomas Piketty wrote: 'Let me return now to the causes of rising inequality in the United States. The increase was largely the result of an unprecedented increase in wage inequality and in particular the emergence of extremely high remunerations at the summit of the wage hierarchy, particularly among top managers of large firms.'[15] Along the same lines, Lawrence Mishel and Alyssa Davis of the Economic Policy Institute (EPI) found in 2015 that:

> The chief executive officers of America's largest firms earn three times more than they did 20 years ago and at least 10 times more than 30 years ago, big gains even relative to other very-high-wage earners … Consequently, the growth of CEO and executive compensation overall was a major factor driving the doubling of the income shares of the top 1 percent and top 0.1 percent of U.S. households from 1979 to 2007.[16]

While there are few systematic studies comparing pay and compensation structures and ratios (due, in part, to the previously discussed comparison issues) there is some evidence in support of the commonsense intuition that publicly owned enterprises likely fare better than their for-profit counterparts on such measures. Due to its unique structure, the electric utility industry offers a case study in the actual compensation of managers in sufficiently comparable privately owned versus publicly owned enterprises. In 2016, Bill

Johnson – CEO of the largest publicly owned power company in the country, the TVA – made a total of $4.9 million in *direct compensation* and $6.45 million in *total compensation* from a base salary of $995,000.[17] By contrast, the median direct compensation for companies in the 'TVA peer group' was $8.18 million.[18] The TVA's $10.6 billion (in 2016) in revenue was roughly equivalent to that of the private corporations Xcel Energy ($11.1 billion in 2016) and Sempra Energy ($10.18 billion in 2016), and more than PPL ($7.5 billion in 2016).[19] In 2015, Ben Fowke, Chairman, President, and CEO of Xcel Energy, made total compensation of $11.5 million; Debra Reed, Chairman, President, and CEO of Sempra, made total compensation of $18.8 million; and William Spence, Chairman, President, and CEO of PPL, made total compensation of $15.5 million.[20] These figures, and the fact that median salaries and wage increases at TVA are similar to those at privately owned utilities, suggests that pay ratios (between top executives and the median employee) at the TVA are significantly lower than their private utility counterparts.[21]

Similar disparities can be found regarding railroads and banks. Joseph Boardman, the former CEO of Amtrak, which has around $3.2 billion in revenue and more than 20,000 employees, made around $350,000 per year (with total compensation of approximately $500,000).[22] By contrast, in 2015 the CEO of Kansas City Southern, a company with $2.4 billion in revenue and only 6,670 employees, made a base salary of $900,000 and received total compensation of $7.9 million – nearly 16 times as much as his public sector counterpart at Amtrak.[23] The CEO of the publicly owned Bank of North Dakota (with around $7.4 billion in assets), Eric Hardmeyer, makes around $260,000 per year.[24] Comparable private banks include Pennsylvania-based Northwest Bancshares, Inc., where in 2015 CEO William Wagner made a base salary of $628,175, and Massachusetts-based BerkshireHills Bancorp, where in 2015 CEO Michael Daly made a base salary of $700,000 per year.[25]

Piketty also referenced changing ownership patterns as a way to reduce inequality, stating that 'more generally, it is important, I think, to insist that one of the most important issues in coming years will be the development of new forms of property and democratic control of capital.'[26] In subsequent discussions of the book, he also acknowledged the importance of returning to the ideas of British Nobel Prize-winning economist James Meade, contending that 'in the book I probably place too much emphasis on progressive taxation, but I do talk about the development of new forms of governance and property structure, but probably not sufficiently.'[27] Meade, for his part, argued for 'property owning democracy' and a form of liberal socialism whereby the state would focus on 'pre-distribution' through changing property rights and employee ownership schemes rather than resorting to traditional redistributive measures.[28] Meade, as historian Noel Thompson recalls:

> Argued too for the extension of public ownership, seeing it as a necessary adjunct to the business of macroeconomic management and as a means of attaining the objectives of greater efficiency and equity. In his *Introduction* he envisioned a situation where the state would own sufficient property to be able not only to ensure 'that the optimum amount of national income is saved' but also 'to achieve a considerable degree of equality in incomes and to finance its ordinary expenditure *without resort to commodity or income taxes*.'[29]

William Edmundson argues that Meade operated from a baseline understanding that public ownership was indisputably superior to private ownership in certain sectors (including railways, utilities, healthcare, education, and more) and that 'what Meade proposed … was a hybrid strategy combining the diffusion and equalizing of property owned privately with an *increase* of state ownership in the British economy as a whole.'[30]

Traditionally, one of the most effective checks on economic inequality has been the existence of strong trade unions. A 2011 study by sociologists Bruce Western and Jake Rosenfeld found that 'unions helped institutionalize norms of equity, reducing the dispersion of non-union wages in highly unionized regions and industries' and that 'the decline of organized labor explains a fifth to a third of the growth in inequality.'[31] Repeated studies have also demonstrated that wages for unionized workers are consistently higher than their non-unionized counterparts. In the 1960s and then again in the 1980s, H. Gregg Lewis found that this 'wage premium' was between 10 and 20 percent.[32] Similarly, in 2013 a report by the US Bureau of Labor Statistics found that throughout the 2000s, unionized workers made between $3.55 and $4.26 more per hour than their non-unionized counterparts.[33]

In addition to wages, benefits are also traditionally higher in unionized workplaces. According to EPI, 'unionized workers are more likely than their nonunionized counterparts to receive paid leave, are approximately 18% to 28% more likely to have employer-provided health insurance, and are 23% to 54% more likely to be in employer-provided pension plans.'[34] As unions have declined, so have benefits such as retirement provision through union and company pension plans. In 2013, the Bureau of Labor Statistics reported that only 18 percent of private sector employees were covered by a defined-benefit pension plan, down from around 35 percent in the early 1990s (during the early 1980s, pension plans covered more than 80 percent of full-time workers in large companies).[35] In many private companies, these defined pension plans have largely been replaced by systems in which individual – rather than corporate – contributions create (or fail to create!) some modicum of retirement income. As EPI points out, 'though many workers are now enrolled in 401(k) plans, these have proven to be a poor substitute, as the typical household approaching retirement has less than two years' worth of income saved in these accounts'[36] (to make matters worse, the large pools of capital that were accumulated by occupational pension schemes were deployed by the financial services industry to undermine the position of unionized workers and export their jobs via overseas investment and mergers and acquisitions – all in the name of the single-minded pursuit of shareholder value).[37]

The importance of unions in reducing inequality is relevant to the discussion of public ownership because in the United States union density has declined from a post-war peak of around 34.7 percent of the labor force in the early 1950s to 10.7 percent today.[38] This decline is almost entirely attributable to the private sector, as currently the public sector (which includes public enterprise) has significantly higher unionization rates than the private sector: 34.4 percent versus 6.4 percent in 2016.[39] 'During the late 1930s and 1940s the US experienced a sudden, steep rise in private sector unionism,' economist Barry Hirsch wrote in 2013:

> It plateaued during the 1950s and then began a long, steady decline. Public sector unionism, however, grew rapidly during the late 1960s and early 1970s following the passage of state collective bargaining laws. Union membership among public sector employees during the last thirty years has grown at about the same rate as has the overall workforce, maintaining a relatively constant share of public sector employment.[40]

Moreover, studies have shown that pay for union members in the public sector is consistently higher than for non-union members. In 2015, for instance, this amounted to around $151 more per week.[41] Also, while defined pension plans have declined precipitously in the private sector, they persist in the public sector. 'The future prospects for DB pension plans in the public sector are more favorable,' the Social Security Administration wrote in 2009. 'Very little of the shift from DB to DC plans has occurred in the public sector.'[42] The public sector also plays a powerful role in reducing economic inequality based on race and gender. 'Historically, the state and local public sectors have provided more equitable opportunities for women and people of color,' a 2012 EPI report maintained.[43] In 2011, women accounted for 59.5 percent of employment in state and local public sectors, compared to 46.7 percent in the private sector, and 48.3 percent of total employment.[44] Similarly, African-Americans accounted for 12.8 percent of employment in state and local public sectors, compared to 10.3 percent in the private sector and 10.9 percent of total employment.[45]

The issues of inheritance, unearned and earned income, and the intergenerational transfer of wealth have long been a focus of those concerned with equality, justice, and fairness in society. It is increasingly understood that a substantial portion of what a person earns today takes the form of a tremendous 'free gift' from society, both past and present – including thousands of years of accumulated knowledge and technology, from mathematics to combustion engines to computer processors.[46] In the 1950s, for instance, the Nobel Prize winning economist Robert Solow demonstrated that just under 90 percent of productivity growth in the first part of the twentieth century was due to technical change (including technology and education).[47] Similar ideas – albeit not always articulated in quite the same manner – go back hundreds of years. Thomas Paine, who emigrated from Britain and became one of America's Founding Fathers, wrote that 'all accumulation therefore of personal property, beyond what a man's own hands produce, is derived to him by living in society; and he owes, on every principle of justice, of gratitude, and of civilization, a part of that accumulation back again to society from whence the whole came.'[48] To address this, Paine proposed that a national fund be established, funded by inheritance taxes, which would then pay out both a capital grant to all people upon reaching adulthood as well as an annual pension after the age of 50.[49] Similarly, in the eighteenth and nineteenth centuries, the great British philosophers Jeremy Bentham and John Stuart Mill argued that inheritance should be limited on the grounds of reducing inequality and achieving economic justice.[50] 'Mill,' Robert Ekelund, Jr. and Douglas Walker wrote in 1996, 'was interested in intertemporal redistributions of wealth and income that would be supportive of a diffusion of property rights and enhanced ex ante equality and opportunity on the part of poor and working class (indeed, all) members of society. These redistributions would flow from hereditary fortunes in concentrated ownership to ever-changing lower classes of society.'[51]

Around the same time in France, the followers of the revolutionary-era political-economic theorist Saint Simon took these arguments one step further and insisted that inheritance should be abolished, and that in a new, non-exploitive order, 'the state, and no longer the family, will inherit the accumulated riches insofar as these form what the economists call production resources.'[52] Drawing on these ideas, Marx and Engels called for 'abolition of all rights of inheritance' in the *Communist Manifesto*. Later, during the First International (The International Workingmen's Association) Marx elaborated and argued for an extension of already existing inheritance taxes and the 'limitation of the testamentary right of inheritance.'[53] Criticizing the Saint Simonians and others, Marx stressed the transitional nature of abolishing inheritance, stating that 'all measures, in regard to the right of inheritance, can therefore only relate to a state of social transition, where, on the one hand, the present economical base of society is not yet transformed, but where, on the other hand, the working masses have gathered strength enough to enforce transitory measures calculated to bring about an ultimate radical change of society.'[54]

In the United States, the discussion of inheritance and unearned income and wealth continued through the early part of the twentieth century. In his 1910 'New Nationalism' speech, for instance, Theodore Roosevelt argued that:

> The really big fortune, the swollen fortune, by the mere fact of its size acquires qualities which differentiate it in kind as well as in degree from what is possessed by men of relatively small means. Therefore, I believe in a graduated income tax on big fortunes, and in another tax which is far more easily collected and far more effective – a graduated inheritance tax on big fortunes, properly safeguarded against evasion, and increasing rapidly in amount with the size of the estate.[55]

In 1916, an inheritance tax (the estate tax) was enacted. However, it has been repeatedly weakened to the point where now only around 0.2 percent of American estates actually pay any estate tax.[56] Recently, however, Piketty has put the question of inheritance back on the table in a powerful way. 'Whenever the rate of return on capital is significantly and durably higher than the growth rate of the economy,' he argues:

> It is all but inevitable that inheritance (of fortunes accumulated in the past) predominates over saving (wealth accumulated in the present) ... If the twenty-first century turns out to be a time of low (demographic and

economic) growth and high return on capital (in a context of heightened international competition for capital resources), or at any rate in countries where these conditions hold true, inheritance will therefore probably again be as important as it was in the nineteenth century.[57]

If, as Piketty suggests, the question of inheritance and its link to increasing inequality re-emerges as a point of contestation as the twenty-first century progresses, the idea of using inheritance taxes as a transition strategy to increased public ownership may become ever more relevant. In 1929, the British political theorist and guild socialist G. D. H. Cole suggested that inheritance taxes should be raised, and deployed 'in such a way as gradually to bring the productive capital of the nation under public ownership as well as public control.'[58] One option for how this could occur would be to strengthen inheritance taxes – for instance, by removing exemptions and raising rates – and directing all revenue collected into a publicly owned fund or series of funds based regionally or locally that would make investments (including equity stakes) in businesses and other assets. This would also mitigate some of the criticisms of estate taxes based on concerns about capital formation and economic growth. Dividends from the fund(s) could then be distributed back to every member of society in the form of a basic income, invested in research and innovation, and/or allocated to socially beneficial purposes, such as funding education, infrastructure, and healthcare. Such an approach crudely combines two of Meade's proposals, the first being that the government should take and hold an ownership stake in a wide variety of companies (without managing them directly) through investment trusts and then distribute the proceeds via some form of a citizen dividend; and the second being a system of inheritance taxation that extends to gifts made during life and incentivizes the broad redistribution of large capital holdings after death.[59]

Public ownership and automation

Whether based on inheritance taxes or other funding mechanisms (such as Meade's proposed capital tax), ideas about such publicly owned funds specifically – and public ownership more generally – are likely to grow in importance given the massively disruptive potential of technological change and automation in the coming decades. According to the McKinsey Global Institute research firm, around half of all the job-related activities people perform around the world are vulnerable to elimination by automation if existing technology is adopted, amounting to some $15 trillion in wages.[60] From driverless cars and trucks to financial services, the potential for automation is expanding to all new industries and sectors – including so-called knowledge work. Related to this question is the issue of the nature of work itself. Already technology is being linked to a rise in precarious work conditions with few protections or traditional benefits (Uber's 'independent contractors' are a classic example). 'What is clear is that the new technologies are disruptive, have increased the ease by which corporations can redesign and relocate production and labour, and have added to the growing inequality and insecurity,' Guy Standing wrote in late 2016.[61]

While many of the media headlines warning of an employment Armageddon are probably exaggerated (there is scant evidence that automation is leading to large-scale job losses in the current economy), and such worries about technological advance under capitalism have repeatedly been present historically, automation and technological change cannot be ignored – especially in an age of widening inequality, increasing political and social turmoil, and the growing threat of climate change. If managed correctly, the further development of the productive forces offers the potential for a fundamental re-evaluation of work and time. 'Technology,' as Derek Thompson wrote in 2015, 'could exert a slow but continual downward pressure on the value and availability of work … Eventually, by degrees, that could create a new normal, where the expectation that work will be a central feature of adult life dissipates for a significant portion of society.'[62] This echoes the famous prediction by John Maynard Keynes in 1930 that, with 'the economic problem' of scarcity finally resolved, in the future people's greatest concern would be how to occupy their free time.[63] However, it is not difficult to imagine the difficulties that could arise if automation and technological change is managed incorrectly. 'The great danger posed by the automation of production, in the context of a world of hierarchy and scarce resources,' *Jacobin*'s Peter Frase writes, 'is that it makes the great mass of people superfluous from the standpoint of the ruling elite.'[64]

Suggesting ways to deal with the anticipated effects of automation and technological change is becoming something of a cottage industry, with proposals ranging from a universal basic income to expanding the earned income tax credit to a job guarantee. However, for some observers, the question comes down to 'who owns the robots?' As economist Richard Freeman puts it, 'if the distribution of capital remains narrow, as it is now, the main beneficiaries of robotization would be a small number of wealthy owners, while the living standards of the vast majority of workers would suffer.'[65] For Freeman and many others, the answer is an expansion of various forms of democratized ownership. For instance, the Labour Party's *Alternative Models of Ownership* report maintains that 'automation has an emancipatory potential for the country's population, but the liberating possibilities of automation can only be realised – and the threats of increased unemployment and domination of capital over labour only countered – through new models of collective ownership that ensure that the prospective benefits of automation are widely shared and democratically governed.'[66]

An increase in public ownership specifically could open up a wide range of possibilities for a broader distribution of the productivity gains from automation. Either directly, via revenues generated from publicly owned and operated companies, or indirectly, through returns generated by one or more publicly owned investment funds with ownership stakes in companies and other assets, a wide variety of programs and initiatives aimed at mitigating the effects of automation and technological change could be instituted and financed – a basic income, job retraining, a reduced work week, a job guarantee program, free education, compensation for unpaid care work, and more. Additionally, public ownership offers the ability to assert democratic control over the process, progression, and pace of automation. The existing Silicon Valley style-creative destruction/disruption method of deploying technological breakthroughs benefits some, but is likely incompatible with a future in which the fruits of those advances are broadly shared.

Public ownership and democracy

Yet another important reason put forward in favor of public ownership relates to democracy – both in terms of reducing the influence of elite individual and business interests in the political system and asserting democratic control over economic decision-making (the latter will be discussed further below). In the United States, it is widely believed, by both scholars and the public, that privately owned corporations are undermining America's democratic system of governance through financial contributions to political candidates and the lobbying of government agencies and legislatures at all levels. This has become especially pronounced in the wake of recent Supreme Court decisions such as *Citizens United* that have loosened restrictions on political expenditures by corporations and other groups. In this context, it is instructive to compare the lobbying and campaign contributions of publicly owned and privately owned enterprises.

Once again, publicly owned and privately owned electric utilities and energy companies serve as a useful comparison. During the 1990s, lobbying by the electric utility sector dramatically increased in connection with political discussions over deregulation, and specifically whether or not the 1935 Public Utility Holding Company Act (PUHCA) should be repealed. That legislation essentially gave utilities a monopoly in a certain geographic area but restricted their activities to that area.[67] On the one hand, it limited competition between utilities that may have driven down prices. On the other hand, it prevented large utilities from rapidly consolidating the utility sector by buying up smaller providers, which in turn could have led to less competition and higher prices. Large privately owned utilities generally favored repealing PUHCA, while smaller privately owned utilities, publicly owned utilities, and cooperatives opposed repeal.[68] In 2005, the large privately owned utilities prevailed and PUHCA was repealed through passage of the Energy Policy Act (EPAct) of 2005.[69] However, EPAct gave the Federal Energy Regulatory Commission (FERC) new and enhanced powers to, among other things, review mergers and acquisitions by electric utilities and holding companies.[70]

In 2014, the electric utility sector spent a total of $121.9 million lobbying the federal government – with the FERC being a prominent focus of their efforts.[71] The top twelve spenders were all privately owned utilities and their trade associations. These were: Southern Co. ($12.34 million); Edison Electric Institute ($8.47 million); American Electric Power ($6.51 million); Duke Energy ($5.87 million); Exelon Corp. ($5.13 million); NextEra Energy ($4.79 million); Energy Future Holdings Corp. ($3.96 million); Entergy Corp. ($3.21 million); General Atomics ($3.2 million); PG&E Corp. ($2.94 million); and Edison International ($2.57 million). By contrast, the first public utility related organization that appeared on the list was the American Public Power Association at 37th, spending just $763,819 – less than 10 percent of the expenditures of the trade association representing privately owned utilities, Edison Electric Institute.[72] All told, publicly owned companies (and their trade associations) accounted for roughly 25 percent of total lobbying entities, and spent a total of just around $7.04 million, a mere 5.7 percent of the sector's total lobbying expenditures.[73] Most telling is that privately owned utilities, energy companies, and their trade associations accounted for just under 90 percent (around $107.1 million) of the electric utility sector's total lobbying expenditures. Even acknowledging the fact that privately owned utilities provide power to around 68 percent of the industry's total customers, the evidence from this sector suggests that private companies lobby more often and spend greater sums than their publicly owned counterparts.[74] 'Municipal and government utilities ... are also active in lobbying elected officials,' the Center for Responsive Politics reported prior to the repeal of PUHCA, 'albeit to a much lesser degree than the wealthy investor-owned utilities.'[75]

Closely associated with the question of democracy is the issue of transparency. On the one hand, knowing how much any enterprise influences the political system, and benefits from it, is important from a public policy (and competition) perspective. On the other, accurate and accessible information about the operation of an enterprise is a critical prerequisite for effective democratic control, oversight, and participation. Whether it is to protect trade secrets, preserve relationships and privileges, prevent reputational damage, or gain an advantage over competitors, most economic enterprises are, by their nature, somewhat secretive and opaque. Over the years, various laws and regulations have been established, forcing companies to adopt basic standards regarding transparency, often to ensure investors have adequate and accurate information. These include releasing information about the company's businesses and management, having financial statements certified by independent auditors, reporting certain lobbying and campaign expenses, and filing information with the government on a periodic basis (which is then made available to the public).[76] Yet, these laws are full of loopholes and exemptions (shell companies, off-shore tax havens, and size thresholds, for example) and in many cases rely on the enterprise to voluntarily release accurate information.

Traditionally, many publicly owned enterprises have been no better – and in some cases worse – than privately owned companies when it comes to transparency. Indeed, many of the governance reform recommendations by consultants and intergovernmental organizations stress the need to raise transparency standards in publicly owned enterprises.[77] However, public enterprise transparency can be relatively easily enhanced and mandated through public policy, if so desired.[78] Take, for instance, the example of Amtrak. The publicly owned railroad is subject to Freedom of Information Act (FOIA) requests and maintains a public record of all FOIA applications; it publicly posts annual reports and audited financial statements, as well as monthly unaudited performance reports; and its various reports and requests to Congress are made public, as are its service, infrastructure, and business planning documents.[79] Congress, through legislation, can mandate increased transparency and determine what information is released to the public at any time. In many cases, publicly owned enterprises at the state and local levels are also subject to both open records laws and open meetings laws – the latter usually requiring that the enterprise announce meetings and publicly post agendas and other documents in advance, allow the public and press to attend the meeting, and publicly disseminate meeting minutes.[80]

Of course, private enterprises could also be forced, through new or existing legislation and regulatory authority, to increase transparency. However, in the existing political-economic context, these efforts are bitterly resisted as an increased regulatory burden and an unwarranted state intrusion into business – and often not implemented unless there is a major crisis or scandal. The 2002 Sarbanes-Oxley Act, for example, included a number of important new regulations and rules concerning corporate transparency. However, it was only passed in the wake of a number of devastating accounting and accountability scandals, the most prominent being the collapse of energy giant Enron.[81] Since its passage, repealing the Sarbanes-Oxley Act has been a priority for conservative politicians, think thanks, and industry lobbyists, and these calls have been growing louder following the election of Donald Trump.[82] Moreover, one of the first pieces of legislation signed by the Trump Administration was a repeal of the Obama era regulation – consistently opposed by industry and their lobbyists – requiring energy companies to disclose payments made to foreign governments.[83] By contrast, increased transparency requirements for public enterprises are often ideologically uncontroversial. For instance, the Passenger Rail Reform and Investment Act of 2015 – which, among other things, imposed new transparency requirements on Amtrak – was introduced by a bi-partisan group in the House of Representatives, including Pennsylvania Republican Bill Shuster and Oregon Democrat Peter DeFazio, and passed 316–101, with 132 Republicans and 184 Democrats in favor.[84] Similarly, in November 2017, the voters of Boulder, Colorado enacted new transparency requirements as part of the effort to municipalize their local electric utility. Frustrated that the city council had conducted many municipalization-related meetings behind closed doors, voters approved a ballot measure that prevents the city council from using executive sessions to discuss the effort. Afterwards, Councilperson Sam Weaver hailed the vote, indicating that he believed that the process would be more transparent in the coming years.[85]

When it comes to democracy, what concerns some academics is how varying deficiencies in democratic political systems affect public and private enterprises and are exploited by them. For example, in 1990 Shapiro and Willig theorized that in imperfect political markets, managers of public enterprises are motivated by both social welfare and private welfare (personal benefits or political pressures) considerations, and 'the less efficient the market, the more weight managers place on private welfare.'[86] In what Megginson calls 'one of the best analyses of the political motivations underlying state ownership,' Leroy Jones suggested in 1985 that when imperfect political markets exist, state owned firms can be used by politicians to transfer wealth and favors primarily from lower-income groups into politically connected groups in the middle and upper classes.[87] Similarly, Peng et al., contend that while most firms 'value political resources and capabilities,' state owned firms will utilize their 'strong connections with officials' to a variety of ends – including enacting policies which, for better or worse, protect their interests.[88] However, one of the important takeaways from these studies is that the degree to which a publicly owned enterprise will positively or negatively interact with the political system has a lot to do with the question of the structuring of the political economic system itself.[89] While this is undoubtedly cause for concern, given the arguably highly degraded state of contemporary American politics, it suggests that in future alternative systems there is no reason why public ownership, properly structured, couldn't in fact be both an important democratic bulwark against the rise of elite money and influence in politics, and avoid many of the negative effects of so-called 'nonmarket-based political ties.'

Finally there is, of course, an enduring argument on the political right, often tracing its lineage to Austrian economists Friedrich Hayek and Ludwig von Mises, that *by definition* public ownership – especially traditional forms of state ownership – is incompatible with political freedom and democracy. For instance, economist Bruce Caldwell, editor of *The Road to Serfdom: Text and Documents – The Definitive Edition*, states that 'though Hayek had many targets in the book, the idea that socialism – state ownership of the means of production – is compatible with political freedom was certainly a chief one.'[90] However, this view is far from unanimous, even on the intellectual Right. In his famous book *Capitalism and Freedom*, Milton Friedman, perhaps the best-known modern proponent of 'free markets' and private ownership, was far more nuanced, suggesting that despite such concerns, in some instances public ownership could be preferential to private ownership, especially if competition was allowed. 'The choice between the evils of private monopoly, public monopoly, and public regulation cannot, however, be made once and for all, independently of the factual circumstances,' he wrote. 'If the technical monopoly is of a service or commodity that is regarded as essential and if its monopoly power is sizeable, even the short-run effects of private unregulated monopoly may not be tolerable, and either public regulation or ownership may be a lesser evil.'[91]

Public ownership and innovation

Another of the principal criticisms of state involvement in the economy in general, and public ownership in particular, is related to innovation. Every American schoolchild is taught that one of the main reasons the Soviet economic model failed was its structural inability to innovate (there are, though, good reasons to doubt much of this conventional account). In politics, economics, and popular culture, the United States is often portrayed as a place where business innovation thrives in spite of the state, and not because of it. The classic, but misleading story, of individual tech entrepreneurs launching the computer age out of their California garages is only the most prominent example. This characterization of the process of innovation in an economy bears at best an uneasy relationship to reality. Going back to Alexander Hamilton and beyond, the United States government has often taken an active role in the development of business and industry. In his *Report on Manufactures* (1791), for instance, Hamilton urged Congress to deliberately encourage and support industrial development.[92] Additionally, his semi-publicly owned First Bank of the United States successfully made loans to individual entrepreneurs and businesses (averaging around 8 percent return on its investments).[93] While both the First Bank and the similarly constituted Second Bank of the United States were ultimately scrapped and the subsidy and incentive portions of the *Report on Manufactures* never enacted, Hamilton's ideas ended up in the ascendant. 'Since its founding fathers, the United States has always been torn between two traditions,' economist Erik Reinert writes, 'the activist policies of Alexander Hamilton (1755–1804) and Thomas Jefferson's (1743–1826) maxim that "the government that governs least, governs best". With time and usual American pragmatism, this rivalry has been resolved by putting the Jeffersonians in charge of the rhetoric and the Hamiltonians in charge of policy.'[94]

In 2013, economist Mariana Mazzucato detailed the extent and impact of such active economic interventionism in her widely-acclaimed book *The Entrepreneurial State: Debunking Public vs. Private Sector Myths*. In her introduction, Mazzucato wrote:

> Across the globe, countries, including in the developing world, look to emulate the success of the US economy. In doing so, they look at the power of 'market-driven' mechanisms, versus what might seem like old-style, State-driven mechanisms in places like Europe or the ex-Soviet Union. But the United States is not what it seems. The preacher of the small State, free-market doctrine has for decades been directing large *public* investment programs in technology and innovation that underlie its past and current economic success.[95]

The Entrepreneurial State painstakingly shows how everything from iPhones (and internet technology generally) to pharmaceutical drugs to fracking technology to renewable energy have their roots in publicly owned research facilities and large public R&D expenditures. 'This book has a controversial thesis. But it is basically right,' the *Financial Times'* Martin Wolf wrote in his review. 'The failure to recognise the role of the government in driving innovation may well be the greatest threat to rising prosperity.'[96]

Activists and politicians alike appear to be re-appraising their ideas about the state's economic role, especially in times of austerity, increasing inequality, and impending ecological catastrophe. In 2012, for instance, President Barack Obama ignited a firestorm of controversy when on the campaign trail in Virginia he stated:

> If you were successful, somebody along the line gave you some help. There was a great teacher somewhere in your life. Somebody helped to create this unbelievable American system that we have that allowed you to thrive. Somebody invested in roads and bridges. If you've got a business – you didn't build that. Somebody else made that happen. The Internet didn't get invented on its own. Government research created the Internet so that all the companies could make money off the Internet.[97]

Conservative commentators pounced, replaying the line 'you didn't build that' over and over again – but they were unable to refute the underlying point. More recently, UK Shadow Chancellor John McDonnell has highlighted Mazzucato's work, stating emphatically that the Labour Party's goal is to create an entrepreneurial state in Britain. 'The state has a role in the economy, working with entrepreneurs and wealth creators, developing and investing in the long term, in patient, long-term investment in research and development and science, helping people develop the products and the markets in that way to create a prosperous society,' he has argued.[98] For McDonnell and others, this does not mean a return to the over-centralized, and over-bureaucratized forms of state intervention prevalent during much of the twentieth century. Mazzucato, for her part, demonstrates the important role of local and regional governments (as well as decentralized networks) in the 'entrepreneurial state,' and McDonnell has called for local councils to create 'entrepreneurial local states.'[99]

Public ownership and the environment

Lastly, there is a growing understanding within the environmental movement that public ownership is a potentially important tool – especially when it comes to the particularly thorny issues of climate change and growth. As we have seen, faced with the intransigence of for-profit fossil-fuel burning corporations, activists and civic leaders in Boulder, Colorado and elsewhere (especially in Europe) have seized on the idea of municipalizing or re-municipalizing local utilities to transition to renewable energy sources and combat climate change. Elsewhere, as was done in Burlington, Vermont, existing publicly owned utilities are being tasked with sourcing 100 percent of their energy from renewable sources. 'Socialization or public ownership ... has the potential of facilitating the shift from fossil fuel energy sources to renewable energy sources and what has come to be known as a "just transition" for workers who will be displaced in the former and transitioned to the latter,' Hans Baer writes in *Global Capitalism and Climate Change*.[100]

What is increasingly concerning many environmentalists is the existence of a so-called 'carbon bubble' in the world economy. Specifically, the current market valuations of the world's for-profit fossil fuel corporations are built upon reserves (oil, gas, coal) that simply cannot be burned if the world is to stand a chance of staying below an acceptable level of climate change.[101] The fear is that either this bubble will force those corporations to continue burning their reserves, thereby dooming planetary civilization, or the bubble will burst, whether through state regulation, public pressure, or cratering demand (perhaps due to reactions to the early onset of climate change effects), destroying the existing world economy. As is discussed further below, some environmentalists and analysts are beginning to float the idea of nationalization (via a buyout) of at least the coal industry, and perhaps even of the fossil fuel sector as a whole.

Also being asked is the related question of whether exponential economic growth on a finite planet can continue indefinitely. While this matter is somewhat complex and controversial, the basic issue is that, historically, economic growth has been accompanied by and predicated on increasing natural resource extraction (fossil fuels, minerals, timber, etc.) and environmental degradation (greenhouse gas emissions, water pollution, species loss, deforestation, etc.). Unless economic growth can be 'decoupled' from resource usage and pollution, then it is ecologically unsustainable and simply cannot continue indefinitely. In 2004, Donella Meadows, Dennis Meadows, and Jorgen Randers released a 30-year update to their groundbreaking 1972 report *Limits to Growth*. In it, they ran 10 computer models for the world through the year 2100, with most resulting in 'overshoot and collapse – the depletion of resources, food shortages, industrial decline, or some combination of these and other factors.'[102] In 2014, Graham Turner of the University of Melbourne tested the 'Limits to Growth' projections against real-world data and found that through 2010 the two matched up pretty well. 'Our research does not indicate that collapse of the world economy, environment and population is a certainty,' Turner and his co-author Cathy Alexander concluded. 'Nor do we claim the future will unfold exactly as the MIT researchers predicted back in 1972 ... But our findings should sound an alarm bell. It seems unlikely that the quest for ever-increasing growth can continue unchecked to 2100 without causing serious negative effects – and those effects might come sooner than we think.'[103]

Private corporations and other for-profit businesses – especially those with shares that are publicly traded – are often forced to adopt a very short-term mindset of immediate profits and performance lest they be punished by shareholders and or find themselves outmaneuvered by competitors. 'Too many CEOs play the quarterly game and manage their businesses accordingly,' Paul Polman, the CEO of Unilever has stated. 'But many of the world's challenges can not be addressed with a quarterly mindset.'[104] This short-termism complicates (or outright prevents) the ability to reduce resource usage or environmental externalities to a sustainable level. 'The corporate sector of society has provided numerous beneficial goods and services for people around the world, but mostly without regard to environmental impacts such as pollution and rapid consumption of finite resources,' biologist Walter Dodds writes. 'Any effort to control the global consequences of human population growth and resource use must consider corporate behavior, which probably is more predictably selfish than the behavior of any other social group. Companies will usually attempt to maximize short-term over long-term profits.'[105] Moreover, there is emerging evidence that if natural resources and environmental externalities were appropriately priced, many companies would not actually be profitable.[106] This further casts doubts on the likelihood that large for-profit private corporations would, or even could, become truly ecologically sustainable.

Public enterprises, on the other hand, are not necessarily constrained by the same short termism. They could, if required, sacrifice immediate economic performance for the longer-term social and economic benefits of reducing resource usage or pollution. They do not necessarily have to grow; they could be confined to a specific geographic area or business line and insulated from certain competitive pressures. They could be tasked with producing higher-quality goods and services (rather than higher quantity) and have limits placed on their ability to advertise (as with the Wisconsin life insurance business discussed above), both of which could help reduce consumerism and the negative impacts of our throw-away culture.[107] Describing the approach of what he calls 'proponents of community economics,' Gabor Zovanyi explains that because 'for-profit corporations are driven by growth and profit imperatives, and as a result ... demonstrate what has been described as "an inexorable, unabatable, voracious need to grow and expand,"' the alternative is 'a local business structure based largely on nonprofits, cooperatives, and public enterprises.'[108] Because these institutions 'are capable of surviving at marginal rates of return,' he adds, they would not be subject to the same growth and resource-use pressures as for-profit enterprises.[109]

In conclusion, the reasons put forward in favor of public ownership can generally be grouped into three overlapping categories: economic – for instance, relating to market failure or generating public revenues that can support public services or reduce the reliance on taxation; distributional (or distributive) – such as reducing inequality or increasing employment; and control – in the form of establishing or re-establishing some form of democratic control over, popular participation in, and transparency of economic and political decision-making at all levels. Related to all of these is the concept of displacement: specifically, creating and developing a range of alternatively structured institutions (such as publicly owned enterprises, worker owned enterprises, non-profits, etc.) that will push out and ultimately replace the traditional, exploitative for-profit corporate forms that are engines of economic extraction, rising inequality, alienation, ecological despoliation, and social atomization. The contemporary and historical experience with public ownership, the implications of the efficiency debate on the structure of public ownership and its relationship to other institutions, and the reasoning behind, and rationale for, public ownership comprise the building blocks upon which a more nuanced understanding of public ownership can begin to emerge, and a theory (or theories) of how public ownership may fit into any alternative future system design can begin to be developed.

Chapter 4
Public ownership and alternative system models

Public ownership is prevalent in all contemporary political-economic systems, but it is also to be found in many if not most modern visions and models of alternative political-economic systems – especially those emanating from the left of the political spectrum. What exactly should be the role of public ownership in any vision or visions of a desirable next system beyond corporate capitalism and state socialism?

It is worth stepping back for a moment to situate this discussion in the traditions of radical political economy and the search for systemic alternatives to capitalism. For as long as there have been organized societies, there have been impulses toward radical alternatives – competing visions of how humanity might better arrange itself around versions of the good life. These include the (sometimes unfairly dismissed) tradition of 'utopian' visions, including early modern examples such as St. Thomas More's *Utopia* and Francis Bacon's *New Atlantis*. In the nineteenth century, ambitious works by so-called 'Utopian Socialists' included blueprints by Robert Owen, Charles Fourier, and Henri de Saint-Simon – not to mention, in an American context, Edward Bellamy's *Looking Backward*.

The dominant strain of Marxian thought on the left tended to reject such exercises – although not entirely. It is also to be found (as my colleague Joe Guinan and I have been exploring) in the 'red thread' of an emerging, disappearing, and then re-emerging tradition of thought on both sides of the great twentieth century division of the left into opposing communist and social democratic camps. It might be summarized as the return, time and again, to the basic appeal of the various forms and applications of *economic democracy* – the original 'Third Way' (before centrist co-optation of the term under Clinton and Blair). On the one hand, this impulse is prominent in the thinking of the dissidents from orthodox versions of Marxism-Leninism in the Soviet bloc that gave rise to some of the most interesting theoretical discussions around market socialism (and the experiments with worker self-management and social ownership in Yugoslavia). On the other, it is an important strain among radical dissenters from social democracy, whether guild socialists or the New Left, who sought refuge from the deadening politics of the top-down bureaucratic welfare state in such directions as workers' control and participatory democracy. As the current order crumbles, these ideas are taking on renewed relevance, albeit in modern and reimagined form, as part of a resurgent left politics on both sides of the Atlantic.

Somewhat paradoxically, the fall of Soviet-style communism (and the turn of Chinese-style communism toward overt state capitalism) has liberated the left from much of the ideological and sectarian straightjacket in which it found itself for a good part of the twentieth century. It is no longer either impermissible or utopian to set about envisioning alternatives to the types of authoritarian, bureaucratic, and top-down state socialist models that predominated in the Eastern bloc. Additionally, in some Western countries – and in the United States in particular – there is increasing popular discomfort with the corporate capitalist model, and a growing hunger for systemic alternatives (especially among the younger generation who, according to a number of recent polls, now have a somewhat higher opinion of socialism than capitalism).[1] Analyzing these visions adds an important forward-looking dimension to discussions about public ownership, and offers important insights into where, why, and how public ownership should and could be deployed in the future.

Since the attempt to reform the Soviet economy in the 1980s (known as *perestroika*), one of the dominant trends in socialist system theory has been *market socialism* in one form or another.[2] Market socialism has its roots in the famous 'socialist calculation debate' (or 'economic calculation debate') between Polish economist Oskar Lange and Friedrich Hayek (together with others on both sides, and building on earlier work) in the early twentieth century.[3] Briefly summarized, Hayek held that entities responsible for economic planning could never compile enough information about costs, available technologies, consumer demands, and other economic indicators to make the millions upon millions of calculations necessary to replicate the allocation function of capitalist markets. Lange countered that if markets for consumer goods and labor were retained within a system of state ownership of the means of production, a central or socialist planning bureau would be able to focus only on the rate of accumulation and the prices and allocation of capital goods – thus greatly simplifying their task.

In order to do this, the planning bureau would establish a preliminary set of accounting values based on the previous prices of capital goods under capitalism, then – with the cost of both capital and labor established – require all state owned enterprises to determine their output using two rules: first, determine the lowest cost method of production (in terms of both capital and labor) at each level; and second, choose a level of output whereby the price (determined from the consumer market) equals the marginal cost. This information (required inputs and levels of output) would be relayed back to the central planning board, which in turn would analyze any shortages or excesses in the consumer market, as well as over-capitalization or under-capitalization in the state owned enterprises, and adjust prices up or down accordingly.[4] This process would be repeated until the economy reached a 'general equilibrium.' 'In this way,' economist Theodore Burczak summarizes, 'a planning board could replicate the pricing and coordination functions of competition in capital goods markets (as well as the markets for other nonlabor factors of production).'[5]

Lange anticipated the criticism that just 'replicating' market structures was not a convincing argument in favor of replacing the existing capitalist system with a planned one, and thus laid out what he saw were the positive implications of such a transition. While inequality would not be eliminated in such a system (due to the continued existence of a labor market), it would be greatly reduced by the abolition of capital ownership (a primary driver of inequality) and the supplementing of incomes by the distribution of profits generated from state owned enterprises (previously appropriated by a narrow class of owners). Moreover, by determining the rate of investment spending, the central planning bureau could smooth out the business cycle, reducing the waste and capital destruction experienced during downturns in a capitalist system. Lastly, the planning board could factor in externalities and benefits in a way that a market could not, thus providing a much more realistic set of prices.[6] In short, Lange envisioned a system based on public ownership of the means of production paired with a labor market, a consumer market, and a planning mechanism. However, as many observers point out, Lange's model sought to approximate the workings of a market rather than institute markets themselves, which sets this model apart from some later market socialist approaches.[7]

In the intervening decades, there have been dozens of variants of what could be (or is) called market socialism.[8] In some of these, public ownership is retained in certain sectors as part of a mixture of traditional ownership forms. In others, traditional ownership forms are retained, but separated from management or control – especially over allocation of the surplus (which is often assigned to the workers). And in still others, some version of social ownership becomes the dominant form, with both traditional private and public ownership eliminated or pushed to the periphery.

One of the most developed modern market socialist proposals is that of Loyola mathematics professor David Schweickart, which he terms *Economic Democracy*. 'Each productive enterprise,' Schweickart writes, 'is controlled by those who work there. Workers are responsible for the operation of the facility: organization of the workplace, enterprise discipline, techniques of production, what and how much to produce, what to charge for what is produced, and how the net proceeds are to be distributed.'[9] A significant feature, however, is that the workers in specific firms do not 'own' the enterprises outright – rather, they are owned by society as a whole.[10] 'In effect,' Schweickart writes, 'workers lease their capital assets from society.'[11] Because markets tend to produce inequality and unemployment, Schweickart also sees a role for a strong welfare state that would provide, among other things, free daycare, free education, and a public pension plan. In these non-market sectors, he explains, 'management is appointed by the appropriate officials,' and workers do not have ultimate control over their workplaces (although Schweickart believes they may be more participatory than their contemporary counterparts).[12] Moreover, he also envisions the government as an 'employer of last resort' that will provide employment if the market sector cannot.[13]

An even more recent model proposed by King's University College professor Tom Malleson envisions cooperatives that are directly owned by their workers operating within a regulated market system. 'The basic functioning of the economy would be straightforward and familiar,' Malleson writes. 'Co-op firms would produce various goods and services to sell on the market. Firms would compete with each other to make profit, and consumers would buy what they desire in response to price signals.'[14] Malleson agrees that in theory 'workplace democracy' can be achieved without direct worker ownership (such as social ownership), but contends that 'it is an empirically robust fact that generally cooperative businesses require collective ownership of the business property to succeed.'[15] However, he also recognizes some of the problems such a system of cooperative ownership would pose, and posits a strong role for public ownership. For enterprises of 'large capital intensity' or national importance (for instance: 'oil, steel, auto, pharmaceutical, etc.') he envisions a structure consisting of state ownership alongside worker–state co-management. The reason for this is two-fold. On the one hand, he argues that cooperatives may not be optimal because most workers likely would not be able to acquire an ownership share given their average incomes and lack of wealth. On the other, if the state were to simply nationalize such industries and turn them over to the workers, it would create massive inequalities between the new worker–owners of these multimillion-dollar enterprises and the rest of society.[16] In Malleson's words, 'this would simply create a handful of new elites.'[17] His solution is that the state would take ownership of these enterprises and they would be jointly managed by representatives of workers and the community.[18]

In most market socialist models, the key component differentiating them from traditional centrally planned state socialist models is, of course, the market (which is not to say, however, that they don't embrace some modicum of planning). For some, ownership forms, while important, are a somewhat secondary concern. As such, several market socialist models envision public ownership as part of a spectrum of possible ownership forms. For instance, in *The Economics of Feasible Socialism* (1983) the late economist Alec Nove described five ownership forms: 1) state enterprises that would be operated directly by the government; 2) 'state-owned (or socially owned) enterprises' that would be autonomous from direct government control; 3) traditional cooperative enterprises; 4) small private companies (with defined limits on scope and scale); and 5) individuals.[19] The first category, or the so-called 'commanding heights,' would include financial institutions as well as other enterprises that 'by their nature operate in large, closely interrelated units, or have a monopoly position, or both' – such as electricity networks, railways, oil companies, steelworks, and chemical producers.[20] Nove's second category of public ownership, socialized enterprises, would exist where 'competition is present, and production decisions "belong" at the level at which production takes place.'[21] Specifically, what would differentiate companies at this level from the next category, cooperatives, is that the state, rather than the workers, would own the means of production and bear all the associated rights and responsibilities.[22] Like other system theorists, Nove allowed for privately owned enterprises to remain, but proposed a limit on their scale. While this would be decided 'democratically,' Nove suggested that it could be based on the number of people employed by such an enterprise or the value of its capital assets, and could be different from industry to industry.

A second tradition ends up in the same place as many market socialist models – a mix of planning and markets and multiple ownership forms – but tends to emphasize ownership forms first and foremost. For lack of a better term, these models can be described as 'pluralist.' Political economist and historian Gar Alperovitz (my colleague and co-founder of The Democracy Collaborative) has developed such a model that he terms the *Pluralist Commonwealth*; '"pluralist" because it involves diverse, plural and decentralized institutional forms of democratizing wealth; [and] "Commonwealth" because common to all the forms at the various levels, though in different ways, is the concept of wealth ownership by the many rather than the few.'[23] Like many market socialist approaches, Alperovitz's model includes a mix of markets and planning, but is based around altering economic ownership patterns as a prerequisite to the establishment of genuine democracy and a culture of community. 'Over time a fundamental shift in the ownership of wealth would slowly move the nation as a whole toward greater equality,' he maintains:

> Among other things the changes would also help finance a reduction in the workweek so as to permit greater amounts of free time, thereby bolstering both individual liberty and democratic participation. As population continues to grow, the model also moves in the direction of, and ultimately projects, a long-term devolution of the national system to a form of regional reorganization and decentralization – a strategic move important not only to democracy and liberty, but to the successful democratic management of ecological and other pressing issues.[24]

The Pluralist Commonwealth's 'mix of wealth holding institutions' includes cooperatives and other employee owned businesses, neighborhood-based corporations, non-profits, and small private businesses.[25] Public ownership plays a prominent role at various scales – especially in the case of banks, utilities, energy companies, healthcare, and transportation. Moreover, the model envisions an expansion of municipal ownership efforts, including the taking of equity stakes in small- and medium-sized private businesses.

Another particularly instructive modern pluralist system model is the 'sketch of a publicly owned economy in the twenty first century' put forward by Andrew Cumbers.[26] While Cumbers describes his model as 'publicly owned' it is also, within the typology employed here, a pluralist model. As noted above, Cumbers takes a more expansive view of public ownership – one that includes worker and employee owned firms. He also envisions the continuation of self-employment and small private firms that would, after reaching a certain size, be required to convert to some form of mutual ownership, as well as a mixture of markets and planning.[27] 'Market competition centered around cooperative or worker-owned enterprises,' Cumbers contends, 'is entirely compatible with Hayek's well-known critique of market socialism.'[28] He identifies six 'broad types' of public ownership, including: 1) full state ownership (FSO) – essentially completely state owned enterprises organized at the national level; 2) partial state ownership (PSO) – enterprises where the national government owns a majority or controlling stake; 3) local or municipal ownership (LMO) – enterprises owned and controlled, either wholly or in part, by sub-departments of the national state (such as municipalities, states, or regions); 4) employee owned firms (EO) – companies owned and controlled by their workers; 5) producer cooperatives (PC) – groupings of smaller businesses comprised of a variety of ownership forms (co-ops or privately owned); and 6) consumer cooperatives (CC) – businesses or entities owned and controlled by specific groups with society.[29]

Cumbers describes a variety of different objectives for public ownership, ranging from reducing inequality through redistributing income and wealth to increasing worker and citizen participation in the economy. However, he warns that 'all forms of public ownership have their advantages and disadvantages, and there will inevitably be trade-offs between the different objectives.'[30] Cumbers applies the three types of public ownership that most closely approximate the narrower definition of public ownership (ownership through the state) to the following sectors: finance, utility industries, public transportation, and public services. For finance, there would be a mix of public ownership forms at various levels, including global (international development and lending), national (monetary policy), and local (funding economic development). Utility industries (such as electricity, water, and gas), public transportation, and public services like health and education, would all be comprised of a mix of national state owned enterprises and local/regional public enterprises.[31] Importantly, Cumbers also institutes a scale requirement for private firms in sectors such as consumer products, private services, and consumer services. 'For those domestic firms operating in these sectors,' he argues, 'beyond a certain size the owners would have the choice of which type of public ownership to transfer to ... In many sectors the small size of the average firm means that there would continue to be plenty of scope for private enterprise and genuine Schumpeterian entrepreneurialism.'[32]

These market socialist and pluralist approaches are not without their critics, especially those operating from a more orthodox Marxist

Table 2 Effectiveness of different forms of public ownership by objective in Andrew Cumbers' 'preliminary sketch of a publicly owned economy in the twenty-first century'

Objective	Form of ownership
Commanding heights	FSO (very positive)
	PSO (positive)
	LMO (positive)
	PC (neutral)
	CC (negative)
	EO (negative)
Local community control	FSO (negative)
	PSO (negative)
	LMO (very positive)
	PC (positive)
	CC (positive)
	EO (positive)
Distributional justice	FSO (very positive)
	PSO (positive)
	LMO (positive)
	PC (negative)
	CC (positive)
	EO (negative)
Environmental sustainability and justice	FSO (very positive)
	PSO (positive)
	LMO (very positive)
	PC (neutral)
	CC (neutral)
	EO (neutral)
Enhance participation/class justice	FSO (neutral)
	PSO (neutral)
	LMO (positive)
	PC (very positive)
	CC (very positive)
	EO (very positive)

Table adapted from Andrew Cumbers, *Reclaiming Public Ownership: Making Space for Economic Democracy* (New York, NY: Zed Books, 2012), p. 165.

orientation. In a late 1990s debate with Schweickart, Bertell Ollman stated that 'the market … is a more important feature of capitalism than is private ownership. Thus, ownership may be transferred to the state (as has occurred with nationalized industries in many countries) or to workers' cooperatives, but if the market remains essentially intact so, too, will most of the problems associated with capitalism.'[33] From a somewhat different perspective, in the late 1980s the Belgian Marxist Ernest Mandel debated Alec Nove over market socialism in a series of exchanges in *New Left Review*. Mandel's criticism of Nove was multi-faceted, but one important component was his assertion that in any form of market economy, workers (producers) would not be free to make their own decisions.[34] Instead of a market-based economy with plural ownership forms, Mandel argued for 'democratically articulated and centralized self-management, the planned self-rule of the associated producers.'[35]

A similar discomfort with markets and traditional ownership forms underpins the *participatory economics* approach most commonly associated with Michael Albert and Robin Hahnel. 'Whatever gains over capitalism have been achieved in attaining market socialism, market socialism still is not an economy that by its intrinsic operations promotes solidarity, equity, diversity, and participatory self-management while also accomplishing economic functions efficiently,' Albert wrote in *Parecon*. 'Instead, all the intrinsic ills of markets – particularly, hierarchical workplace divisions, remuneration according to output and bargaining power, distortion of personality and motives, and mispricing of goods and services, etc. – persist, while only the aggravating presence of private capital is transcended.'[36] However, participatory economics does offer a vision of 'social' ownership that is similar to that which is envisioned by some market socialists. Hahnel explains that while individual private property ownership would continue, the entirety of the means of production would be owned by everyone in society equally.[37] In Albert's formulation:

> We simply remove ownership of the means of production from the economic picture. We can think of this as deciding that no one owns the means of production. Or we can think of it as deciding that everyone owns a fractional share of every single item of means of production equivalent to what every other person owns of that item. Or we can think of it as deciding that society owns all of the means of production but that it has no say over any of the means of production nor any claim on their output on that account.[38]

Such social ownership (often combined with worker self-management/ governance) is hard to evaluate in that it is, essentially, a theoretical negation of traditional forms of ownership (private, public, or cooperative).[39] For instance, a 2005 United Nations report on property rights in the former Yugoslavia stated that:

> Views on how to interpret 'social ownership' differ among former Yugoslav academics. Most of these views, however, were based on the

premise that social ownership was a new socio-economic category and tenure system, which could neither be fully explained nor grasped by traditional civil law criteria ... Questions as to who the holder of such social-owned property was, and who – in the name of society – had a right of disposal over it, were subject to much debate.[40]

In vastly simplified terms, as much as the 'state' – through representative (or otherwise) political bodies at various scales – acts as the 'agent' of society regarding the exercise of ownership rights and responsibilities, social ownership could be considered a form of traditional public ownership. By contrast, if the ultimate authority for exercising those rights and responsibilities lies with the firm's workers, it could be considered a form of worker or collective ownership. In his reading of the Yugoslav model of social ownership, Robert Dahl commented that:

> Since Yugoslav society is an entity with no means of acting except through its specified institutions, all the rights, powers, and privileges ordinarily associated with ownership must be lodged in specific institutions ... Among the institutions that speak authoritatively on this question in Yugoslavia, the Party and the government of the state – whether of the federation or of the republics – are crucially important. Because the structure, duties, and authority of the self-managed enterprises are determined by statutory and constitutional law, sovereign authority over the enterprises seems to rest de jure with the state and de facto with the leadership of Party and state. As a result, ownership of enterprises by 'society' is almost entirely symbolic.[41]

Another variant of this non-market, social ownership model is the 'participatory democratic planning' approach articulated by economist Pat Devine. His model seeks to 'enable the *ex ante* coordination of investment to take place through negotiation,' rather than via markets or central planning.[42] To do so, Devine makes a distinction between market exchange ('the sale/purchase of the output of existing productivity') and market forces ('the process through which changes in the structure of productive capacity brought about by investment and disinvestment are coordinated in capitalism (and market socialism)').[43] Devine articulates a vision of social ownership based around the concept of affected interests – essentially that individuals should be able to influence the decisions that affect their lives.[44] However, unlike other proposals which remain vague on the question of what exactly social ownership might look like in practice, Devine offers an instructive snapshot. In his model, representatives of various groups – including workers, other enterprises in the industry, suppliers, consumers, local government, local residents, and advocacy organizations (such as environmental groups) – would have seats on the board of each enterprise and 'negotiate over strategic policy decisions and monitor the activities of the internally self-managed workforce.'[45]

It is probably fair to conclude that the vast majority of alternative system proposals emanating from the political left, to say nothing of a fair number from the right (fascism, of course, has traditionally included a substantial degree of state ownership), envision retaining or expanding public ownership in one form or another.[46] Those discussed above represent a tiny fraction of the total.[47] A fundamental problem confronting alternative system theorists, however, is how to walk the line between articulating a developed and desirable alternative that inspires positive action, and avoiding a disempowering utopianism that fails to clearly and realistically demonstrate how that alternative could emerge. Public ownership is one of the structural elements that connect many alternative systemic theories to contemporary and historical reality, and through this connection transition strategies and possibilities emerge. Alternative system theorists also sometimes simply ignore the power and motivations of the institutions and individuals that benefit from and underpin existing systemic arrangements. Yet the history of revolution – from France to the American colonies to Russia to Cuba to Chile and beyond – amply demonstrates that attempts to comprehensively restructure political-economic systems are often vigorously (and violently) opposed by entrenched interests, and the inevitable confrontation with those interests risks derailing or compromising the underlying restructuring efforts, and potentially sending the entire effort spiraling in unwanted directions. By focusing on how institutions are organized – including who owns, manages, and benefits from them, and how they interact with other socio-economic structures – some of the possibilities and pitfalls for systemic change can be identified. Public ownership, with its concrete historical and contemporary record, will likely remain a critically important element in efforts at political-economic institutional design in pursuit of a viable and desirable next system, whether in the United States or elsewhere.

Chapter 5

Toward a framework of public ownership for the twenty-first century

In order to begin bridging the gap between real-world experience with public ownership and its potential role in future political-economic systemic alternatives, it is useful to develop a framework whereby public ownership can be expanded and scaled up from existing levels across a variety of economic sectors. The aim at this stage is not to articulate the full workings of a systemic alternative to capitalism – as we have seen, there are many such models, starting from a variety of perspectives (even that of public ownership). Rather, it is to identify where and in what economic sectors public ownership might be necessary, recommended, and possible; to speculate as to what structure or form public ownership could or should take in each of these areas; and to suggest ways in which an expansion or reconceptualization of public ownership can play a role in the transition to an alternative system.

At the outset, a few clarifications, assumptions, and definitions are required. First and foremost, while capitalism is undoubtedly a global economic system, within it there exist many variants and varieties – Nordic social democracy, Chinese state capitalism, and American 'free market' capitalism, to name but a few. As such, the experience of – and possibilities for – public ownership will vary greatly depending on the version of capitalism concerned, to say nothing of the distinct historical experiences and cultural differences that accompany it. Furthermore, while some future system models may dispense with the nation-state (or its subdivisions) as the dominant political jurisdiction, in both the current and possible transitional context, the nation remains the primary site where changes to political-economic arrangements will occur (even acknowledging the expansive role of transnational and supranational organizations like the World Bank, WTO, IMF, OECD, and EU). With all this in mind, the analysis that follows will be primarily based on the political-economic system, arrangements, and transformative opportunities that exist currently in the United States.

Second, while the current economic system in the United States is, in the classical sense, predominantly market-based, it is far from a 'free market' in the conventional understanding of the term. As Karl Polanyi wrote in *The Great Transformation*, the great paradox of free-market thinking is that 'even those who wished most ardently to free the state from all unnecessary duties, and whose whole philosophy demanded the restriction of state activities, could not but entrust the self-same state with the new powers, organs, and instruments required for the establishment of laissez-faire.'[1] Thus, in reality, the 'free market' system inevitably includes a heavy element of government policies, regulation, administration, and accompanying interventions at various levels – in some cases approximating a haphazard attempt at soft planning. While future systems may utilize a more explicit mix of markets and planning – or even dispense with markets altogether – this analysis will operate from the perspective that a regulated market economy will continue to exist in the United States, at least for now. In fact, this was exactly the situation envisioned by Marx. *The Communist Manifesto* lays out a transitional program which includes, among other things, the expansion of public ownership with regards to: credit ('centralisation of credit in the hands of the state, by means of a national bank'); transportation and communication ('centralisation of the means of communication and transport in the hands of the State'); and manufacturing and agriculture ('extension of factories and instruments of production owned by the State; the bringing into cultivation of waste-lands, and the improvement of the soil generally in accordance with a common plan').[2] 'The immediate result of introducing these measures would be a mixed economy, combining socialism with capitalism,' as the late political philosopher Stanley Moore wrote in *Marx Versus Markets*.[3]

Lastly, it would be extremely difficult to analyze the possibility for public ownership in every single industry in a national economy the size of that of the United States. By way of illustration, the index file for the North American Industry Classification System has around 20,000 entries.[4] Historically, some theorists have avoided this by establishing a broad general scheme for how public ownership should be deployed across the economy. For instance, in their 1980 book *Economic Democracy*, Martin Carnoy and Derek Shearer suggested establishing a new public holding company that would purchase a stake (10–20 percent in most cases) in at least one company in any industry that was exhibiting high levels of concentration.[5] The holding company would also help finance new local, state, and regional public enterprises across a variety of sectors (as well as worker and community owned companies).[6] Similarly, in his landmark work *Small Is Beautiful*, British economist E. F. Schumacher maintained that all enterprises above a 'minimum size' should be 50 percent publicly owned.[7] While such approaches offer important insights, especially regarding a possible transition strategy, they are insufficient when trying to develop a more comprehensive understanding of where and why public ownership is or is not necessary or desirable in a modern economy. Instead, what follows is an (imperfect) attempt to broadly delineate certain economic 'sectors' that are particularly pertinent to the discussion about expanding public ownership for various reasons. These sectors do not necessarily correspond to other official or unofficial categorizations, and they are subject to overlap (for example the 'chemicals' sector and the 'manufacturing' sector). Furthermore, some important sectors will be discussed only briefly in this analysis, or not at all. In other words, what follows is not intended to be either comprehensive or prescriptive; it seeks only to perform an initial survey of the terrain as a starting point to guide further exploration and discussion.

Utilities

The utility sector – including electricity, water, sewer, and gas – is widely accepted as being one of the most conducive to public ownership. The services this sector provides are essential to the functioning of any modern society and there has, historically, been widespread opposition to the concept of extracting private profit from such basic functions. As we have seen, in the early twentieth century, taking utilities into public ownership was a cornerstone of both the socialist and progressive movements (to the degree that municipal socialism is often called 'gas and sewer socialism'). The all-public and cooperative electric power system in Nebraska, for instance, is an example and legacy of public opposition to for-profit private corporations in the utility sector. Similarly, commitments to public ownership in the 2017 British Labour Party manifesto, the ongoing municipalization effort in Boulder, Colorado, and the general retreat from water privatization around the United States (and elsewhere in the world) demonstrate that such sentiments remain widespread. Market failure, or perceived market failure, is a primary driver of these concerns – especially as it relates to poor service, lack of service in rural or disinvested communities, inadequate investment and modernization, and high end-use costs for consumers. From an economic perspective, many utilities in their current form are the classic example of natural monopolies, given their high fixed costs (such as electricity wires, water pipes, treatment facilities, etc.), centralized coordination needs (such as an electrical grid or water system), economies of scale, high barriers to competitors entering the industry, and a tendency toward oligopoly and monopoly when competition is involved.[8] As such, competition tends to make little economic sense, and even in the specific industries where ownership is more mixed (such as electric utilities), providers – be they privately, publicly, or cooperatively owned – still rarely compete with one another in the same geographic area.[9]

However, across the utility sector, for-profit companies and investors have, for many years, aggressively pursued deregulation and/or privatization. In the electricity industry there has been a longstanding effort to loosen many of the restrictions regarding ownership consolidation, rate increases, and competition. As previously discussed, in 2005, after many years of aggressive lobbying by private corporations, the Public Utility Holding Company Act of 1935 was repealed. According to an American Public Power Association brief during the repeal fight, 'the SEC's aggressive enforcement of PUHCA resulted in the creation of a financially sound electric utility industry free from the abusive practices of the 1920s and 1930s.'[10] 'However,' it warned:

> Partial repeal of PUHCA by Congress with its Energy Policy Act of 1992, combined with almost nonexistent SEC enforcement in the last decade, has resulted in the return of many of the pre-PUHCA era problems. Today, consumers and investors are not being protected from utility companies' financial manipulations and anticompetitive practices. The Enron story is an excellent illustration, as its dramatic rise has been revealed as a fraud.[11]

While not necessarily leading to widespread ownership changes, deregulation of the electricity sector has, thus far, been considered a disaster by many observers. 'Electricity deregulation is a failure,' the *American Prospect*'s Robert Kuttner wrote in 2008. 'Adjusted for the price of fuel, the retail cost of electricity has increased at a faster rate after deregulation than before. Deregulation has invited merger and market power, not competition.'[12] More recently, in July 2016, Gerry Anderson, the CEO of for-profit DTE Energy, agreed, stating that the 'claim that deregulated markets are "generally working to lower prices for consumers" is simply not accurate ... Furthermore, customers in deregulated states have experienced significant price volatility, which often led to temporary price freezes, price caps and other forms of market intervention.'[13]

The state of Nebraska and the long history of publicly owned utilities in the United States in general shows that a fully publicly owned (or publicly and cooperatively owned) and decentralized utility sector could be both feasible and efficient. Moreover, the serious issues that have occurred related to deregulation and competition in the electricity industry (and with privatization in the water industry) lend weight to the argument that utilities should be a sector in which for-profit companies are not allowed to operate. However, this is not to say that the existing structure of centralized, vertically integrated utility monopolies should be the only option. For instance, regarding electricity, John Farrell of ILSR (which has been at the forefront of efforts to democratize energy networks for decades) maintains that 'it no longer makes sense to preserve last century's forms of utility ownership and control in a century where cost-effective technology enables widely distribut[ed] production and ownership of electricity.'[14] Farrell proposes that the local distribution system – currently owned and operated by public, cooperative, or private utilities – be operated by an independent manager who would enable a wide array of new democratized and clean energy efforts to contribute to power generation and transmission (such as individual or community owned solar and wind facilities). 'The grid could be owned as a commons, like the roads or municipal water supply, or not,' Farrell writes. 'But it must be built and operated to facilitate maximum economic opportunity for electric customers.'[15]

A variant of this already exists in Nebraska (and elsewhere). By and large, new wind power facilities in the state are owned and operated by private companies who then sell the electricity generated to the state's publicly owned utilities through what is called 'Power Purchase' agreements (although the largest wind facility in the state, Ainsworth, is still publicly owned).[16] Inverting this model, the Labour Energy Forum in the UK has suggested that publicly owned offshore wind turbines wouldn't necessarily have to sell electricity directly to consumers (rather, they could sell to separately constituted supply companies).[17] Hamburg, Germany, first set up its own green 'utility' company and then (via a re-municipalization referendum) also took the grid operator (TSO) into public ownership as a separate entity.[18]

It is therefore feasible to imagine an electricity system that is both publicly owned and allows for energy democracy and a transition to distributed renewable energy production. For instance, one possible model for further exploration (especially with regards to viability and a cost-benefit analysis) is as follows: Publicly owned companies or cooperatives could own power generation facilities (these might be partnerships of various publicly owned utilities within a region), while other independent publicly owned institutions could own and manage the local grids. Electricity could be supplied to end consumers by yet a third publicly owned company (the 'utility'), which would have a local quasi-monopoly and would purchase directly from the generation company (or generate its own electricity). In such a network, individuals and groups of individuals (such as consumer cooperatives) could participate in the renewable energy transition by opting out of the utility's service and producing their own electricity to be distributed through the publicly owned grid. The independent grid management company would balance supply and demand to ensure that both individuals and the utility company remain economically viable, and would deal with interconnection processes, equitable access, and maintenance. For-profit companies, while likely banned from owning the grid and supplying customers directly (thus protecting the public and the environment from abusive corporate practices and ensuring local control over vital services), could potentially be allowed to invest in certain generation projects as minority shareholders alongside publicly owned companies or cooperatives.

The story of how Nebraska became an all-public power state provides a precedent for how public ownership could be expanded across the sector. In the 1920s and 1930s, Nebraskans began organizing a grassroots campaign against the large corporate holding companies that were buying up all their local publicly owned utilities and cooperatives. They bypassed the corporate-influenced state legislature and took a revenue bond-financing proposal for the creation of publicly owned utilities straight to the voters, who approved it overwhelmingly. This was the catalyst that was needed for a ripple effect, and subsequent state and federal laws followed – including the state's Enabling Act (1933), which allowed a small percentage of eligible voters in an area to petition for a decision on a publicly owned utility. By 1949, the process of expanding and scaling public ownership was complete. Popular movements currently mobilizing around energy democracy, water security, local control, climate change, and reducing corporate influence could effect similar far-reaching changes – starting with local efforts to resist privatization, deregulation, and corporate consolidation, which could then lead to innovative strategies such as municipalizing existing privately owned utilities (as in Boulder, Colorado), banning private ownership of utilities, and creating new publicly controlled and democratized networks for the delivery of utility services.

Banking and finance

The financial sector, and the role it plays in allocating capital, is the heart of today's capitalist system in both theory and practice. That there are fundamental economic flaws in the structure and organization of the American financial system is a relatively uncontroversial statement in the wake of the devastating financial crisis and recession of the late 2000s. As a result of that crisis, the term 'too-big-to-fail' has entered popular discourse as a way to explain and understand more opaque concepts such as 'systemic risk' and 'moral hazard.' Collectively, these terms describe a financial sector that was – and very much still is – so large and so systemically important vis-à-vis the rest of the economy that it is virtually guaranteed that the public, through the government, would be forced to step in and bail it out in times of crisis, economic difficulty, or heightened risk.

In addition to 'too-big-to fail,' there is also the more fundamental issue of *financialization* and how the financial sector interacts with and supports the rest of the economic system. 'Financialization,' Gerald Epstein of the Political Economy Research Institute (PERI) states, 'means the increasing role of financial motives, financial markets, financial actors and financial institutions in the operation of the domestic and international economies.'[19] While there have been many documented effects of financialization – from incentivizing short-termism and speculative investing to increasing risks for workers and less affluent investors – of particular importance in the current political-economic context are the plethora of studies in recent years that have demonstrated the profound influence it has had on increasing inequality, especially in the United States.[20]

Mainstream proposals to rein in and restructure the financial sector in the wake of the financial crisis have generally focused on re-regulating the industry and/or breaking up the largest institutions. Proponents of re-regulation often focus on two concepts: 1) reversing the repeal of Glass-Steagall, the New Deal-era legislation that for decades separated investment banking and various forms of speculative activity from ordinary commercial banking functions; and 2) preserving and strengthening the Dodd-Frank financial reform legislation that was enacted in 2010 in the aftermath of the Great Financial Crisis. 'Despite the progress we've made since 2008, the biggest banks continue to threaten our economy,' Democratic Senator Elizabeth Warren of Massachusetts stated in 2015 when introducing a new bill to restore Glass-Steagall. 'The biggest banks are collectively much larger than they were before the crisis, and they continue to engage in dangerous practices that could once again crash our economy. ... [This act will] rebuild the wall between commercial and investment banking and make our financial system more stable and secure.'[21]

For others, re-regulation does not go far enough, and breaking up the banks – which became a rallying cry during the insurgent 2016 presidential campaign of Vermont Senator Bernie Sanders – is preferable. In 2010, during debate on Dodd-Frank, Senator Sherrod Brown, a Democrat from Ohio, and Senator Ted Kaufman, a Democrat from Delaware, advocated breaking up the banks. At the time, Brown asserted that their proposed amendment 'prevents megabanks from controlling too much of our nation's wealth,' and that 'if we're going to prevent big banks from putting our entire economy at risk, we need to place sensible size limits on our nation's behemoth banks. We need to ensure that if banks gamble, they have the resources to cover their losses.'[22] In supporting the Brown-Kaufman amendment, banking expert Simon Johnson connected the effort to the issue of the financial sector's political-economic power, stating that 'in the American political system – where the power of major banks is now so manifest – there is no way to significantly reduce the risks posed by these banks unless they are broken up.'[23]

Beyond these unsuccessful mainstream proposals to reform and restructure the banking system lie more comprehensive and radical approaches – many of which propose some element of public ownership. For instance, in the midst of the crisis in September 2008, former Goldman Sachs adviser (and now chief economist at Citigroup) Willem Buiter wrote:

> Is the reality ... that large private firms make enormous private profits when the going is good and get bailed out and taken into temporary public ownership when the going gets bad, with the taxpayer taking the risk and the losses? If so, then why not keep these activities in permanent public ownership? There is a long-standing argument that there is no real case for private ownership of deposit-taking banking institutions, because these cannot exist safely without a deposit guarantee and/or lender of last resort facilities, that are ultimately underwritten by the taxpayer.[24]

During his presidential campaign, Bernie Sanders, in addition to advocating the break-up of the big banks, also put forward a plan to establish a postal bank in the United States, along the lines of similar such institutions existing in most other countries (one 2013 report found that only 7 percent of sampled postal systems worldwide do not offer some banking services).[25] '[We] need to give Americans affordable banking options,' Sanders argued. 'Post offices exist in almost every community in our country. One important way to provide decent banking opportunities for low income communities is to allow the US Postal Service to engage in basic banking services, and that's what I will fight for.'[26] Essentially, postal banking could, depending on its structure and range of services, become a viable public option for the financial sector. As we have seen, another precedent for this in the United States is the publicly owned Bank of North Dakota which, importantly, demonstrates that sub-national publicly owned banks can operate efficiently and at the same time stabilize and support local economies and communities (as we have also seen, a similar system of local and regional publicly owned banks – the Sparkassen and Landesbanken – operates with great success in Germany).

However, establishing a postal bank and/or scaling local or regional public banks only addresses one half of the equation. The other half is what to do with the large Wall Street financial corporations that currently dominate the economy and the process of allocating capital. One possibility would be to put forward and organize for legislation requiring the government to take an ownership stake with full voting rights in any financial institution that has to be bailed out or rescued due to its own fraudulent or speculative activities (which happens with extraordinary frequency; the government has been forced to bail out and/or temporarily nationalize leading financial institutions several times in recent decades, including Franklin National Bank in the 1970s, Continental Illinois National Bank and Trust Company in the early 1980s, the savings and loan industry in the late 1980s, and many of the leading Wall Street banks in the late 2000s).[27]

As we saw above, the government's response to the 2008–2009 financial crisis involved the strange, illogical, and purely ideologically driven reluctance to conduct what should have been a transparent and straightforward nationalization of much of the US banking sector. That approach has confounded many experts, then and now. At the time, Bo Lundgren, the former Swedish Minister of Fiscal and Financial Affairs who had engineered his own government's response to a financial crisis in the 1990s, commented that the structure of many of the bailouts was a problem. 'If you go in with capital,' he told the *New York Times*, 'you should have full voting rights.'[28] The prospective legislation could also require the government to investigate, in a transparent manner and with public input, the possibility of longer-term public ownership.

During the financial crisis, many commentators who professed support for short-term nationalization were emphatic in their rejection of long-term public ownership. For instance, economist Adam Posen stated in 2009 that 'nobody in their right mind wants the government to be in the banking business any longer than it needs to be.'[29] However, such judgements – rolled out in this case alongside the usual roster of bogeymen including 'Lenin, Chavez, and Mitterrand' – deliberately ignore the extensive, and often highly successful, experience with public banking around the world (some of which was covered earlier).

One such proposal for long-term public ownership came in conjunction with the run-up to the government bailout of Franklin National Bank in 1974. A year earlier, Democratic Congressman Henry Reuss of Wisconsin, then a high-ranking member of the House Banking Committee, suggested that Franklin National should be nationalized and run as a publicly owned bank. By law, the bank would have focused on making 'socially desirable loans' (such as low- and moderate-income housing, local government needs, and 'productive investments'), and would have been prevented from speculative loans and currency trading. The company's board would have been independent, and all profits would have been returned to the public.[30]

Today, any legislation mandating ownership in exchange for bailouts could result in a publicly owned financial sector in very short order. This is due to the fact that most leading banking experts agree that another financial crisis is inevitable – more a question of *when* than *if* – and when it occurs the weak regulations put in place by Dodd-Frank are unlikely to prevent the need for another massive public bailout. In early 2016, President of the Federal Reserve Bank of Minneapolis and architect of the 2008 bailout Neel Kashkari made headlines when he stated that 'no rational policymaker would risk restructuring large firms and forcing losses on creditors and counterparties using the new tools in a risky environment, let alone in a crisis environment like we experienced in 2008. They will be forced to bail out failing institutions – as we were.'[31] Kashkari continued that it was time to 'seriously consider bolder, transformational options,' including taxing leverage to reduce systemic risk, breaking up the large banks, and turning large banks into public utilities.

Going beyond these largely regulatory approaches, legislation authorizing public ownership instead of bailouts could also reduce systemic risk as the threat of nationalization would, if structured appropriately, serve as a powerful disincentive to owners and managers of financial corporations engaging in risky, speculative, or fraudulent business practices. If and when the nationalization of large financial institutions actually occurred under this new legislation, it could have numerous additional political, economic, and social benefits, such as reducing wealth and income inequality, financialization, and political interference. Perhaps more so than in any other sector, increasing public ownership in the financial sector would lead in the direction of a fundamental systemic shift (as is recognized by most alternative system theorists). However, as Portuguese economist Nuno Teles points out, increasing 'public ownership of banks is necessary but not sufficient.'[32] In addition to reducing systemic risk and supporting the real economy, public ownership in the financial sector must also open up the possibility of financing ownership transitions (public or collective) and improving access to capital in a wide variety of other economic sectors.

Such institutions must also be internally democratized and made democratically accountable. Teles suggests multi-stakeholder management arrangements (something that will be discussed further below).[33] One real-world example is Banco Popular (BPDC), Costa Rica's third-largest bank. Formed by the government to support economic development more than 40 years ago, BPDC is now a hybrid publicly owned enterprise and cooperative. The bank has a democratic assembly made up of 290 representatives selected (on the basis of representing various economic and social sectors) from among the bank's member–owners. Any worker holding a savings account for over a year receives an ownership share. The assembly, in turn, advises on the bank's strategic direction and selects four of the company's board members, with another three appointed by the government. Moreover, the bank is committed to a nationwide, popular consultative process when it comes to its strategic direction, requires 50 percent of board members to be women, and directs a portion of revenues to social projects through its Social Bank subsidiary. The bank has also become a leading financier of ecological sustainability in the country in conjunction with its 'triple bottom line' approach seeking economic, social, and environmental returns.[34]

Healthcare

In many countries, healthcare systems are, and have been for generations, public in one form or another, and for the most part universal. It is therefore difficult for many people around the world to conceive of a different approach in a sector that is so fundamental to the functioning of society and the economy (to say nothing of life itself). Infamously, however, the US healthcare system is a patchwork, piecemeal system of private, public, and nonprofit institutions – and as a result it produces higher costs, more inequality, and worse health outcomes. For instance, a 2015 study by the Commonwealth Fund revealed that among 13 high-income countries, the United States was the only one without a 'publicly financed universal health system,' and yet (in per capita terms) 'spends more public dollars on health care than all but two of the other countries.'[35] Moreover, while healthcare spending *in total* was significantly higher than all the other countries, health outcomes across a variety of indicators were worse.[36] The healthcare sector is critically important in any political-economic analysis, not only one related to public ownership, because it is both extremely large economically and also projected to grow steadily as the population ages during the twenty-first century. For instance, according to the Centers for Medicare and Medicaid Services, US healthcare spending is expected to rise from 17.5 percent of GDP in 2014 to 20.1 percent just by 2025.[37]

The ownership structure in the American healthcare system is complex and the result of the country's unique historical, cultural, and political development. There are roughly 4,862 registered community hospitals in the United States. Of these, 2,845 are nonprofit, 1,034 are for-profit, and 983 are publicly owned (there are also 212 federal publicly owned hospitals).[38] For-profit hospitals tend to cater to well-insured patients and offer more specialized services in order to generate profits for shareholders, while publicly owned hospitals often provide more general services to low-income and uninsured individuals (in a sense, they often act as the provider of last resort). Nonprofit hospitals fall somewhere in the middle.[39] This structure likely plays a role in persistent and rising health inequality in the United States. In 2016, it was reported that health inequality between the rich and poor has risen dramatically in recent generations. For men born in 1920, the life expectancy gap between the top 10 percent of earners and the bottom 10 percent was six years; for men born in 1950, it was up to 14 years. For women born in 1920 it was 4.7 years; for women born in 1950, it was 13 years.[40] Moreover, for-profit hospitals have a long history of being investigated for Medicare fraud and other types of fraudulent and abusive billing practices (and have paid hundreds of millions of dollars to settle such cases), which is unsurprising, given their need to generate profits for shareholders at all costs.[41] Studies have also shown that in addition to having higher costs, for-profit hospitals have higher death rates, further contributing to the United States' poor comparative performance in terms of health outcomes.[42]

In the health *insurance* industry, while four of the top five health insurance companies in the country are for-profit, nonprofit companies cover about half of all people enrolled in a private health insurance plan.[43] Additionally, around 36 percent of all Americans are covered by public plans such as Medicare and Medicaid.[44] Yet, even with this variety of options, around 28.5 million people still do not have health insurance (down from around 41 million before passage of the Affordable Care Act, also known as Obamacare, in 2010) – primarily due to cost.[45] Even for those Americans with insurance, costs continue to rise as premiums increase and employers shift to higher deductible plans. A 2016 report from the Commonwealth Institute found that:

> Many families feel pinched by their health care costs: despite a recent surge, income growth has not kept pace in many areas of the U.S. Employee contributions to premiums and deductibles amounted to 10.1 percent of U.S. median income in 2015, compared to 6.5 percent in 2006. These costs are higher relative to income in many southeastern and southern states, where incomes are below the national average.[46]

Given the clear limitations of the American healthcare sector, as well as the comparative outcomes and costs vis-à-vis other developed countries, some form of a more comprehensive publicly financed and or owned healthcare sector is likely both preferable and inevitable. In discussing the mounting problems associated with the 'Obamacare' health insurance exchanges – where people can shop for insurance provided by for-profit or nonprofit companies and apply for a subsidy from the government based on their income – former US Secretary of Labor Robert Reich commented in August 2016 that:

> In the short term, Obamacare can be patched up by enlarging government subsidies for purchasing insurance, and ensuring that healthy Americans buy insurance, as the law requires. But these are band aids. The real choice in the future is either a hugely expensive for-profit oligopoly with the market power to charge high prices even to healthy people and stop insuring sick people. Or else a government-run single payer system – such as is in place in almost every other advanced economy – dedicated to lower premiums and better care for everyone. We're going to have to choose eventually.[47]

In recent years, there have been both top-down and bottom-up attempts to move in the direction of a single-payer system. With regards to the former, a so-called public option – whereby the government would operate a public insurance plan that would compete with for-profit and nonprofit companies – was very close to being enacted as part of the Affordable Care Act, before being removed as part of a deal to secure support from health insurance companies and moderate Democratic politicians. For many 'healthcare for all' advocates, the public option was a critical first step. 'Progressives supported [the public option] as a voluntary transition toward single-payer insurance,' Helen Halpin and Peter Harbage recall.[48] Recently, political scientist Jacob Hacker has argued that resurrecting the public option is critical to the long-term success of Obamacare. 'A public option,' he writes, 'would increase coverage and create greater insurance competition at a time when some insurers (most recently, Aetna and Oscar) are pulling back. It could also use its bargaining power to push back against drug makers, medical device manufacturers, hospital systems and other health care providers that have become increasingly consolidated.'[49] From the bottom up, several states – notably Vermont, Colorado, and California – have seriously considered setting up single-payer systems at the state level. For a variety of reasons, not least of which is the political will required to make the final decision to implement such a radical economic overhaul, these efforts have not, as of yet, succeeded.[50]

However, just establishing a single-payer healthcare system does not answer the question of what role public ownership would or should play in the sector. Even within single-payer systems worldwide there are big differences with regards to the mix of ownership forms. For example, Canada has what is often termed a National Health Insurance Model. Public financing accounts for around 70 percent of healthcare spending and individual out-of-pocket expenses account for 30 percent; however, the majority of hospitals are community-based nonprofit institutions with varying degrees of government control and oversight (including setting budgets, approving large-scale expenditures, and closing facilities), and the majority of doctors work as independent private practitioners who contract their services.[51] Britain, on the other hand, has a National Health Service Model, whereby most hospitals and medical facilities are publicly owned and many doctors are government employees (with a small sector of private facilities and private doctors).[52]

Given that nonprofit and publicly owned hospitals in the United States already account for 78 percent of registered hospitals, in the event of a transition to a single-payer (or otherwise publicly financed) system, it is not hard to conceive of also converting all (or most) existing for-profit hospitals and large healthcare facilities to either nonprofit or public ownership, thereby reducing health inequality and reducing some cost pressures. The example of Denver Health (reviewed earlier) demonstrates that these publicly owned entities can have innovative ownership and management structures that enhance efficiency, public service, and accountability. Along the lines of the systems that exist in countries like Canada and Germany, doctors could also remain independent operators who would run small family practices, contract their services to larger institutions, or become direct employees of publicly owned or nonprofit health institutions.

Pharmaceuticals and chemicals

Like health insurance companies, the pharmaceutical industry is particularly controversial in the United States. An August 2016 Gallup poll found that just 28 percent of Americans had a positive view of the pharmaceutical industry, compared to 51 percent who had a negative view – ranking it lowest out of any of the 24 industries surveyed.[53] In particular, Americans hold pharmaceutical companies largely responsible for rising healthcare and prescription drug costs. A September 2016 Politico/Harvard poll, for instance, found that 70 percent of Americans blamed drug companies for rising costs, compared to 60 percent who blamed insurance companies.[54] This has been bolstered by a litany of public scandals linked to pharmaceutical companies and their seemingly tone-deaf executives. These include, in recent years, the notorious cases of Martin Shkreli and Heather Bresch. Shkreli was the brash and abrasive young CEO of Turing Pharmaceuticals who bought and then raised by more than 5,500 percent the price of a drug used to treat toxoplasmosis, and was subsequently indicted for fraud regarding actions he took at his former company.[55] Bresch is the CEO of Mylan and the daughter of West Virginia Senator Joe Manchin. In 2013, she spent millions of dollars lobbying Congress to recommend that all schools stock the life-saving medical device EpiPens, all while steeply increasing the price of the EpiPens from $104 in 2009 to $609 in 2016. (She also performed a corporate inversion to move the company's residence to the Netherlands in order to avoid US taxes.)[56]

There is widespread concern that the pharmaceutical industry has become singularly focused on profits and shareholder value, to the detriment of patients, the healthcare sector generally, and society as a whole. This is supported by many statements from pharmaceutical company executives themselves. For instance, J. Michael Pearson, CEO of Valeant Pharmaceuticals, explained in 2015 that 'if products are sort of mispriced and there's an opportunity, we will act appropriately in terms of doing what I assume our shareholders would like us to do.'[57] There is also widespread agreement that the pharmaceutical industry is at least partially to blame for the opioid and heroin epidemic that has swept the country in recent years. 'For decades, certain pharmaceutical companies misled the FDA about the risks of opioid dependence in an effort to sell more of the drugs,' CNN Chief Medical Correspondent Dr. Sanjay Gupta writes, 'and three top executives from Purdue Pharma even pleaded guilty to those criminal charges.'[58] Similarly, in 2014, Dr. Nora Volkow addressed the Senate Caucus on International Narcotics Control and asserted that among the several factors at play for the dramatic rise in opioid and heroin addiction is 'aggressive marketing by pharmaceutical companies.'[59] Alex Lawson, Executive Director of the national coalition Social Security Works, goes even further, stating that the epidemic is 'a consequence of the pharmaceutical industry using ever more aggressive tactics to push doctors to prescribe high-level opioids for all manner of complaints,' and that 'it is the American drug cartels – some of them doing business as Purdue Pharma, Johnson & Johnson, and Endo Pharmaceuticals – that bear ultimate responsibility for the opiate epidemic.'[60]

In addition to the abuses that have occurred under the existing, mostly for-profit model, the pharmaceutical industry is also both capital intensive and of national strategic importance – which makes it a candidate for public ownership under a variety of alternative systemic proposals (Malleson specifically references the industry in this regard). Moreover, Big Pharma – and its ability to generate private profit – is already heavily reliant on the government. 'More so than most other investor-owned industries,' political economist Uwe Reinhardt wrote in 2001, 'the drug industry is a creature of government, because it cannot exist for long without government protection of its economic turf.'[61] This includes protecting drug company patents, restricting imports of lower-priced drugs, and limiting the ability to resell drugs. It also involves substantial government financing and support for pharmaceutical research and development. A 2011 Columbia University study found 'direct government funding to be important to research and development for the most innovative new drugs,' and argued that 'taxpayers should not have to pay twice for publicly funded research – once through taxes, and once through monopoly prices or restricted access to drugs.'[62]

The pharmaceutical industry and the biopharmaceutical industry are two of the major examples in Mariana Mazzucato's research on the 'entrepreneurial state' (reviewed above). 'Large pharma, small biotech, universities and government labs are all parts of the ecology,' she writes, 'but it is especially government labs and government backed universities that invest in the research responsible for producing the most radical new drugs.' She goes on to cite the former editor of the *New England Journal of Medicine*, Marcia Angell, who 'has argued forcefully that while private pharmaceutical companies justify their exorbitantly high prices by saying they are due to their high R&D costs, in fact it has been state funded labs and research that are responsible for two-thirds of the new molecular entities that have been discovered in the last ten years.'[63]

In addition to concerns about residents paying exorbitant costs for products they already paid to develop, there is the related argument that the economic benefits of publicly funded research should accrue to the public at large rather than to a small, wealthy elite. One vehicle for achieving this would be public ownership. Publicly owned pharmaceutical companies already exist in a number of countries around the world. In February 2016 the government of South Africa joined this list, announcing that it had established a company called Ketlaphela to help supply the AIDS-stricken country's public health system with anti-retroviral drugs.[64] In the United States, one or more publicly owned pharmaceutical companies could be established to either compete with existing for-profit companies across all product lines or given the task (free of competition) of producing high-need, high-demand, or high-importance products (such as those on the FDA's drug shortage list).[65]

It is also conceivable, contingent on an analysis of economies of scale, that each state or region could have one or more such publicly owned pharmaceutical companies focused on producing low-cost drugs that match the unique health needs of area residents. These publicly owned companies could be intentionally linked to the existing network of publicly funded research facilities to ensure the public benefits from such investments in the form of lower costs for drugs, revenues to support further research, and support for social services that have been demonstrated to improve individual health outcomes. For instance, additional revenues could be directed to help prevent and treat prescription drug addiction in local communities. At a minimum, the public – perhaps through a public investment company or fund – should receive a share of the patents (and the profits derived from them) in accordance with the amount of public funding received during the research and development process.

Chemical producers similarly play a critically important role in the United States (and any advanced) society. In 2015, the chemical products sector alone had a gross output of around $791 billion, equivalent to roughly 4.3 percent of GDP.[66] However, according to the American Chemistry Council, a trade group for the industry, 'developing and producing the products of chemistry creates a ripple effect, responsible for nearly six million American jobs and nearly 26 percent of America's GDP.'[67] While chemicals undoubtedly have many societal benefits, they also have tremendous consequences in the areas of public health and the environment. For instance, a 2009 Centers for Disease Control and Prevention report found that 212 different artificial chemicals can be found in most Americans.[68] Given that toxicity is measured by levels of exposure (as well as absorption and clearance), this may not in and of itself be problematic.[69] However, many of the long-term health effects of this chemical accumulation are unknown. In some areas, there is clear evidence linking chemical exposure to a wide range of deteriorating health trends, especially when it occurs at vulnerable times of human development. For instance, several studies have linked early-life chemical exposure to the 'later diagnosis of breast and testicular cancer, learning and developmental disabilities, and Alzheimer's disease.'[70]

Chemicals also have well-documented environmental impacts. Rachel Carson's famous 1962 book *Silent Spring* exposed the American public to the dramatic effect pesticides were having on the environment, and is widely credited with ushering in the modern environmental movement along with the banning of DDT. 'Along with the possibility of the extinction of mankind by nuclear war,' she wrote, 'the central problem of our age has ... become the contamination of man's total environment with such substances of incredible potential for harm – substances that accumulate in the tissues of plants and animals and even penetrate the germ cells to shatter or alter the very material of heredity upon which the shape of the future depends.'[71] Similarly, the widespread use of chlorofluorocarbons (CFCs) during the twentieth century created a hole in the earth's ozone layer, and were subsequently phased out as part of the 1987 Montreal Protocol (though they are still produced and used in some developing countries). Chemicals are especially troublesome for aquatic life. For instance, there are toxic 'dead zones' in many major bodies of water across the world tied to fertilizer and pesticide runoff, along with animal waste and sewage, from agricultural areas. One of the largest is in the Gulf of Mexico and can be up to 7,000 square miles, depending on conditions.[72]

Until recently, most chemicals in the United States evaded regulation. In the four decades following passage of the Toxic Substances Control Act in 1976, the Environmental Protection Agency (EPA) tested only a few hundred chemicals and regulated a mere handful. Moreover, more than 60,000 chemicals were 'grandfathered in' when the law was enacted.[73] In June 2016, bipartisan legislation was passed amending the law and requiring the EPA to determine the risk of all existing and new chemicals and accelerate the testing and regulation of those chemicals.[74] However, the law also preempts states from testing chemicals ahead of the EPA and prohibits states from restricting or regulating chemicals the EPA has made a ruling on or deemed safe.[75] This is a direct challenge to states like California that in recent decades have taken the lead on such chemical testing and regulation.

Moreover, the for-profit chemical industry has a long and well-documented history of influencing, capturing, and using the regulatory system – particularly the EPA – to its advantage. For instance, in the 1980s, 13 EPA officials – including its Administrator, Anne McGill Burford – were forced out after a Congressional investigation into possible collusion with Dow Chemical around downplaying the safety hazards and the extent of dioxin contamination in Michigan waterways.[76] A quarter of a century later, in 2008, it became clear that Dow was continuing to use its considerable political influence to avoid responsibility for the dioxin contamination when the Bush Administration forced EPA regional director Mary Gade to resign. Gade had invoked emergency powers to order Dow to clean up record levels of dioxin contamination near one of its plants. According to a *Chicago Tribune* investigation, 'Dow responded by appealing to officials in Washington' and Gade was told to quit or be fired. 'There's no question this is about Dow,' Gade was quoted as saying in the article.[77]

These serious environmental and public health externalities (which also raise questions about the efficiency of private chemical production inasmuch as they are not appropriately priced in), along with the economic and societal importance of the sector and its demonstrated exploitation of political-economic power to avoid regulation, suggests that public ownership in some form may be appropriate. Like pharmaceutical companies, this could be structured in different ways and at various scales. While it will be discussed further later, it is worth noting in passing that both the historical record and empirical studies suggest that public ownership alone will likely not solve the issues of environmental, health, and other externalities in sectors such as these. Unless publicly owned enterprises are democratized, decentralized, and transparent, they will likely replicate some of the same patterns with regards to environmental despoliation and the use of political power to avoid responsibility (the environmental record of the Soviet Union, for instance, was far from stellar, as former residents of Chernobyl and the Aral Sea region can attest). Additionally, environmental and public health goals would need to be embedded in the mission of newly created or converted publicly owned entities in this sector. For instance, these companies could be tasked with creating, mass-producing, and selling environmentally safe alternatives to chemicals currently being made by for-profit corporations.

Transportation

Transportation is yet another sector where public ownership has traditionally been both beneficial and necessary to the functioning of an advanced economy. The transportation system can be roughly divided into two components – infrastructure and services (sometimes referred to as 'fixed' and 'variable' costs respectively). In the first, public ownership is usually dominant. As we have seen, in the United States this includes ports, airports, roads and highways, and bridges. Public ownership of such transportation infrastructure enables generally equal access for individuals and businesses, extends the network to most parts of the country, and helps distribute the enormous direct and indirect economic benefits more evenly. Moreover, in most cases high capital costs, economies of scale, and the need for network coordination make transportation infrastructure a natural monopoly and generally unsuitable for high levels of competition. In the second, the provision of transportation services, ownership structures are more mixed.

One example of these two components interacting can be seen in the air transportation industry. Here, services are provided predominantly by private, for-profit companies that pay to use the publicly owned infrastructure (airports, air traffic control centers, etc.). These carriers are subsidized by the government to varying degrees in order to maintain service levels across the network (for instance, to provide air transportation access to rural areas where it would be unprofitable for private companies to operate) and have been bailed out by the government in times of economic crisis.[78] Another example is the more than four million miles (as of 2013) of public roads in the United States, defined by the Bureau of Transportation Statistics as 'any road under the jurisdiction of and maintained by a public authority (federal, state, county, town or township, local government or instrumentality thereof) and open to public travel.'[79] In addition to individual use, service on these roads is provided by a mix of privately owned and publicly owned enterprises (e.g., privately owned and publicly owned buses).

Regarding roads, it is important to note two important and connected developments. First, as of 2015 there were around 5,932 miles of toll roads (including bridges and tunnels) across 34 American states and Puerto Rico.[80] While many of these toll roads are operated by states or publicly owned transportation agencies (thus allowing revenues generated to be reinvested in public road maintenance or new public road creation), a hybrid form of ownership has emerged in recent years. These are public–private partnerships (PPPs) whereby private, for-profit corporations provide up-front capital investment for new or existing transportation infrastructure development and then enter into long-term leases with the government to collect revenues from the operation of that infrastructure (a related development is the leasing of existing revenue-generating infrastructure – such as parking meters and toll roads – to private corporations in exchange for an up-front fee).[81] While the underlying infrastructure remains in public ownership, the long-term leases (in some cases up to 99 years) and the onerous terms often essentially amount to privatization under a different name. The American experience with PPPs in infrastructure has, in several cases, been catastrophic for individuals, businesses, and state finances. A 2011 report by the Brookings Institution, for instance, found that 'in practice [PPPs] have been dogged by contract design problems, waste, and unrealistic expectations.'[82]

In many cases, it would be more economically beneficial to the public, especially in the long run, to use existing bond-financing measures and to retain direct public control over the collection of toll revenue. For instance, in 2015, transportation officials in Virginia estimated that by forgoing a PPP for the expansion of Interstate 66 (including the addition of toll lanes) and instead using traditional financing mechanisms, the state would recoup $200 to $500 million over 40 years, which could be reinvested in other transportation projects. 'We would welcome a partner on this deal. But it's not going to be driven by ideology,' Virginia Transportation Secretary Aubrey Layne said at the time. 'Our numbers show right now it's better for the Commonwealth to do this as a publicly financed deal.'[83]

Virginia's newfound hesitation regarding PPPs is not without cause. An early adopter of such projects, the state had been left holding the bag on a number of previous long-term arrangements that benefited neither state finances nor local residents. One example is the Dulles Greenway, a toll road near Washington, D.C. nicknamed the 'Champagne Highway' due to its extraordinarily high rates and severe underutilization (in a region crippled by chronic traffic problems).[84] Local, mostly Republican, officials have tried in vain for years to either force the private owners to lower the toll rates or have the state nationalize the road.[85]

A somewhat more atypical ownership structure exists in the railroad industry. Here, the legacy of privately owned passenger railroads and their failure during the post-war period has left a system that is almost an inverse of the traditional model. As we have seen, the publicly owned company Amtrak exclusively provides inter-city passenger rail service in the United States. However, 72 percent of the track used by Amtrak is owned by other entities, including private, for-profit freight rail corporations and state and local governments.[86] This structure throws up a host of impediments to effectively expanding passenger rail service across the country – especially the deployment of high-speed rail which, in a continental system as large as the United States, is important with regards to both reducing travel times (and the attendant economic benefits this would have) and cutting carbon emissions (as airline travel is one of the more carbon-intensive modes of transportation).[87] Not coincidently, in the only part of the United States that currently has anything approximating high-speed rail (the Northeast Corridor), *both* the infrastructure and the service are publicly owned (mostly by Amtrak, although some sections are owned by other public transit agencies).[88] In areas where Amtrak does not own the rail infrastructure, the prospects for high-speed rail (or even reliable regular rail transport) are remote. 'Outside of the Northeast Corridor, the railroad infrastructure is generally owned by freight companies,' journalist Matthew Yglesias writes. 'Amtrak is just piggybacking on the spare capacity. That means the technology isn't optimized for passenger rail needs. But it also means passenger train scheduling needs to take a back seat to freight priorities.'[89]

Most local transit systems also have a structure where both the infrastructure and services are publicly owned. The way this ownership is manifested varies widely. In Boston, for instance, the Massachusetts Bay Transportation Authority (MBTA) is owned and operated by the Massachusetts Department of Transportation (MassDOT) and overseen by the MassDOT board (appointed by the state's governor).[90] In the San Francisco area, the Bay Area Rapid Transit (BART) District's board is comprised of a representative from each of the system's nine districts across multiple political jurisdictions.[91] The largest public transit system in the country, the Metropolitan Transportation Authority (MTA), is a public-benefit corporation chartered by the State of New York.[92] It is overseen by a 17-member board nominated by the Governor of New York. Four board members are recommended by the Mayor of New York City, and one each by the county executives of seven adjacent counties (although four of these seven members collectively receive only one vote).[93] Additionally, there are a number of non-voting board members representing commuters and workers.[94]

There are numerous reforms to publicly owned local transit systems that could make them more accountable, transparent, and democratic (some of which will be reviewed below). However, in terms of ownership, the integrated structure of publicly owned infrastructure and service delivery generally works well and should likely be preserved. In some cities, however, years of underinvestment, inadequate funding, and, in some cases, poor management have led to rising cost pressures and deteriorating service quality. To deal with this, several transit systems are considering, or have implemented, pseudo-privatization programs. In Boston, for instance, MBTA has outsourced parts warehousing and cash management, and is considering the same for bus maintenance and customer service.[95] While costs have indeed come down, they have been at the expense of workers as union jobs have been replaced and the threat of privatization has been deployed to lower pay and reduce benefits system-wide.[96] Following Boston's lead, WMATA in Washington, D.C. is considering a similar approach – possibly including outsourcing station managers and track inspectors on a soon-to-be-opened stretch of new track (which raises serious safety and quality questions). In these cases, rather than engage in a race to the bottom that hurts workers and consumers, public transit systems should consider alternative approaches. On the revenue side, public ownership and development of land around transit stops could be further utilized. When it comes to costs, transit systems could engage in public-public partnerships with their workers and other stakeholders to increase efficiency and reduce costs rather than treating them as hostile adversaries.[97]

In terms of inter-city rail, an integrated, publicly owned structure should likely be expanded as part of a comprehensive strategy to enhance passenger rail (and specifically high-speed rail) access, reliability, and service – which, as we have seen, is recognized by people across the ideological spectrum as being essential to stabilizing the economies and demographics of local communities. Perhaps most importantly, the nation's rail *infrastructure* should be taken into public ownership, perhaps gradually, to allow for this expansion. Once the infrastructure is publicly owned and overseen, it would be possible to allow various entities to provide services. For instance, rather than a single, centralized, publicly owned passenger rail company, there could be several regional publicly owned companies that provide service in designated areas but do not directly compete (it is also conceivable, although probably not advisable given the experience of rail service privatization in the UK, that private companies could be given the opportunity to operate certain rail franchises).

With regards to the nation's road infrastructure, PPPs and other backdoor privatization efforts should be resisted and reversed. While upfront payments and new and expanded roads are attractive to often cash-strapped states and municipalities, in the long run taxpayers and users will usually be better served by returning to traditional financing mechanisms – especially in low-interest-rate environments such as have existed for many years in the United States (in the case of the Dulles Greenway, the interest rate on the bond secured by its private owners was around 14 percent, compared to the 4 percent interest rate the state pays on its bonds).[98] Moving beyond this, it may be in the public interest to enter into new public–public partnerships to finance these types of infrastructure projects. This might include large public pension funds with trillions in assets (or other 'publics' such as union pension funds) providing the upfront capital investment in exchange for long-term stable returns. The $300 billion California Public Employees' Retirement System (CalPERS) is one such pension fund moving in this direction. In May 2016, it announced that its Infrastructure Program had made its first US transportation investment, buying 10 percent of the private company that operates the Indiana Toll Road.[99] Moreover, a recent bill passed by the California legislature (but vetoed by Governor Jerry Brown) would have allowed the state to identify local infrastructure projects for CalPERS to invest in and act as a guarantor if the investment did not yield the expected rate of return.[100] The United States could also consider the example of other nations and create a large public sovereign wealth fund (similar to those that exist in a handful of US states) that could be used to invest in local, regional, and national infrastructure projects. Already US infrastructure is being eyed as a lucrative opportunity by foreign entities, including Qatar's sovereign wealth fund, which has announced that it plans to invest up to $10 billion in such projects.[101]

Air transportation offers another interesting possibility for the expansion of public ownership. As we have seen, around the world many airlines are either completely or partially publicly owned – including some of the fastest growing and best-rated carriers based in the Middle East. While the creation or purchase (perhaps in exchange for bailout funds, as in the case of banks) of a publicly owned flag carrier or carriers may be preferable – especially to compete with such entities operating abroad – at the very least a publicly owned carrier could be formed that would take over the already subsidized and loss-making routes that for-profit carriers would otherwise not operate (an 'airline of last resort,' for lack of a better term). In addition to ensuring that affordable service is maintained for all communities, such a public enterprise would allow for-profit airlines to focus their resources, potentially lowering costs for consumers and allowing them to be more competitive with foreign companies on lucrative international routes.

Energy

While there is considerable overlap between the energy and utility sectors, this section focuses primarily on enterprises that extract and produce energy-related resources, as opposed to those that generate and transmit electricity. Essentially, this means the oil, gas, and coal industries, and, to a lesser extent, the uranium-mining industry. In these industries, the rapidly shrinking timeframe needed to avoid catastrophic climate change suggests the need for dramatic and comprehensive, rather than piecemeal and incremental, change. At this point, it is well-demonstrated that the large, for-profit fossil fuel corporations pose a fundamental political and economic impediment to efforts to adequately address climate change.

In 2010, for instance, corporate lobbying played a significant role in getting the Democrat-controlled Senate to drop a cap-and-trade climate bill already passed by the House of Representatives.[102] Seizing upon the public and political concern over stubbornly high unemployment at the time, gas and coal companies and their allies went on the offensive. During debate over the legislation, National Petrochemical and Refiners Association (NPRA) Executive Vice President and General Counsel Gregory M. Scott argued that 'the draconian carbon reduction targets and timetables in this bill would trigger destructive change in America's economic climate. This would add billions of dollars in energy costs for American families and businesses, destroy the jobs of millions of American workers, and make our nation more dependent on foreign energy sources.'[103] Among others, the American Petroleum Institute chipped in with television, radio, and print ads featuring ordinary Americans criticizing the possibility of increased energy taxes.[104] It is estimated that the oil and gas industry spent $163 million lobbying against the bill after it had passed the House (and $250 million altogether over an 18-month period).[105] In 2009 alone, the oil and gas industry spent nearly eight times as much opposing the bill as environmental groups and their allies did supporting it. One company alone, Exxon-Mobil, spent more than all the environmental groups put together.[106] 'The opposition outspent us, and they took it to a new level this time,' Nathan Wilcox of Environment America lamented.[107] Greenpeace spokesperson Joe Smyth agreed, stating, 'we as a community are not going to be able to out-lobby [oil and gas], or other industries. We need to take our fight elsewhere.'[108]

Moreover, this corporate obstruction on climate-change issues is not limited to lobbying elected officials. In 2015, an investigation by *InsideClimate News* revealed that Exxon-Mobil's decades-long efforts to deny the science and obstruct the politics of climate-change mitigation occurred even though its own scientists had known about, rigorously studied, and warned about the issue from 1977 onwards.[109] As Bill McKibben puts it, 'had [Exxon's] leaders merely stated directly what they knew to be true, [they] could have ended the pretend debate over climate change as early as the 1980s.'[110] In his 2009 book *Heat*, investigative journalist George Monbiot revealed that Exxon-Mobil alone 'lists 124 organizations which have taken money from the company or work closely with those which have,' and these organizations 'take a consistent line on climate change: that the science is contradictory, the scientists are split, environmentalists are charlatans, liars or lunatics, and if governments took action to prevent global warming, they would be endangering the global economy for no good reason.'[111] One of the goals of funding multiple groups, Monbiot explained, is to make it seem that climate skepticism and doubt is widespread.[112] Steve Coll, a journalist at *The New Yorker* and author of *Private Empire: Exxon Mobil and American Power*, concurs, revealing that Lee Raymond, Exxon's CEO until 2005, 'believed that [climate change] was a hoax, in effect, that the earth was not warming at all. … So he not only went after the treaty bargain, but funded, often in the early years surreptitiously, campaigns to attack the science that were carried out by nonscientific groups, often by free-market ideologues.'[113]

And, of course, such activities are not limited to Exxon. In the early 1990s, Exxon joined with other corporations and groups such as BP, Shell USA, Texaco, and the American Petroleum Institute as part of the now defunct Global Climate Coalition. Financed by fees from its member corporations and trade groups, the organization embarked upon a lobbying and public relations campaign intended to discredit climate science – even as its own scientists and experts were warning that global warming and the potential impact of human emissions of greenhouse gases could not be disputed.[114] This activity is not confined to the past. Recently, the corporate-backed Western Petroleum Association led a high-profile fight against California's attempts to pass innovative climate-change legislation at the state level.[115]

Intricately linked to the efforts of fossil fuel corporations to block or stall political progress on climate change is the emerging economic issue of stranded assets (sometimes called 'sunk carbon costs,' 'unburnable carbon,' or the 'carbon bubble'). As we have seen, investors, public officials, and others are beginning to realize that if all the proven reserves of fossil fuel companies were to be used, the world would blow past every measure of 'acceptable' temperature increase and experience the full and catastrophic effects of runaway climate change. The London-based think tank Carbon Tracker Initiative has estimated that as much as 80 percent of the proven fossil fuel reserves of for-profit, publicly traded fossil fuel corporations will have to be left in the ground to reduce the likelihood of temperature rises above 2° Celsius – around a $20 trillion write-down, according to John Fullerton of the Capital Institute, an ex-JP Morgan Managing Director.[116] In September 2015, Mark Carney, Governor of the Bank of England, became one of the most senior officials in the world to embrace this reality when he warned an audience at Lloyds Bank that efforts to combat climate change would 'render the vast majority of reserves "stranded" – oil, gas and coal that will be literally unburnable.'[117]

In other words, if climate change is to be avoided (or mitigated) major oil and gas companies are facing the prospect of financial implosion. A recent illustration of this can be found in what has already happened to the American coal industry. In 2015 and 2016, several coal companies collapsed, including Peabody Energy – once one of the world's largest coal companies – which had lost 99 percent of its value since 2011.[118] 'The Coal Industry is Bankrupt,' John Brinkley declared in an April 2016 article for *Sierra Magazine*.

Brinkley went on to cite numerous industry and market experts who agreed that the industry was basically finished because of climate-related legislation, environmental activism, and the rise of cleaner gas and renewables as energy alternatives. Hundreds of coal-fired power plants are scheduled for closure, hundreds more have been blocked from opening, and nations across the world are reducing their coal imports. One coal industry analyst, Matthew Miller, was quoted as saying that it is 'unlikely that another coal-fired electric power plant will be built in the United States.'[119]

This raises the prospect of public ownership in these industries to manage their transition in an orderly fashion, limiting the environmental and social damage they cause on the way down. In June 2016, New York University Professor Stephen Kass proposed that in the case of coal-fired power plants, 'the federal government could buy the plants and close them.'[120] Kass envisions a program that would use the federal government's *eminent domain* powers to compulsorily purchase and then close all coal-fired power plants over a 10-year period – thus achieving greater and quicker carbon-reduction benefits than the regulatory approach that was put forward under President Obama's Clean Power Plan. In Kass's estimation, the plan could be supported by plant owners and workers, given that the alternative they are facing is terminal decline and bankruptcy. A similar argument could be made with regards to the coal *mining* industry, given that most of those companies are already in bankruptcy proceedings or careening rapidly toward them. In fact, Kass uses the example of Peabody Energy and states that 'coal-plant owners and institutional investors, as well as their lenders, are locked in to deteriorating assets that are losing the competition against natural gas and renewable energy sources – and facing increased regulation of pollutants independent of climate change initiatives. These parties might welcome a graceful exit from coal.'[121] Immediately nationalizing the coal companies that are in bankruptcy (or already heading toward it) would remove a still-powerful political impediment to addressing climate change, and, if paired with an aggressive phase out/conversion plan (discussed further below), would be an important step forward to lowering carbon emissions to acceptable levels and increasing human health (it would also prevent new buyers from purchasing the companies' assets and continuing coal production).

Nationalizing the big oil and gas corporations would be much more expensive and politically controversial – although it is no less necessary from a climate-change perspective. One estimate is that, absent any devaluation that may occur as a result of additional environmental regulation, awareness of stranded assets, or lowering of demand, it would cost around $1.15 trillion to purchase the top 25 publicly traded oil and gas companies along with most of the remaining publicly traded coal companies.[122] Adding some smaller publicly traded companies and certain privately held companies would likely raise this amount to somewhere in the $2 trillion range, not counting associated costs such as environmental cleanup, job retraining, and healthcare and retirement for workers. This seems like a large sum until it is set beside, say, the wars in Iraq and Afghanistan, now estimated to have cost around $5 trillion, including $1.7 trillion in direct war appropriations.[123]

Perhaps the biggest cost, however, would be replacing fossil fuels with renewable energy.[124] Together with colleagues at the Democracy Collaborative, I have proposed one possible public ownership option for the US fossil fuel industry that begins to address both the cost and transition issues as a basis for further exploration. Rather than fund the buyout program through conventional public expenditures, the federal government could simply create new money via the Federal Reserve, as it did with its roughly $3.5 trillion 'Quantitative Easing' program between 2008 and 2014 (which, counter to conventional wisdom, did not lead to runaway inflation).[125] The money could then be used to buy up, over a period of time, the stock of fossil fuel corporations and capitalize a publicly owned Green Investment Bank (or series of state-level banks). Fossil fuel investors could also be given the opportunity to roll their investments over tax-free to Green Investment Bank bonds or eligible renewable energy company stock. The bank(s) would then facilitate the massive, new investment in renewable energy (and conversion or replacement of existing generation facilities) necessary to maintain a sufficient supply of energy while the fossil fuel companies are steadily decommissioned over a period of perhaps several years. If supply and demand remain relatively balanced during the decommissioning process, energy prices for consumers should also remain somewhat stable. However, if an imbalance does occur for any reason, and prices for consumers begin to rise, profits generated by the publicly owned fossil fuel corporations during the decommissioning process (perhaps collected from the beginning and put into an investment fund) could be distributed in the form of an energy rebate.[126]

Public ownership in the oil and gas industry has been seriously proposed at various points in American history. For instance, in the 1970s, faced with rising energy costs, Democratic Senators Adlai Stevenson III of Illinois, Edward Kennedy of Massachusetts, and

George McGovern of South Dakota – together with consumer advocates and union leaders – backed legislation to create a Federal Oil and Gas Corporation that would extract, refine, transport, and sell fossil fuel resources. Senator Stevenson argued that because most existing reserves were on public land, they were 'owned by the people' and 'should be developed for the people.' The private oil and gas industry was, obviously, deeply opposed to the idea, and lobbied heavily against it. The CEO of Exxon, M. A. Wright, wrote to Stevenson stating that 'it is likely that creation of a Federal Oil and Gas Corporation would be the first step towards a total nationalization of the industry.'[127] At that time, nationalization was being considered to increase production because of shortages; today, nationalization should be considered in the context of the need to reduce, and eventually eliminate, the extraction of fossil fuels.

While removing a powerful political impediment to badly needed policy changes is important, public ownership of fossil fuel enterprises alone will not be sufficient to address the threat of climate change. As we have seen, around the world most oil and gas resources are already extracted by publicly owned enterprises. Like for-profit corporations, these enterprises are also sitting on top of massive, unburnable reserves. Moreover, in many countries the enormous revenues generated by publicly owned fossil fuel companies are used to subsidize various other economic sectors and pay for social services. A report by the Natural Resource Governance Institute, for instance, found that in 36 out of 45 countries, 'governments rely on [state owned petroleum or mining companies] to provide a range of services – from infrastructure construction to social services to fuel subsidies.'[128] At best, these companies wield tremendous political-economic influence, and at worst are engines of corruption and cronyism. Therefore, any nationalization effort targeting fossil fuel companies would have to be deliberately augmented by a more comprehensive, publicly managed conversion program to renewable energy. Investments would need to be shifted, workers retrained and redeployed, research and development re-focused, and so on – all in a way that maintains a constant supply of energy to meet existing and increasing demand. Moreover, given that fossil fuel extraction is often geographically concentrated in certain regions, the program would need to include significant re-allocation of resources and targeted economic development strategies in order to prevent a re-run of the catastrophic deindustrialization of the Rustbelt and deepening regional socio-economic imbalances, the political consequences of which are still coming home to roost in today's America.

Fortunately, public ownership is compatible with, and perhaps even a prerequisite for, such a comprehensive, complex, and ambitious strategy of economic planning. The array of renewable energy enterprises resulting from such a program of nationalization and conversion could, for the variety of reasons related to public benefit and control already noted, be kept in public ownership at various scales (local, regional, or national), or spun off to worker, community, or nonprofit ownership.

Defense

In 1961, President Dwight Eisenhower (who was also a retired five-star army general) gave his now famous 'military industrial complex' speech, officially his farewell address to the nation, from the White House as he prepared to leave office. Eisenhower noted that the development of a large-scale defense (armaments) industry was relatively unprecedented in American history, yet now its political-economic influence 'is felt in every city, every State house, every office of the Federal government.' 'In the councils of government, we must guard against the acquisition of unwarranted influence, whether sought or unsought, by the military industrial complex,' Eisenhower continued. 'The potential for the disastrous rise of misplaced power exists and will persist.'[129] Eisenhower's warning went essentially unheeded, and in the more than 50 years since, the US defense industry has grown in both power and influence. According to the Stockholm International Peace Research Institute's Arms Industry database, in 2014 seven of the top 10 (and four of the top five) arms companies around the world were American (Lockheed Martin, Boeing, Raytheon, Northrop Grumman, General Dynamics, United Technologies, and L-3 Communications).[130] Combined they had total sales of around $291.2 billion and employed 705,000 people.

The political power of these corporations is legendary.[131] 'Although the defense sector contributes far less money to politicians than many other sectors,' the Center for Responsive Politics reports, 'it is one of the most powerful in politics.'[132] In many cases, this power now overrides military requirements and suggestions. During the Cold War, policymakers generally respected the military's judgement on procurement decisions. As Eugene Gholz and Harvey Sapolsky wrote in 1999, 'today, however, contractors and congressional representatives have cemented the military-industrial ties that critics feared during the Cold War.'[133] For instance, in recent years, despite being told repeatedly by the army that it is not needed, Congress has appropriated nearly a half billion dollars to developing an upgraded version of the Abrams tank to be produced by General Dynamics.[134] And in May 2014, the House and Senate Armed Services Committees rejected most of the defense cuts proposed by the military's post-war re-organizational plan. 'As they have in past years,' the *Washington Post* reported, 'lawmakers preserved funding for myriad of programs and platforms … including several the Pentagon has come to see as expendable in an era of leaner budgets.'[135]

More so than perhaps any other sector, the defense industry is almost completely reliant on public support. This includes government contracts, subsidies, research and development, and bailouts. For instance, in 2015, Lockheed Martin had total revenue of $46.1 billion, and it was reported that it received government contracts worth $36.2 billion – the most of any company in any industry.[136] Moreover, the public advocacy group Good Jobs First reports that since 1996, the company has received more than $1.4 billion in local, state, and federal subsidies.[137] And, in 1971, the government set the precedent that large defense corporations are too important to fail when it bailed out Lockheed – which was spiraling toward bankruptcy as a result of cost overruns, the winding down of the Vietnam War, and the bankruptcy of Rolls-Royce, the British engine manufacturer.[138] In essence, the defense sector is the epitome of what political scientist and critic Michael Parenti calls 'the practice of using the public's money and resources to bolster private profits.'[139]

Because of this, taking the defense industry into public ownership has long been advocated by an array of observers, from mainstream journalists and academics to peace advocates and alternative system thinkers. Outraged by war profiteering during the First World War, a variety of groups and social movements took up the cause of defense industry nationalization during the 1930s.[140] In 1969, economist John Kenneth Galbraith wrote in a long essay in the *New York Times* that we should 'recognize the reality of things, which is that the large specialized defense contractors are really public firms' and that 'by no known definition of private enterprise can these specialized firms or subsidiaries be classified as private corporations … The process of converting the defense firms from *de facto* to *de jure* public enterprises would not be especially complicated.' His proposal is worth quoting at length:

> The defense industry is highly concentrated. If a company or subsidiary exceeded a certain size and degree of specialization in the weapons business, its common stock would be valued at market rates well antedating

the takeover and the stock and the debt would be assumed by the Treasury in exchange for Government bonds. Stockholders would thus be protected from any loss resulting from the conversion of these firms to *de jure* public ownership. Directors would henceforth be designated by the Government and the firms, subject to any needed reorganization and consolidation, would function thereafter as publicly owned, nonprofit corporations.[141]

More recently, Charlie Cray, currently a senior research specialist at Greenpeace focusing on corporations and democracy (among other things), has written extensively about taking the defense industry into public ownership. 'It is hard to imagine an industrial sector better suited for federal chartering than the nation's defense and security contracting firms,' Cray and his coauthor Lee Drutman wrote in 2005. 'The existence of these firms is predicated upon federal policy goals with the largest receiving major income streams through federal contracts.' Converting these companies to public ownership (along with making them nonprofit) would, they contend, have a variety of benefits:

> It would reduce the entities' impetus for aggressive lobbying and campaign contributions. Chartering the defense contractors at the federal level would in effect allow Congress to ban such activities outright, thereby controlling an industry that is now a driving force rather than a servant of foreign policy objectives. As public firms, they would certainly continue to participate in the policy fora designed to determine the nation's national security and defense technology needs, but the profit driven impetus to control the process in order to best serve corporate shareholders would be eliminated. Thus, by turning defense and security firms into full public corporations, we would replace the criteria by which their performance is judged from quarterly earnings targets to criteria that is more consistent with the national interest.[142]

Much as with the fossil fuel industry, merely taking defense companies into public ownership would be unlikely in and of itself to sufficiently address larger systemic concerns – in this case, the moral imperative to secure peace, end imperialism, and address pressing social needs. For this, public ownership should be paired with a plan for the conversion of production to civilian purposes. For more than 50 years, this effort to convert defense-related facilities was led intellectually by the late Seymour Melman, an economist at Columbia University. Economic conversion, as Melman put it, was 'the formulation, planning and execution of the organisational, technical, occupational and economic changes required to turn factories, laboratories, training institutions, bases and other facilities from military to civilian use.'[143] In 1976, economic conversion was successfully added to the Democratic Party platform; in 1977, former Democratic presidential nominee George McGovern sponsored a Defense Economic Adjustment bill; and in the late 1980s, several economic conversion bills were on the verge of being consolidated and pursued in Congress. After the effort was defeated by concerted defense corporation lobbying, Melman lamented that 'a historic opportunity had been destroyed.'[144]

Following the fall of the Soviet Union, many observers began questioning why the promised 'peace dividend' had failed to materialize. 'The United States has a long history of opposing large, standing armies. After every previous war, including Vietnam, we expeditiously dispatched troops, shuttered bases, mothballed or scrapped equipment, and canceled defense contracts ... So why has the United States failed to demobilize since the Cold War?' Ann Markusen asked in 1997.[145] While recent efforts to reduce the size of the US military (in terms of personnel and bases) have been relatively successful, the defense industry remains incredibly large – especially as compared to that of other nations. The United States continues to spend more on defense than the next eight countries combined, including Russia and China.[146]

One of the problems with such an effort is resistance from affected workers and communities – something that becomes evident whenever military bases are slated for closure. One farsighted precedent for addressing this problem was developed in the United Kingdom. In the mid-1970s, unionized workers at Lucas Aerospace refused to accept that unemployment was the only option in the face of government defense spending cuts and instead generated a highly sophisticated defense conversion plan of their own. 'Workers' skills and facilities would be converted to production of social benefit: wind turbines, hybrid car engines, cheap heating systems and medical products such as kidney machines,' writes Phil Asquith, one of the shop stewards involved in the effort. The idea was embraced by leading figures in the Labour Party (which included supportive language in its 1976 conference program), unions, and a variety of civil society organizations.[147] While the Lucas Plan (as it became known) was never implemented due to strong resistance from management, it was nominated for the Nobel Peace Prize in 1979 and has served as a beacon of possibility ever since.[148] Meanwhile, economic conversion efforts in the United States were also beaten back by corporate opposition. Combining such a participatory conversion plan with the nationalization of defense industries could offer hope of overcoming the limitations such approaches have experienced on both sides of the Atlantic.

Telecommunications and information technology

As advanced nations continue to transition in the direction of the so-called 'knowledge' or 'information' economy, telecommunications has emerged as a critical strategic sector. Specifically, the United States economy is already heavily reliant on internet and mobile phone networks, and their importance will only continue to grow. Leaving aside how crucial these networks are to virtually every other industry, it has been estimated that by 2015 the 'internet sector' alone accounted for around 6 percent of GDP, more than many other sectors combined.[149] Currently, the telecommunications sector in the United States is dominated by large for-profit corporations. In the cable (or broadband) industry, these include Comcast, AT&T, Time Warner, and Verizon. In the wireless carrier industry (mobile phone networks), these include AT&T, Verizon, Sprint, and T-Mobile (a subsidiary of Deutsche Telekom, which is around 31 percent publicly owned by various German government entities). In both industries, the trend is toward increased consolidation and concentration of corporate power. 'Most Americans probably believe the communications sector of the economy has room for innumerable competitors,' Harvard's Susan Crawford writes in *Captive Audience: The Telecom Industry and Monopoly Power in the New Gilded Age*. 'But they may be surprised at how concentrated the market for the modern-day equivalent of the standard phone line is. These days what that basic transmission service is facilitating is high-speed access to the internet. In that market, there are two enormous monopoly submarkets – one for wireless and one for wired transmission. Both are dominated by two or three large companies.'[150] This consolidation is understandable given that communications is arguably a natural monopoly. As Crawford explains, setting up a telecommunications system is capital intensive and most of today's dominant players have historically received substantial government support.[151]

The problems with this oligopolistic structure in the telecoms sector are well documented. On the one hand, it results in abusive practices and higher costs for individual consumers, businesses, organizations, and governments. Writing about the wireless industry's 'longstanding industry norms' of restrictive contracts, termination fees, overage charges and other 'unfriendly practices,' Columbia Law School's Tim Wu argues that:

> Our current approach, focused near-exclusively on monopoly, fails to address the serious problems posed by highly concentrated industries. If a monopolist did what the wireless carriers did as a group, neither the public nor government would stand for it. For our scrutiny and regulation of monopolists is well established – just ask Microsoft or the old AT&T. But when three or four firms pursue identical practices, we say that the market is 'competitive' and everything is fine. To state the obvious, when companies act in parallel, the consumer is in the same position as if he were dealing with just one big firm. There is, in short, a major blind spot in our nation's oversight of private power, one that affects both consumers and competition.[152]

On the other hand, an oligopolistic telecommunications sector also contributes to so-called market failures that leave wide swathes of the country (both geographically and socio-economically) with inferior or unaffordable service. According to a 2015 White House report supporting the establishment of local, publicly owned internet networks, around 50 million Americans simply did not have access to high-speed internet, including many residents of rural areas.[153] Furthermore, of the roughly 30 percent of American households that did not have a broadband internet connection, nearly 40 percent cited prohibitive costs.[154] On top of this, American internet is far slower and more expensive than most other advanced countries. 'Given that duopolies presently dominate both the wired (Comcast, Time Warner) and Wireless (Verizon, AT&T) U.S. markets,' Victor Pickard writes, 'it is reasonable to assume that a lack of competition plays an important role in this predicament.'[155]

Like other sectors where it is critically important for both economic and social reasons that core infrastructure remains public and accessible to all users, telecommunications is a sector where public ownership is demonstrably appropriate. For these reasons, and others, publicly owned telecommunications companies are prevalent around the world. Going forward, what is needed, Pickard and others contend, is a reconceptualization of communications infrastructure as a public good or service, and an embracing of 'the government's affirmative role in providing for society's communications needs – especially as systemic media market failure becomes increasingly evident.'[156]

Many observers, activists, and policymakers are supporting the rapid development of local, publicly owned communication networks, especially in those communities underserved or ignored by the for-profit telecommunications oligopoly. Crawford suggests a structure whereby local, publicly owned networks (supported and defended by the federal government) would exist alongside for-profit corporations. 'Municipally controlled fiber networks will route around the second-best installations now sold to residents by incumbent cable companies,' she writes.[157] However, these for-profit companies would also be radically restructured as public utilities (private entities that are subject to 'public supervision and control'). The reason for this, Crawford states, is that 'only large corporations with extensive resources are capable of initially mass-producing communications infrastructure at low prices; economies of scale are needed.'[158] Of course, the ability of corporations operating as public utilities to use their political-economic power to eventually capture the regulators, secure deregulation, and eliminate competition is well understood. If economies of scale are indeed necessary in this sector and decentralized, local publicly owned networks are insufficient, regional or national public enterprises could conceivably play the same role as the highly regulated, for-profit corporations Crawford suggests.

These decentralized public ownership efforts intersect with the hopes of many techno-optimist (or techno-utopian) alternative system thinkers that communications networks will enable a radical restructuring of the economy and democratization of political and economic power. 'A new communications/energy matrix is emerging,' Jeremy Rifkin writes:

> And with it a new 'smart' public infrastructure. The Internet of Things (IoT) will connect everyone and everything in a new economic paradigm that is far more complex than the First and Second Industrial Revolutions, but one whose architecture is distributed rather than centralized. Even more important, the new economy will optimize the general welfare by way of laterally integrated networks on the Collaborative Commons, rather than vertically integrated businesses in the capitalist market.[159]

The seeds of 'the commons society to come,' Michel Bauwens similarly suggests, can already be seen in the rise of free software, peer-to-peer production, code and design, open design, and more.[160]

However, for both the existing and future commons economy (and society) to flourish, a widely accessible and equitable communications system is a prerequisite. 'Infrastructure that is kept open and accessible to all can help guarantee that there is competition and innovation in the marketplace ... [Yet] the internet may be the most significant piece of infrastructure now endangered,' David Bollier notes.[161] In the fight over so-called 'net neutrality,' big corporate Internet service providers (ISPs) have for years been seeking the right to charge users different prices for different levels of internet access. Aligned against them have been consumer groups, activist organizations, and millions of citizens (along with other corporations, like Google, Amazon, and Netflix, who would lose out if net neutrality rules were scrapped).[162] With the election of President Trump – and his elevation of net neutrality opponent Ajit Pai, a former Verizon associate general counsel, to the position of Chair of the Federal Communications Commission – prospects for preserving net neutrality through regulatory action appear dim.[163] 'Only one option remains that can guarantee an open internet,' David Morris of ILSR argues: 'owning the means of distribution.' 'Thankfully an agency exists for this,' he continues: 'Local government.'[164]

Manufacturing

No economic sector captures the imagination of the public, policy-makers, and alternative system theorists quite like manufacturing. Especially in the United States, manufacturing is seen and portrayed as the engine that built national economic power and a strong and vibrant middle-class and labor movement. The widespread and widely reported decline of manufacturing in the United States since the 1970s has produced an existential crisis for workers and communities in many parts of the country, the social and political repercussions of which are still being felt acutely. Manufacturing employment fell from around 19 million in 1979 (18.6 percent of labor force) to just around 12 million in early 2017 (7.7 percent of the labor force).[165] More shockingly, much of this decline happened in just seven years (2000 to 2007), in the wake of the instituting of permanent normal trade relations (PNTR) with China.[166] The socio-economic consequences of manufacturing job losses on big cities like Detroit and Cleveland are well known. However, the impacts have been equally profound in smaller communities. 'While large legacy cities were engines of our nation's growth for almost a century, smaller cities made important marks on our history as well,' a recent Federal Reserve Bank of Boston report contends. 'Smaller cities face challenges similar to those of larger cities, such as job and population loss, which are often compounded by their smaller size and regional location.'[167]

In 2008 *Forbes Magazine* published a report on America's dying small towns. Number one on the list was Bensenville, Illinois, a village south of Chicago. Between 2000 and 2015, that town's population fell by more than 10 percent.[168] Kenneth Johnson, a senior demographer at the University of New Hampshire, outlined the economic causes of the decline, stating that 'much of the low-level manufacturing work has gone overseas, or the jobs have shifted to the outer edges of the metro area. What's happening is, you have industrial jobs replaced by service jobs.'[169] A 2011 report from the *Associated Press* related the story of Moundsville, West Virginia. Between 2000 and 2015 the town's population dropped 11 percent.[170] 'This place ain't dead yet, but it's got about half a foot in the grave,' said Bob Frees, a local resident interviewed for the *AP* story. 'The big-money jobs are all gone. We used to have the big mills and the rolling plants and stuff like that, and you could walk out of high school when you were 16 or 17 and get a $15-an-hour job.'[171] Bringing back well-paid manufacturing jobs has become a mantra for politicians of all stripes, not least Donald Trump. However, without a serious industrial strategy it is doubtful in this era of globalization and increased automation that large numbers of manufacturing jobs will be coming back of their own accord, and those that do are likely be either lower wage or require advanced skills and education beyond those that most manufacturing workers currently possess.

Yet while manufacturing jobs are declining, manufacturing itself is still a crucial and vibrant economic sector. According to a 2012 report by the Manufacturing Institute, between 1980 and 2011 the rate of profitability in the sector averaged 12.5 percent and was at a record high.[172] In 2015, the National Association of Manufacturers reported that manufacturing's contribution to the economy was nearly 30 percent higher than in 2009 and accounted for around 12.1 percent of GDP.[173] And more recently it was revealed that while manufacturing output is up by more than 20 percent since the end of the Great Recession, employment has risen by just 5 percent.[174] Therefore, it appears, perhaps unsurprisingly, that the proceeds from increased productivity in the manufacturing sector are not being redistributed or shared with local communities to an extent sufficient to counterbalance the overarching effects of manufacturing job losses and ongoing deindustrialization.

It is also important to note that small firms now dominate US manufacturing, with three quarters of the roughly 250,000 firms in 2014 employing less than 20 workers.[175] Moreover, many of these smaller, local manufacturing firms are privately held, with baby-boomer owners who, over the next 15 years, will be retiring as part of the so-called 'silver tsunami.'[176] With few other options other than to sell to competitors or vulture-like private equity firms, there is the distinct possibility of further large-scale manufacturing-related job loss, plant closure, and economic dislocation in local communities across America in the next two decades.

Public ownership, alongside worker ownership, could play a role in both alleviating the local economic implications of the imbalance between manufacturing productivity and employment and the threat of further transition-related community economic dislocations. In the current economic context, state and local economic development agencies (along with municipal governments) play an important role in subsidizing and incentivizing manufacturing (and other) companies as a business attraction and retention strategy. As many observers have documented, this process is seriously flawed, can weaken local revenue collection, and often results in a race to the bottom of competitive subsidization among neighboring jurisdictions. Research by Good Jobs First has shown that the state and local subsidies deployed in such 'smokestack-chasing' strategies total around $70 billion a year, an expense that, in 2005, Susan Christopherson judged to be almost 'a complete waste of taxpayer money.'[177]

Alternatively, those resources could be far better spent by charging local economic development agencies and/or local public banks with the task of investing directly, and taking ownership stakes, in these smaller local manufacturing firms. This would ensure that a portion of company profits is distributed back to the local economy, perhaps in the form of increased investment in other job-creating activities (including other manufacturing firms), education and job training (including the skills needed for workers to secure higher-paid positions in more automated manufacturing facilities), and infrastructure (including high-speed internet networks necessary for local economic development). Already, state and local development agencies are involved in similar activities with a number of firms across multiple economic sectors. For instance, Susan Clarke and Gary Gaile revealed in 1998 that more than half of the cities they surveyed were making direct investments in local businesses.[178] Inasmuch as the public would begin taking actual ownership stakes in such companies, this could also serve as a powerful mechanism to keep companies from relocating (or threatening to relocate) to other communities or offshore. It could also serve as a way to keep manufacturing companies locally owned when their previous owners are seeking to retire. Local development agencies or public banks could purchase the firms from their retiring owners and/or use their financial muscle to help the workers in those firms purchase their workplaces (in the latter case, the public could choose to retain an ownership stake alongside workers or be bought out by the worker-owners over time).

Using economic development agencies or other public entities as the vehicle to make and manage these types of investments could also be a way to address the previously discussed question of managerial autonomy. Representative political bodies could task these permanent autonomous entities with broad goals (such as profits, service, or employment) and criteria (such as geographic limitations) governing the investment strategy, but would not be involved in the individual investment decisions or the day-to-day exercise of the public's ownership stake. Taking this a step further, the governance structure of these autonomous public agencies could include representatives of various stakeholder groups (community, labor, business, environment, government) and involve a mix of direct election and appointment. Such multi-stakeholder boards would be better placed – in that they would be informed by a much wider range of interests and socio-political understanding – to determine whether to increase or decrease investments in certain companies or to vote for or against specific business decisions (such as relocating production abroad or laying off workers). Also, this structure of potentially hundreds of autonomous local public agencies making investments in a wide variety of companies could actually help to preserve and enhance competition and innovation – something that, as we have seen, may be important given the lack of natural monopoly in many manufacturing industries.

Of course, economies of scale do exist in manufacturing (and other sectors), necessitating some larger companies. However, generally speaking, the argument for the existence of larger corporations is often overstated. As Gar Alperovitz likes to point out, H. C. Simons, one of the conservative founders of the Chicago School – and a teacher of Milton Friedman – wrote in the early part of the twentieth century that 'few of our giant corporations can be defended on the ground that their present size is necessary to reasonably full exploitation of production economies.'[179] Similarly, another founder of the Chicago School, Jacob Viner, noted that the manufacturing of many goods often worked as well in very small countries as it did in large, continental systems such as the United States.[180] More recently, Thomas H. Naylor and William H. Willimon stated that 'the so-called law of increasing returns to scale, which misled us into believing that average costs would decrease with increases in company size, turns out to be a myth.'[181]

In other words, some of the manufacturing that is automatically assumed to require very large, vertically integrated companies could perhaps be accomplished by the smaller public or worker owned companies described above. Historically, one of the driving forces behind the increasing size of companies in manufacturing and other sectors was the efficiencies gained from greater administrative coordination – especially regarding the integration of production with marketing and distribution.[182] For a manufacturing sector comprised of smaller firms (be they publicly owned, worker owned, privately owned, or some combination of all three) to replace some work now done by large corporate players, the coordination problem will have to be addressed.

One classic option is the 'network model' found in the Emilia Romagna region of Italy. 'Italy has not cultivated the model of the big, stand alone corporation and has on the contrary developed strong networks of small and medium size enterprises (SMEs), highly specialized in certain lines of business,' economic historian Vera Zamagni recently observed in an interview about the region. 'Networking is the alternative to full integration, to reap economies of scale and scope. If and when mergers and the building up of a single integrated firm is not acceptable either on technical grounds (need for specialization) or on cultural ones (no propensity to work in a big business), networks can provide the necessary cuts in transactions costs.'[183] The development of this network model of production in Emilia Romagna was aided in its early stages by the creation in 1974 of a majority publicly owned economic development agency called Ente Regionale per la Valorizzazione Economica de Territorio (ERVET). ERVET's mandate was to 'act as a policy tool to implement economic and industrial policies, translate regional programming into actual projects, and design and implement innovative projects together with the local economic actors.'[184] To accomplish this, ERVET established a network of specialized subsidiaries that provided local firms with a variety of services and support ranging from certification to marketing to business development.[185]

Beyond this, where large manufacturing companies are truly needed for economic reasons, public ownership strategies may also be applicable. E. F. Schumacher, for instance, wrote that 'when we come to large-scale enterprises, the idea of private ownership becomes an absurdity. The property is not and cannot be private in any real sense.'[186] For Schumacher, transitioning large enterprises to public ownership did not simply mean transferring the existing 'bundle of rights' that makes up ownership from private hands to the state. It meant re-conceptualizing those rights and determining which should be placed where (this will be discussed further below). It is beyond the scope of this work to determine what the optimal scale of enterprise is in every manufacturing (or other) industry. However, it is useful to recall that the US government defines a 'large' company as being one with more than 500 employees. Under this definition, there are no more than 3,800 such manufacturing companies in the entire country.[187]

In the context of manufacturing, it is also important to raise the 'employer of last resort' concept promulgated by many political-economic theorists. In recent years, this has been closely associated with Modern Monetary Theory (MMT) and its prominent advocates L. Randall Wray, Stephanie Kelton, and Pavlina Tcherneva (among others). 'The employer of last resort (ELR),' Tcherneva writes, 'is a proposal for a federally-funded program in which the government employs all of the jobless who are ready, willing, and able to work in a public sector project at a base wage,' and has numerous economic benefits.[188] The real-world ELR precedents often pointed to are the Works Progress Administration (WPA) and the Civilian Conservation Corps (CCC) established during the Great Depression, when the government, at modest cost, employed millions of people to build bridges, roads, airports, parks, and other public facilities (in addition to providing other services). With most experts agreeing that the nation's infrastructure is now in dire need of repair, replacement, and modernization (to say nothing of the need for a massive expansion of affordable housing in some areas, plus community regeneration, restoration of ecosystem services, social care, and the like) a publicly owned, locally administered employer of last resort construction enterprise like the WPA and or CCC could fit the bill.

Agriculture and retail

As with manufacturing, real or perceived economies of scale have been used to justify increased consolidation in both the retail and agricultural sectors. 'Mergers and acquisitions (M&A) have resulted in the consolidation of retail chains, thereby substantially altering the retail competitive arena,' Ruth Bolton, Detra Montoya, and Venkatesh Shankar wrote in 2009. 'The financial rationale for consolidation is that retailers can maintain or strengthen their competitive positions in the marketplace by increasing their size, thereby lowering costs (by improving their bargaining position vis-à-vis manufacturers), expanding revenues from consumers and markets, and gaining market share across channels and formats.'[189] The classic example most economists point to is the giant retailing behemoth Wal-Mart (now the largest private employer in the United States).[190] 'Although retailing, in general, has relatively limited opportunities to benefit from economies of scale, Wal-Mart has prospered by leveraging scale where it matters,' Timothy Laseter and Elliot Rabinovich write.[191] Specifically, this has involved building a global distribution network that allows it to reduce costs across supply, transportation, and facilities.

Of course, Wal-Mart's rise to dominance in the retail industry was also driven by ruthlessly exploiting its growing economic and political power to destroy competitors, squeeze suppliers, and bulldoze through social, environmental, and economic regulations. In the *Big Box Swindle*, Stacy Mitchell contends that:

> The reigning assumption is that mega-retailers have attained their market dominance solely because of consumer choices. But corporate chains have been aided and abetted in no small part by public policy. Federal, state, and local policies have created an uneven playing field. It began in the late 1950s with accelerated depreciation, which fueled the explosion of shopping malls, and picked up speed in the 1980s and 1990s, as policymakers funneled billions of dollars in development subsidies to big retail chains, opened up tax loopholes that gave large retailers a decided edge over local competitors, and failed to adequately police abuses of market power. This favoritism has been driven in part by the political power of the chains and retail development industry, and by the persistent myth that big-box stores boost employment and tax revenue. But it also flows from a double standard pervasive among policymakers, who insist that small businesses be subject to the rigors of the free market, while granting their biggest competitors a leg up in the name of the public good.[192]

A similar dynamic is at play with the rise of online retail giant Amazon. Famously, Amazon for years rarely turned a profit, preferring to subsidize growth and increase market share (at the expense of its competitors) in anticipation of massive profits down the road – a strategy that has largely succeeded.[193] Furthermore, in the early days when it was trying to establish itself, Amazon exploited a legal loophole that allowed online retailers to avoid collecting sales tax (which all local retailers had to collect, thus increasing the total price to consumers of the goods sold). Because they were only required to collect sales taxes in states where they had a physical presence, the company would deliberately locate its warehouses in sparsely populated states near those with large populations (Nevada next to California, for instance).[194]

Moreover, even when states which did have physical facilities (like Texas) tried to collect the tax, Amazon would contest the effort, claiming that its distribution centers were not retailing facilities and were, as subsidiaries, separate legal entities. A 2011 report in *Governing* found that:

> At every turn, Amazon has gone to great lengths to block state collection efforts. In states that claimed nexus because Amazon affiliates were located there, Amazon ended relationships with those businesses and, in turn, pursued litigation in the state. In states where it had facilities, it threatened to pull them out, thereby raising the specter of eliminating jobs. And where Amazon wanted to open facilities, it insisted on a free pass on tax collection.[195]

For Mitchell and others, the decimation of small, independent retailers at the hands of global retailing corporations (be they predominantly physical, as in the case of Wal-Mart, or online, as in the case of Amazon) has serious implications for local economic stability, politics, culture, and the environment.

In many ways, these concerns echo those articulated by observers worried about the incredible consolidation and centralization of the agriculture industry. 'At all stages of the food system – from seeds and other inputs to food processing and retail food sales – market power is concentrating in an ever-smaller number of corporate firms,' the Worldwatch Institute warns. 'This trend is transforming how the world produces food, squeezing millions of farmers between a small group of input suppliers and an equally concentrated group of commodity purchasers.'[196] In the United States, the number of farms continues to fall (from around 6.8 million in 1935 to just over 2 million today), and large farms (both family and corporate owned) now account for around 84 percent of the value of production.[197] In many agricultural industries, an oligopoly of large companies controls processing and distribution, and uses either direct contracts or market power to severely limit the options of smaller producers (to negotiate better prices, sell to other vendors, employ different farming techniques, etc.). According to the Worldwatch report, 'virtually all U.S. poultry is produced under contract, as are close to 60 percent of hogs, cotton, rice, fruit, and dairy.' In the beef-packing industry, just four companies are responsible for around 80 percent of US production.[198] In addition to these restrictive contracts with suppliers, this market power allows the companies to both secure deregulation as it affects their operations and increase regulation of their potential smaller competitors. Moreover, as Elanor Starmer of the Agribusiness Accountability Initiative states, 'evidence suggests that on par, the economies of rural communities have not benefited from the presence of these large packing plants,' due to automation, de-unionization, subsidies, and the exploitation of migrant labor.[199]

Neither the agriculture or retail sector appears, on its face, conducive to widespread public ownership. The idea that local governments, for instance, would take direct ownership stakes in small farms or shops is likely undesirable; collective ownership in the form of worker cooperatives and other worker-ownership schemes seems more appropriate. However, from the perspective of supporting small businesses, local economies, and communities – especially regarding coordination issues – history demonstrates that public ownership can indeed play a role. For instance, as previously mentioned, North Dakota still operates a large, successful (it receives no taxpayer subsidies and returns large amounts of money to the state treasury) publicly owned mill and elevator that competes with private facilities. The publicly owned mill and elevator was conceived in an era of corporate consolidation and abuse in the agricultural sector not dissimilar to that existing today. 'Actual creation of the North Dakota Mill and Elevator Association was the result of a long battle waged by farmers and progressives in an attempt to break the grain trade monopoly and have some control over pricing and grading of grain,' the State Historical Society of North Dakota recalls.[200] Similar publicly owned processing and distribution facilities could be organized at the state level across a variety of agricultural sectors and exist, as does the North Dakota Mill and Elevator, as a public option that supports small farmers by weakening the oligopolistic hold of large corporations.

Similarly, in the retail sector, public ownership could be used to strengthen local and/or collectively owned small businesses. For instance, public ownership of commercial land and facilities can be used to support local business development and generate revenue for the municipality. In a recent report examining how rising commercial rents are imperiling small businesses across the country, Stacy Mitchell and coauthor Olivia LaVecchia detail how some cities are making publicly owned land and real estate available to locally owned businesses in a variety of ways.[201] In relating the story of one such effort in Austin, Texas, Mitchell writes that 'having a public-ownership stake can make all the difference.'[202] As we have seen in the case of Faneuil Hall, the Burlington waterfront, and various transit-oriented developments, public ownership of land and facilities is not uncommon in the United States and could be greatly expanded upon and more consciously linked to the support of small retail businesses – especially if the massive subsidies local and state governments currently provide to large corporations are redirected to such efforts. Another option for how public ownership could support small retail (and other businesses) is with regards to warehousing and transportation. Currently, smaller companies that do not have their own warehousing and transportation infrastructure often use so-called 'public warehousing' companies to provide those services. As the name suggests, these companies are essentially providing a publicly benefiting service, and there is no reason why such companies could not also be publicly owned (at the local or regional level) – thus, potentially, lowering costs for small businesses and making the services more widely available.

Education and beyond

As mentioned at the outset, this brief sectoral survey leaves some obvious gaps in the terrain of the economy as a whole. One of the most evident is education, which hasn't been covered in part due to great organizational variances across the thousands of jurisdictions that make up the continental American nation. However, it would be unsatisfactory to conclude without at least touching on this critically important sector. The American education system is a patchwork in every sense of the word. Throughout the pre-school, primary school, secondary school, and higher education systems there exists a variety of ownership forms – including public schools, for-profit private schools, nonprofit private schools, homeschools, faith-based schools, etc. – as well as financing mechanisms (often based on local property taxes) and regulatory approaches. The result is a system that is, in many estimations, one of the most unequal in the advanced world.[203] Poorer Americans – especially racial minorities – are falling behind their wealthier white peers at astonishing rates, while educational outcomes across the board lag behind those of other advanced countries.

Neatly coinciding with the resurgence of 'free market' rhetoric beginning in the 1970s, there has, in recent decades, been increasing pressure to address these issues through privatization in one form or another. Milton Friedman himself, an early proponent of so-called 'school choice,' wrote in 1995 that a 'radical restructuring' was needed and could only be achieved by 'privatizing a major segment of the educational system.'[204] This has led to, among other things (such as vouchers), the rise of charter schools and for-profit universities. Charter schools are publicly funded schools run by private organizations, many of them for-profit entities (some of which are considered great investment opportunities for hedge funds). While charter schools continue to enjoy support from numerous powerful and wealthy boosters (Bill Gates, Betsy DeVos, and the Walton family, to name a few) evidence against them is beginning to mount. Beyond very serious questions as to whether many charter schools are benefiting their students academically, the industry as a whole is riddled with fraud, lacks accountability and transparency, generates private profits on the backs of taxpayers, impoverishes public school systems, and, critically, can contribute to the re-segregation of the education system and deepening inequality.[205]

Similarly, for-profit universities and colleges – which have experienced exponential growth over the past two decades – are increasingly coming under scrutiny for substandard performance (e.g., low graduation rates and poor job prospects), exorbitant costs (which are driving students deeper into debt), and manipulative recruiting and advertising practices.[206] After two large for-profit chains (Corinthian Colleges and ITT Technical Institute) collapsed amidst allegations of widespread fraud, the Obama Administration pushed through new rules that tied government support (in the form of federal student aid dollars) to the earnings of students post-graduation.[207] However, following the election of President Trump and his appointment of pro-privatization zealot Betsy DeVos as Education Secretary, for-profit universities and colleges have made a comeback. The Obama-era rules have been halted, a former for-profit university 'dean' has been appointed to lead government oversight of the industry, and new fraud claims are being left uninvestigated.[208] Not coincidentally, the stock prices of many for-profit colleges have surged since the 2016 election.[209]

As in other sectors, the viability of for-profit ownership in education is predicated on high levels of direct public financial support. Most for-profit schools, and even some private nonprofit ones, would collapse without it. This is the great lie behind privatized education. Because the service is an essential societal need and must remain broadly accessible, the public continues to shoulder a great deal of financial responsibility, but forfeits control – enabling all sorts of wealth extraction and rent-seeking opportunities. Instead of more privatization, for-profit ownership in the sector should be abolished, which could be relatively easily done in most cases by simply withdrawing public support from such entities. Nonprofit private schools could continue to exist to the extent that they can support themselves without public subsidies, but at some point their role in exacerbating wealth and racial inequality should be seriously examined. However, this alone wouldn't solve the many interconnected problems facing the education sector. What is needed is a fundamental re-evaluation of how much society values education and equitable access to it. An increase and reinforcement of public ownership in the sector will likely need to be accompanied by changes to how schools are funded, how teachers are compensated, how students are taught, and who participates in governing and administering the system. This need to think beyond ownership transitions goes for all sectors, not just education.

Conclusion
Systemic crisis and democratic public ownership

Public ownership is not a panacea. It is, however, a far more prevalent, viable, and adaptable economic form than the dominant neoliberal free market ideology of the past several decades would have us believe. It is also an important potential solution, or element in a solution, to many of the most pressing difficulties – economic, social, and ecological – we are facing in the United States and elsewhere in the early part of the twenty-first century. As we have seen, most movements and theorists actively seeking a more equitable, sustainable, and democratic political-economic system have been led to support elements of public ownership in one form or another. However, simply returning to the traditional top-down managerial forms public ownership often took in the past is demonstrably insufficient. As Carnoy and Shearer put it sharply in 1980, 'the transfer of ownership to the government does not automatically guarantee the establishment of an egalitarian, democratic society.'[1]

The historical record of many of the large, centralized, and bureaucratized state owned enterprises that sprung up during the middle part of the twentieth century on such issues as transparency, environmental sustainability, and democratic accountability leaves a lot to be desired. The TVA's rather checkered record on environmental issues and lack of democratic accountability is a salutary reminder of this in the US context. The TVA has long been criticized for failing to live up to its own promises of 'grassroots democracy,' with many of its development projects, including those concerned with navigation, flood control, and electric power, largely directed from above with little local participation. While the administration of the power program through municipal and cooperative systems did allow local residents to determine their own rates and quality of services, autonomous boards held substantial decision-making power which significantly curtailed local control. Given these constraints, Victor Hobday stated in 1960 that 'a suggestion today that TVA's power operations have increased citizen's participation or

Conclusion: Systemic crisis and democratic public ownership

have encouraged anything resembling a town meeting would evoke laughter anywhere in the Valley.'[2] Of particular concern to many critics, particularly the late Philip Selznik in his classic work *TVA and the Grassroots*, is that while the TVA uses the rhetoric of grassroots participation to rally political support, it actually collaborates with (or co-opts) powerful local interests and leaves existing power relationships unchanged.[3]

Throughout the twentieth century, public ownership was often used merely as a way to improve distributional outcomes within existing economic arrangements rather than as the basis of a more expansive effort at economic democratization. However, as Andrew Cumbers writes, 'current global inequities and injustices are brought about as much by the appropriation of economic decision-making by elite groups as by distributional outcomes. In this sense, the quest for democracy means nothing if it does not include the ability to participate in the key decisions about economic life.'[4] For this reason, Cumbers titled his landmark 2012 book *Reclaiming Public Ownership: Making Space for Economic Democracy*. Similarly, Pat Devine contends that public ownership as traditionally conceived is merely a stepping stone toward more democratic and participatory institutions.[5] In Devine's formulation, whether or not public ownership (or any other form of ownership) qualifies as social ownership depends on the degree to which decisions regarding the 'use made of the means of production' are made by 'those most affected.'[6] Leaving aside for now terminology and the matter of who qualifies as 'those most affected,' for public ownership to truly become the basis for a more equal, participatory, and sustainable political-economic system – one that embraces more than just a distributional justice framework – it must be fundamentally re-conceptualized, re-structured, and re-invigorated. It must, in short, be 'democratized.'

Fortunately, one of the great strengths of public ownership is its capacity for adaptation and redeployment. 'Private ownership of the means of production,' E.F. Schumacher contended:

> Is severely limited in its freedom of choice objectives, because it is compelled to be profit-seeking, and *tends* to take a narrow and selfish view of things. Public ownership gives complete freedom in the choice of objectives and can therefore be used for any purpose that may be chosen. While private ownership is an instrument that by itself largely determines the ends for which it can be employed, public ownership is an instrument the ends of which are undetermined and need to be consciously chosen.[7]

Many theorists, Schumacher included, start the process of reimagining public ownership with the concept of decentralization. As Cumbers notes, public ownership has traditionally fallen short when it comes to economic democracy because of excess centralization, bureaucratization, and top-down management.[8] Devine provides additional detail for the bill of complaint, writing that:

> The threat to personal freedom from the concentration of political and sometimes economic power in the state, the paternalism of nationalized industries and welfare state provision, the inefficiency of statist command planning, the power and lack of social accountability of large corporations, have between them led to a search for ways of decentralizing political power and economic decision-making.[9]

In addition to guarding against such threats, decentralization is more generally seen as a way of enabling stakeholders to access various decision-making processes, and is a core component of efforts to increase participatory or direct democracy in modern societies.[10] As John McDonnell has stated, 'decentralisation and social entrepreneurship are part of the left ... democracy and decentralisation are the watchwords of our socialism.'[11] Two components of decentralization are relevant to the discussion of democratizing public ownership – *geographic* (spatial) and *functional*, for want of better terms.

The first, geographical decentralization, is relatively straightforward and, for our purposes, can refer to the physical location, scale, scope, and governance of publicly owned enterprises. The World Bank provides a serviceable overview:

> Where it works effectively, decentralization helps alleviate the bottlenecks in decision making that are often caused by central government planning and control of important economic and social activities. Decentralization can help cut complex bureaucratic procedures and it can increase government officials' sensitivity to local conditions and needs. Moreover, decentralization can help national government ministries reach larger numbers of local areas with services; allow greater political representation for diverse political, ethnic, religious, and cultural groups in decision-making; and relieve top managers in central ministries of 'routine' tasks to concentrate on policy. In some countries, decentralization may create a geographical focus at the local level for coordinating national, state, provincial, district, and local programs more effectively and can provide better opportunities for participation by local residents in decision making. Decentralization may lead to more creative, innovative and respon-

sive programs by allowing local 'experimentation.' It can also increase political stability and national unity by allowing citizens to better control public programs at the local level.[12]

In other words, from the perspective of democratic participation and accountability, the principle of subsidiarity appears relevant – namely that wherever possible smaller, local publicly owned and controlled enterprises will be more desirable than larger regional or national publicly owned enterprises.[13]

At the same time, larger-scale economic organization, as we have seen, is both ubiquitous and necessary for a variety of reasons. 'Nobody really likes large-scale organisation,' Schumacher argued, citing Franz Kafka, 'Yet, it seems, large-scale organisation is here to stay.'[14] This reality brings the second component of decentralization to the fore. When larger-scale enterprises and coordination is necessary, efforts can be made to decentralize in other ways.'[15] In this regard, Cumbers, for one, prefers the term *decentering* over *decentralization*. Similarly, Schumacher puts forward the concept of 'smallness *within* large organisation,' and calls for large enterprises to 'consist of many semi-autonomous units, which we may call *quasi-firms*. Each of them will have a large amount of freedom.'[16] In this way, even within large publicly owned enterprises decision-making could be dispersed and made more participatory. Another version of this would include smaller publicly owned companies being temporarily brought together into a larger publicly owned company on a project-by-project basis – a variant of the network model discussed earlier.

This *functional* decentralization intersects with another important component of democratizing public ownership: *worker participation*. Often referred to as worker self-management, this desire to increase the ability of workers within enterprises to direct their own workplaces and participate in decision-making is a cornerstone of economic democracy and, as we have seen, almost every alternative system vision emanating from the left. '*If* democracy is justified in governing the state,' Dahl famously wrote in *A Preface to Economic Democracy*, 'then it must *also* be justified in governing economic enterprises.'[17] Self-governing enterprises, he noted, have been linked to a number of economic, civic, and individual benefits.[18] While contemporary empirical evidence to support this hypothesis is somewhat mixed, Dahl held out hope for the long-term, writing:

> I cannot help thinking that if their experiment in self-management lasts a hundred years, Yugoslavs will be different in important ways from what

they would have been had they continued to live in a command society that was authoritarian not only in politics but in economic life as well. And might not we Americans be different, if in the 1880s we had adopted self-governing enterprises rather than corporate capitalism as the standard solution?[19]

It is well understood from historical experience that merely transitioning from private ownership to public ownership does little to enhance worker participation within firms or in the operations of the economy as a whole. 'Changing the ownership of production (to public or social ownership) is not sufficient to change relations in production,' Carnoy and Shearer wrote. 'Public enterprise is an important reform in and of itself ... But power relations within firms (and, by implication, power relations in the society as a whole) may remain hierarchical and relatively undemocratic even after such reforms.'[20] In many countries, especially in Europe, various strategies to improve worker participation in publicly and privately owned firms alike have been developed with varying degrees of success (the most famous of which is probably Germany's 'codetermination' system). Most often, this has taken the form of worker representation on company boards (usually through the intermediation of a trade union). Currently, 19 of the 28 European Union member states (plus Norway) provide for worker representation at the board level of a firm. How this is manifested varies widely from country to country, and depending on the type of the enterprise (public or private), its size, and what industry it is in, among other factors. For instance, in some countries worker representatives sit on supervisory boards rather than boards of directors; in some, worker representatives account for as many as half the board seats, while in others workers may be entitled to a solitary representative; and in some, worker representatives are prohibited from participating in certain decisions (such as collective bargaining).[21]

For many theorists, however, self-management ought to be more robust and expansive than some of these formulaic versions of codetermination and co-management. For instance, political scientist Philip Resnick argued in 1994 that 'workers' control is rooted in a larger left tradition that goes beyond the limited measure of worker participation proposed under certain industrial consultation schemes.'[22] The literature on self-management is voluminous, and much of it is beyond the scope of this book. However, the relationship of self-management to ownership – and especially to public ownership – is of particular relevance. Increasingly in the modern era, worker self-management is being articulated as worker *ownership*,

Conclusion: Systemic crisis and democratic public ownership

or collective ownership in the original Pannekoek formulation. Especially in advanced capitalist countries, advocates and theorists often suggest that one of the best ways to enable the democratic participation of workers is to confer upon them ownership of the enterprise in some form or another. For example, Resnick suggested that worker participation must be 'effectively coupled' with control, and that 'in practice, workers' control would be based upon equal ownership – one worker, one vote – over all enterprises beyond a certain asset size.'[23] More recently, employee-ownership proponents Joseph Blasi, Richard Freeman, and Douglas Kruse have stated that 'the way forward is to reform the structure of American business so that workers can supplement their wages with significant capital ownership stakes and meaningful, capital income and profit shares. This will give them the potential for greater participation in decision making to increase the value of their firms and the opportunity for sharing the fruits of their performance.'[24]

However, for others, worker self-management is *the* important design principle and can be achieved within various ownership forms. 'How should self-governing enterprises be owned?' Dahl asked. 'Four possibilities are particularly relevant: individual ownership by members of an enterprise; cooperative ownership of an enterprise by all its employees; state ownership; or ownership by "society".'[25] Similarly, for economist Richard Wolff, worker self-management, in the form of so-called 'Worker Self Directed Enterprises' (WSDEs), is the key innovation. 'Various ownership arrangements can coexist with WSDEs,' Wolff writes. 'The salient point is that the internal organization of surplus production, appropriation, and distribution in WSDEs is different from and can coexist with various forms of ownership of means of production.'[26]

Both Dahl and Wolff have offered ways in which worker self-management could work within a framework of public ownership. Dahl highlighted the early suggestion of Oxford political theorist and market socialist David Miller that 'after acquiring ownership of an industry the state could then lease the firms to the employees, who could then operate them as self-governing enterprises.'[27] As we have seen, this is similar to David Schweickart's Economic Democracy model in which workers lease their 'capital assets' from society. Wolff presents another version of this, stating that 'the state might own the means and make them available to WSDEs. If so, the arrangement might involve only centralized state ownership or perhaps some mixture of state, regional, and local governments owning various kinds and quantities of productive property.'[28]

In his analysis of the different ownership possibilities, Dahl suggested that the advantage of combining public ownership with worker self-governance is that 'this solution symbolizes the public nature of economic enterprises, in contrast to ownership by employees, whether individually or cooperatively, which still retains a strong flavor of private ownership.'[29] This introduces a third component of democratizing public ownership. Specifically, workers are but a subset of society as a whole – in the United States, for instance, less than half of the total population is currently employed. While in some cases the interests of workers may align with other groups in society (retirees, environmentalists, the unemployed, children, people with disabilities, workers in other industries, etc.), in others they likely will not and the workers will act, as Dahl suggested, like private owners concerned primarily with their own well-being and prosperity. Therefore, publicly owned enterprises should include some broader societal representation in the management structure. In traditional public enterprises, appointees of the state take on this responsibility as representatives of society. However, given the deficiencies of top-down, bureaucratic forms of management, this is not sufficient from a democratic standpoint.

This raises the prospect of more direct forms of community representation, such as the multi-stakeholder boards that, as Devine suggests, are a way to organize 'social-ownership' at the enterprise level. Another model, suggested by Alec Nove (building on the work of Radoslav Selucký) is 'tripartite supervision, with management responsible to the state, the users *and* the workforce.'[30] Still another is the communal ownership of 'social property enterprises' (EPS) in Venezuela. Here, communal parliaments – made up of recallable representatives from all local communal councils and EPSs in a specified geographic area – make decisions relating to production, distribution, surplus, investment, and employment.[31] Recently, Peter Gowan and Mio Tastas Viktorsson have put forward a variant of the famous Meidner Plan dating from 1970s Sweden. Briefly, the Meidner Plan envisioned several large wage-earner funds that would, every year, receive 'profit-related payments from firms in the form of voting shares.'[32] Eventually, these funds would become the majority owners of most companies. The wage earner funds were to have been administered by workers through their union representatives. Gowan and Viktorsson suggest that, instead, the state should own the funds but grant their boards (which would be made up of both government and worker representatives) 'substantial operational autonomy.' Below the board level, there would be committees for each industry whose members would be a mix of board appointees, worker representatives, and other stakeholders, 'such as consumer groups, local authorities, and environmental or minority group representatives.' This structure would be accompanied by representative councils at the firm level that would give workers additional influence over management decisions (and act as the vehicle for representation at the wage earner fund level).[33]

Of course, these models conflict with pure versions of worker self-management or control. 'There is a subtle question that we all have to handle in any sort of democratized society,' anthropologist David Graeber contends:

> Which is how do you square the problem of one principle which says all those people engaged in a project should have say over how that project is done, and the second principle which is all those people affected by a project should have some say in how that project is done. One of them, if you take it exclusively, leads to pure workers' control, the other leads to a sort of general direct democracy on every level. Well clearly some compromise between the two principles has to be worked out, and it just seems reasonable that if there is a factory then people in the surrounding community really don't care about their vacation policy, but will probably want to have some say over what they dump in the river.[34]

Similarly, George DeMartino contrasts a 'strong definition' of appropriative justice – where workers in a firm, or perhaps even just a small subset of those workers, would have appropriative rights – with a 'weak definition' that could include a much broader understanding of who should enjoy those rights (including the community as a whole).[35] Commenting on DeMartino's favoring of the 'weak definition,' Theodore Burczak writes that 'while he does not spell out the exact nature of this communal appropriation, it is hard to imagine how it would not involve some sort of democratic government acting as the agent of appropriation.'[36]

Related to both decentralization and community participation is the overarching question of the state itself. For many modern leftists and system theorists, the state (especially the capitalist state) represents an obstacle to genuine democracy, participation, and social or mutual ownership – an obstacle that must be both confronted and weakened by developing autonomous, decentralized, and self-sufficient institutions outside of the state from the ground up. As Cumbers suggests, there is a tendency in some traditions to dismiss engagement with the state entirely and of trying instead to work outside of both the state and capitalist structures, leading to a rejection of traditional forms of public ownership and state support.[37] One alternative, as Hilary Wainwright has demonstrated, is a participatory restructuring of the state.[38] Wainwright points to various experiments (including the Greater London Council – GLC – during the 1980s, where she led the Popular Planning Unit) and 'in and against the state social movements' to suggest how increased participation and unlocking the practical knowledge of state workers and users of public services can facilitate a 'deepening of democratic control of state resources' and provide a way to democratize public institutions (rather than privatize them as has been the traditional solution).[39]

One of the examples Wainwright and many others highlight is the widely heralded participatory governance effort in Porto Alegre, Brazil. After the Worker's Party (PT) won municipal elections in 1988, the city began to institute a participatory budgeting program that enables residents to make certain decisions regarding public spending (regional assemblies first debate and vote on priorities, then elect representatives to a city-wide council). 'The participatory budgeting process demonstrates that ordinary citizens can effectively participate in technical and complex decision making,' Maureen Donaghy writes.[40] Subsequently, participatory budgeting has spread throughout Brazil and the world. It is currently estimated that there have been more than 250 such processes in just North America (New York City and Chicago being among the most prominent in the United States).[41] Participatory budgeting, and the countless other experiments with participatory governance, planning, and politics around the world in recent decades, is evidence not only that people can effectively participate, but that there is also a desire and hunger to do so.

Elsewhere in Latin America, there have also been more comprehensive experiments. Discussing the failed 1992 coup in Venezuela (which was the precursor to the Bolivarian revolution), George Ciccariello-Maher writes that:

> The goal ... was not simply to seize the state but to immediately replace it with something very different ... For [guerrilla commander] Kléber [Ramírez Rojas] ... this new alternative state was in fact no state at all. Instead, building communal power meant dissolving political power into the community itself; it meant a 'broadening of democracy in which the communities will assume the fundamental powers of the state.[42]

However, the experience of the Venezuelan communes with regards to the state has, in Ciccariello-Maher's words, 'been far more complex.'

Conclusion: Systemic crisis and democratic public ownership

'The real question,' he continues in the context of an interview with Andrés Antillano (a 'longtime militant' and leader of a participatory research project), 'is how to deal with the challenges of co-optation by and dependency on the state, and how best to use the funds to deepen self-management. There is no easy answer, Antillano insists: "You can do politics against the state or with the state, but you would be fucked trying to do politics without the state."'[43]

To begin to square some of these problems, to use Graeber's phrase, it is instructive to briefly review the concept of ownership generally, and the theory of ownership as a 'bundle of rights' more specifically. In a 1961 essay titled 'Ownership,' A. M. Honoré built on earlier work and suggested that 'ownership comprises the right to possess, the right to use, the right to manage, the right to income of the thing, the right to the capital, the right to security, the rights or incidents of transmissibility and absence of term, the prohibition of harmful use, liability to execution, and the incident of residuarity: this makes eleven leading incidents.'[44] With this in mind, it is possible to see how E.F. Schumacher could write that '"nationalisation" is not a matter of simply transferring this bundle of rights from A to B, that is to say, from private persons to "the State", whatever that may mean: it is a matter of making precise choices as to where the various rights of the bundle are to be placed.'[45]

This also intersects with the more fundamental need to re-appraise the question of property rights. Recently, David Ellerman has argued that the 'fundamental myth about property rights' is 'the idea that the rights to the product (and, incidentally, the management rights over production) are part and parcel of "the ownership of the means of production" (to use the Marxian phrase).'[46] Ellerman uses the example of a corporation that leases its factory to another company to point out that:

> The legal party who ends up appropriating (i.e., having the defensible claim on) the produced assets is the party, sometimes called the 'residual claimant,' who was the contractual nexus of hiring (or already owning) all the inputs used up in production (and thus who 'swallowed' those liabilities). Since that party is determined by who hires what or whom (and power relations in the market certainly affect that outcome), the property rights to the product are not part of some prior bundle of rights to a capital asset or to a corporation.[47]

Ellerman's central point is that at the 'root' of the 'problem in our economic system' is employment itself. 'If the neo-abolitionist proposal were accepted that the contract for the renting of human beings be recognized as invalid and be abolished,' he continues, 'then production could only be organized on the basis of the people working in production (jointly) hiring or already owning the capital and other inputs they use in production.' In other words, instead of capital renting labor, labor would rent or own capital and would therefore be the residual claimant on the goods and/or services produced (inverting the fundamental myth).[48] The result, in Ellerman's formulation, is a 'democratic firm' operating within a 'private property market of such firms' called "economic democracy".'[49] In all this, he is echoing a concern articulated by my Democracy Collaborative colleague and business journalist Marjorie Kelly. 'Ownership, that bundle of concepts we also label property rights, is ... [an] antique tradition that has remained impressively intact,' she writes in *The Divine Right of Capital*.[50] 'Curiously – or perhaps appallingly – the law of master and servant remains the law in employer–employee relationships today, as a living fossil of the notion of ownership.'[51] In *Owning Our Future*, Kelly suggests that the important question is not whether ownership can be 'disaggregated' (it can be), but for what purpose.[52] As we have seen, theorists such as Schweickart, Wolff, and Dahl believe ownership should or could be disaggregated in a way that certain rights are conveyed to workers, while others are retained by the public at large (or by representatives of the public).

Related to this discussion about disaggregation is the issue of the functional divide between ownership and management in modern capitalist corporations (with the classic work in the field remaining Adolph Berle and Gardiner Means' 1932 book *The Modern Corporation and Private Property*).[53] Recently, Seth Ackerman of *Jacobin* has described how this can be applied to the question of restructuring public ownership. 'What is needed,' he writes:

> Is a structure that allows autonomous firms to produce and trade goods for the market, aiming to generate a surplus of output over input – while keeping those firms public and preventing their surplus from being appropriated by a narrow class of capitalists. Under this type of system, workers can assume any degree of control they like over the management of their firms, and any 'profits' can be socialized.[54]

By accepting that the ownership and management of enterprises can be separate, engaging with the concept of ownership as a 'bundle of rights,' and re-appraising property rights, a variety of options emerge regarding how the democratization of public ownership could be

Conclusion: Systemic crisis and democratic public ownership 143

implemented within the overarching framework of decentralization, worker self-management and governance, and direct community participation.

What 'democratized' public ownership would look like in practice is likely variable from firm to firm, and industry to industry, over time. However, beyond such a highly unsatisfactory answer, one speculative framework might be as follows. Each wholly or majority publicly owned enterprise above a certain size could have a board of directors comprised of a mix of appointed and elected stakeholder representatives. For instance, representatives could be appointed by government (at whatever appropriate level or levels), directly elected by consumers or residents, appointed or elected by workers through either a trade union or work council, appointed or elected by environmental organizations (a very important role, given that the natural world cannot represent its own interests yet is massively impacted by business decisions), and appointed or elected by various other NGOs (based on the specific industry and geography). The exact mix of board representation would be dependent upon industry, size, geography, or capital needs and/or could be decided democratically (through a referendum or deliberative process). Boards could be subject to racial, gender, and age-diversity requirements, term limits, and a mandate to decentralize as much as possible, both physically and functionally. Enterprises as a whole could also be subject to certain requirements regarding transparency (such as open meetings and open records), popular consultation (especially with regards to relocating/closing facilities and mergers and acquisitions), and more egalitarian pay ratios between senior managers and the lowest-paid worker (such as the maximum ~9 to 1 ratio operative in the famous large-scale Mondragón cooperative network in Spain).[55]

The boards could consult with government policy-makers and planners (at various levels and at regular intervals) regarding long-term goals and strategic objectives, but would likely have operational autonomy (including decisions to hire and fire management). Internally, each enterprise could have a worker's council or assembly to maximize worker participation in day-to-day decision-making (workers could also continue to be represented by labor unions in contract negotiations with management). These councils or assemblies could also become the vehicle by which workers elect representatives to the board. When it comes to profits, each firm could – as in Schweickart's proposal – be required to pay a capital assets tax back to the state (at the appropriate level of jurisdiction) and then decide how to allocate the remainder with regards to re-investment in the business, higher wages and benefits for workers, or lower costs for consumers.[56] Alternatively, how much of a firm's profit is to be returned to the state could vary depending on different enterprise classifications based on their societally agreed *raison d'être* (for instance, profit maximization, consumer benefit, job creation, environmental performance, etc.). For minority publicly owned enterprises (where, for instance, the public owns a small percentage of a company), a publicly owned fund at the appropriate scale could exercise ownership rights and responsibilities (and there could be a multitude of such funds nationally). Those funds could be managed by multi-stakeholder boards, have operational autonomy, and be subject to many of the same requirements as the publicly owned enterprise boards.

Against the whirlwind

Little has been said thus far about the mounting political, social, economic, and ecological crisis – a systemic crisis – that is increasingly threatening to engulf the current system of corporate capitalism in the United States and around the world. This crisis may simply be the culmination of decades-long processes and difficulties finally coming to a head. 'We are no longer sure,' wrote the late Giovanni Arrighi several decades ago in his survey of *The Long Twentieth Century*, 'that the crisis of the 1970s was ever really resolved.'[57] This still holds true today. Long-term social-economic trends – including compounding inequality, persistent poverty, increasing financialization, and declining unionization – are intersecting dangerously with new structural changes, including low growth, expanding automation, fixed ecological limits (climate danger and water scarcity being but two), and fallout from a series of disastrous imperial military adventures, including the creation of a massive refugee and migration crisis. All this deepening pain and anger is combining in what amounts to a potentially explosive political-economic powder keg. The neoliberal consensus consisting of globalization, economic liberalization, privatization, austerity, and monetary orthodoxy that appeared unassailable just a few years back is now (depending on which country one looks at) either fraying at the edges or already in tatters, as technocratic elites struggle to retain political control in the face of a widespread and growing popular backlash.

Even for those who have long anticipated such a crisis, the speed with which events are unfolding is dizzying. In a nine-month period between June 2016 and March 2017, Great Britain voted to leave

Conclusion: Systemic crisis and democratic public ownership 145

the European Union, Scotland announced its intention to hold a second referendum on independence from Great Britain, voters in the United States emphatically rejected the establishment political duopoly and 'threw the bums out' by electing Donald Trump to the presidency, and Austria and the Netherlands only narrowly avoided the ascension of far-right leaders as heads of state and government. In France in April and May, the establishment political parties of the center left and center right were routed in the presidential elections, with a new left-wing alliance led by Jean-Luc Mélenchon putting in a strong showing and resulting in a final round run-off between two political insurgents, far-right Marine Le Pen and independent Emmanuel Macron. The subsequent collapse of Macron's popularity following his victory does not bode well for the future. The medium-term future of the European Union itself hangs in the balance, with Greece in particular still mired in an inescapable debt crisis, both exacerbated and ignored by European elites, and international lenders threatening to send the country crashing out of the Eurozone.

Across the Northern heartlands of neoliberalism, fascism is very clearly on the rise, with long dormant white supremacist and neo-Nazi groups emerging from the shadows and political violence escalating – including the bombing of refugee centers in Europe, the burning of mosques in the United States, and the massacre of Muslim worshippers in Canada. The early period of the Trump presidency was marked by a seemingly endless series of dangerous new developments that point in the direction of further years of tumult if not full-blown constitutional crisis. The new generation of globalizing neoliberal trade agreements – the Trans-Pacific Partnership (TPP) and the Transatlantic Trade and Investment Partnership (TTIP) – are dead in the water, and even the North American Free Trade Agreement (NAFTA) seems unlikely to survive in its current form, given shenanigans around the erection of a wall on the Mexican border and the even more virulently anti-immigrant turn of US policies. Meanwhile, climate science is under attack at every level of the federal government, and the country's international climate change commitments are being systematically junked. Implementation of Trump's 'Muslim ban' as proposed on the campaign trail has been attempted, statements have been made about bringing back torture, and aerial bombardments (accompanied by inevitable civilian casualties) have increased across the Middle East, all but guaranteeing bloody confrontation at home and abroad. And casual allegations of allegedly massive voter fraud have been tossed around (and far more convincing evidence of voter suppression ignored), threatening to further undermine the public's already fragile faith in America's democracy. At every step thus far, the Trump Administration has been faced with resistance. In one interesting early development, staff at various government agencies (and even within the White House) defied administration efforts to muzzle them by 'going rogue' on social media, perhaps prefiguring new potential organic moves in the direction of working 'in and against the state.'

We may now have entered into what my colleague Joe Guinan and I have termed 'a Polanyi moment' – the point at which the unsustainable social and ecological impacts of market liberalism push the system up against its limits, and a backlash sets in.[58] Polanyi identified such a 'double movement' in the terminal end-point of the previous, Victorian era of globalization and the consequent chaos and destruction of the first half of the twentieth century. Today, the vast disruptive power of untrammeled market capitalism unleashed upon people, communities, and the biosphere now requires a massive 're-embedding' of the economy in society and nature if we are to avoid another catastrophic spiral into fascism and environmental collapse. The gap between positive theoretical visions of future alternative institutional arrangements and our terrifying contemporary reality must now be closed – and quickly. It is imperative that the left not cede to the neo-fascists the political rallying ground of anti-elitist populism against a system increasingly seen as rigged in favor of the very rich. In particular, it must not abandon its core principles and radical ambitions in an attempt to mount an impossible defense of the indefensible – and rapidly vanishing – neoliberal consensus.

Returning to the subject of this book, that neoliberal 'consensus' has been at best quietly tolerant of public ownership in those instances where it supported profitability and financial extraction. More often, however, it has been outright hostile to it in almost all forms. The building *legitimation crisis* (to use Habermas' term) that neoliberalism is currently experiencing opens the door to reappraisals and new understandings – including of public ownership. The Financial Crisis and subsequent Great Recession of the late 2000s may well come to be remembered as a major historical turning point in this regard. As a highly leveraged and imploding financial sector threatened to bring down the entire global economy, the myth of the infallibility of free markets and the private sector was laid bare for billions to see. Governments around the world hurriedly stepped in with various hasty nationalization schemes to ward off disaster – usually accompanied by piously hypocritical pronouncements of their 'temporary' nature – further deepening popular awareness and

Conclusion: Systemic crisis and democratic public ownership 147

distrust of the cronyism and corruption at the heart of contemporary capitalism. This has reinforced the longstanding disconnect between people's everyday experience with public ownership and the hegemonic ideology of the innate superiority of the private.

In the United States, public ownership – especially at the local and subnational level – remains vibrant and broadly popular. From local, low-cost power, to various modes of transport, to land, housing, and schools, Americans interact with public ownership every day, with little more than the occasional griping. Even for those who have bought into neoliberal talking points about government being the 'problem' and the 'superiority' of private business, there is usually little appetite for the handover of, say, a county's publicly owned electric or water utility or a city's public transport system to extractive for-profit corporations. This is equally the case when it comes to privatizing large regional and national state owned enterprises like the US Postal Service or the TVA.

At the very outset of the Trump Administration, this resilient bedrock of popular support for actually existing public ownership was demonstrated yet again, this time in the case of public lands. Seeking to exploit their newly acquired political control of all branches of the federal government in Washington, Republicans in Congress forced through changes to gut the requirement that transfers of federal land must not decrease federal revenues or increase federal debt. In a follow-up measure, Utah Representative Jason Chaffetz, a Republican, introduced legislation to sell off 3.3 million acres of federal land across 10 Western states (as well as an accompanying bill to strip federal land management agencies of law enforcement authority). The proposed legislation immediately caused a firestorm of intense criticism and public protest from a cross-party coalition of conservationists, hunters, and outdoorspeople across the West, leading to Chaffetz's hasty withdrawal of the bill in early February 2017. 'I'm a proud gun owner, hunter and love our public lands,' he wrote. 'Groups I support and care about fear it sends the wrong message ... I look forward to working with you. I hear you and [the proposed bill] HR 621 dies tomorrow.'[59]

We may now be finding that the concept of public ownership is finally breaking free of what Cumbers calls the two competing and unrealizable dogmas of the twentieth century – 'a centralized and planned version of socialism and a free market unregulated capitalism.'[60] On the one hand, it can be now be convincingly argued that traditional bureaucratized, centralized, and hierarchical forms of public ownership are not the only (or desired) alternative to private ownership, and that democratized and decentralized forms of public ownership can and should be a component of any alternative to corporate capitalism. On the other hand, it is also increasingly possible to demonstrate that the oft-repeated mantra of relative inefficiency is a red herring designed to mask a tremendous transfer of public wealth and assets to a small group of privileged individuals – and that the empirical and theoretical literature does not, and never has, supported the theory that private ownership is inherently economically superior to public, collective, or social ownership.

With this liberation, however, comes a very real risk that a repurposed public ownership may be co-opted by the rising tide of right-wing populism, whether through a reappearance of Trump's 'America First' economic agenda (largely abandoned in office) in a trillion-dollar infrastructure investment plan or in the newfound post-Brexit taste for state interventionism and industrial policy of Theresa May (and some of her likely successors) in the British Conservative Party. As with issues of trade and globalization, the left must not surrender public ownership to these forces; it must center democratized forms of public ownership as part of its vision for the future, its transition strategies, and its resistance efforts.

The first steps in this challenge are identifying where and how public ownership could be implemented or scaled up in the existing economy; why it should be so; and how it should be designed or reformed to further the goals of economic democracy, participation, transparency, efficiency (however defined), and sustainability. This must not remain solely the work of utopian systemic design, valuable as that is. The developing crisis – and the emerging reality of a hard-right political turn in the United States and many other parts of the world – demands that we pay careful attention to existing political-economic arrangements (especially ownership patterns) and debates. For example, as 'rebel cities' emerge as a critical line of defense for progressive forces in the Trump era, their financial situation – already weakened by the Great Recession – may be further imperiled by punitive withholdings of federal dollars. In this context, it may be possible to make the case for rapidly deploying public banking and other public enterprise at the municipal level in order to provide new, independent sources of revenue, capital, and jobs.

The next system will not be the last system, or the ideal system – as my colleague Gar Alperovitz likes to say. Now more than ever it is critical that we develop viable and actionable expansion and transition strategies for a plausible and practical vision of a more democratic economy capable of attracting real support against the

Conclusion: Systemic crisis and democratic public ownership

backdrop of a rising tide of popular anger and an anti-democratic turn among technocratic ruling elites. One central element in such a vision is the concept of a renewed and democratized public ownership in all its forms, which must now be embedded within the larger framework of economic democracy and the evolutionary development of a more just, equitable, and sustainable next system of political economy. In this way, we on the left can once again set about our historic task of constructing in earnest the kind of possible future world in which we'd actually want to live.

Notes

Preface

1 Jason Horowitz and Liz Alderman, 'Chastised by E.U., a Resentful Greece Embraces China's Cash and Interests', *New York Times*, August 26, 2017, accessed November 30, 2017, www.nytimes.com/2017/08/26/world/europe/greece-china-piraeus-alexis-tsipras.html.
2 For an excellent summary of the financialization of Thames Water, see: John Allen and Michael Pryke, 'How Thames Water Will Pay Next to Nothing for a £4 billion Tunnel', *The Conversation*, July 2, 2014, accessed November 30, 2017, https://theconversation.com/how-thames-water-will-pay-next-to-nothing-for-a-4-billion-tunnel-28684.
3 OECD, *Slovenia: Overview* (Paris, France: OECD Economic Surveys, 2017), p. 11.
4 I use the term 'progressives' here to describe all those of a social democratic and socialist disposition who share a commitment to social and climate justice, tackling inequalities and searching for alternative and more democratic institutions for running the economy.
5 My thinking is in line with Gar Alperovitz's call for a Pluralist Commonwealth in this regard. See: Gar Alperovitz, *Principles of a Pluralist Commonwealth* (Washington, D.C.: The Democracy Collaborative, 2017).
6 For a more recent updating of these ideas, see: Andrew Cumbers, 'Diversifying Public Ownership: Constructing Institutions for Participation, Social Empowerment and Democratic Control', *Next System Project*, April 18, 2017, accessed November 30, 2017, https://thenextsystem.org/diversifying-public-ownership.
7 Andrew Cumbers, *Reclaiming Public Ownership: Making Space for Economic Democracy* (New York, NY: Zed Books, 2012).
8 Jacques Rancière, 'Ten Theses on Politics', *Theory and Event*, vol. 5, no. 3 (2001).
9 Mark Blyth, *Austerity: The History of a Dangerous Idea* (New York, NY: Oxford University Press, 2013); Matthias Matthijs, 'Powerful Rules Governing the Euro: The Perverse Logic of German Ideas', *Journal of European Public Policy*, vol. 23, no. 3 (2015).
10 Andrew Cumbers, *Reclaiming Public Ownership*.

Introduction

1 Adam Becket, 'Jeremy Corbyn's Labour Conference Speech in Full', *Business Insider*, September 27, 2017, accessed October 25, 2017, www.businessinsider.com/full-text-of-jeremy-corbyns-labour-conference-speech-2017–9.
2 Harriet Agerholm and Louis Dore, 'Jeremy Corbyn Increased Labour's Vote Share More Than Any of the Party's Leaders Since 1945', *Independent*, June 9, 2017, accessed November 27, 2017, www.independent.co.uk/news/uk/politics/jeremy-corbyn-election-result-vote-share-increased-1945-clement-attlee-a7781706.html.
3 Stephen Castle, 'Jeremy Corbyn Says U.K. Labour Party Is Ready to Govern', *New York Times*, September 27, 2017, accessed November 27, 2017, www.nytimes.com/2017/09/27/world/europe/uk-jeremy-corbyn-labour.html?_r=0.
4 Joe Guinan and Thomas M. Hanna, 'Privatisation, a Very British Disease', *openDemocracy*, November 5, 2013, accessed December 1, 2017, https://www.opendemocracy.net/ourkingdom/joe-guinan-thomas-m-hanna/privatisation-very-british-disease.
5 'For the Many Not the Few: 2017 Labour Party Manifesto', *Labour Party*, 2017, accessed October 27, 2017, http://labour.org.uk/wp-content/uploads/2017/10/labour-manifesto-2017.pdf.
6 'Alternative Models of Ownership', *Labour Party*, 2017, accessed October 27, 2017, http://labour.org.uk/wp-content/uploads/2017/10/Alternative-Models-of-Ownership.pdf.
7 'I come at this report with an agenda: I believe that free enterprise policies are a key driver of prosperity. Sadly though, it appears that a large proportion of British voters do not share this view,' the Legatum Institute's Senior Fellow Matthew Elliott laments in his foreword. See: Matthew Elliott and James Kanagasooriam, *Public Opinion in the Post-Brexit Era: Economic Attitudes in Modern Britain* (London, UK: Legatum Institute), October 2017, pp. 3 and 15.
8 George Eaton, 'How Nationalisation Made a Political Comeback', *New Statesman*, September 29, 2017, accessed October 27, 2017, www.newstatesman.com/politics/uk/2017/09/how-nationalisation-made-political-comeback.
9 Joshua Kurlantzick, *State Capitalism: How the Return of Statism Is Transforming the World* (New York, NY: Oxford University Press, 2016), p. 1.
10 Robin Blackburn, 'Finance for Anarchists', *New Left Review*, no. 79 (2013).
11 John Marangos, *Consistency and Viability of Socialist Economic Systems* (New York, NY: Palgrave Macmillan, 2013).
12 G. E. M. de Ste. Croix, *The Class Struggle in the Ancient Greek World* (London, UK: Duckworth, 1981), pp. 3–4.
13 Karl Marx and Frederick Engels, *The German Ideology: Part One with Selections from Part Two and Three and Supplementary Text*, ed., C. J.

Arthur (New York, NY: International Publishers, 1970); Ken Morrison, *Marx, Durkheim, Weber: Formations of Modern Social Thought* (London, UK: Sage Publications, 2006), pp. 52–53.

14 'In theory ...' Pennsylvania State University economist Jan Prybla wrote in his 1969 book *Comparative Economic Systems*, 'the two extreme tools of resource allocation are: individual ownership of all the means of production, and public ownership of all the means of production.' See: Jan S. Prybyla, 'Meaning and Classification of Economic Systems: An Outline', in Jan S. Prybyla, ed., *Comparative Economic Systems* (New York, NY: Meredith Corporation, 1969), p. 11.

15 Peter Wiles, *The Political Economy of Communism* (Cambridge, MA: Harvard University Press, 1962), pp. 4–12.

16 Robert A. Dahl and Charles E. Lindblom, *Politics, Economics, and Welfare*, 1953, Reprint (New Brunswick, NJ: Transaction Publishers, 2000), pp. 9–11.

17 George DeMartino, 'Realizing Class Justice', *Rethinking Marxism*, vol. 15, no. 1 (2003).

18 Cat Hobbs, 'Privatisation is a Rip Off that Has Gone on Long Enough – And the Public Knows It', *New Statesman*, October 24, 2017, accessed October 27, 2017, www.newstatesman.com/politics/economy/2017/10/privatisation-rip-has-gone-long-enough-and-public-knows-it.

19 Musacchio and Lazzarini describe these models as being part of a resurgence of 'state capitalism.' The two models they identify are: 1) the 'Leviathan as a majority investor model,' in which 'the state is still the controlling shareholder, but SOEs have distinct governance traits that allow for the participation of private investors,' and 2) 'Leviathan as a minority investor model,' in which 'the state relinquishes control of its enterprises to private investors but remains present through minority equity investments by pension funds, sovereign wealth funds, and the government itself.' See: Aldo Musacchio and Sergio G. Lazzarini, *Reinventing State Capitalism: Leviathan in Business, Brazil and Beyond* (Cambridge, MA: Harvard University Press, 2014), p. 2.

20 Branko Milanović, *Liberalization and Entrepreneurship: Dynamics of Reform in Socialism and Capitalism* (Armonk, NY: M. E. Sharpe, Inc., 1989), p. 154.

21 'About the Company – Corporate Governance: Shareholders', *Telia Company*, March 6, 2017, www.teliacompany.com/en/about-the-company/corporate-governance/shareholders/; 'Shareholders', *TeliaSonera*, accessed March 6, 2017, http://annualreports.teliasonera.com/en/2015/governance/shareholders/; 'Shareholdings as of September 30, 2017', *Telia Company*, accessed November 20, 2017, www.teliacompany.com/en/investors/share-related-information/shareholdings/.

22 Omar Shah and Scott Campbell, 'End of the Golden Era? The European Courts Move To Promote Greater Free Movement of Capital within the EU by Attacking "Golden Shares"', *Eurowatch*, February 15, 2007.

23 Anton Pannekoek, 'Public Ownership and Common Ownership', *Western Socialist*, November 1947, accessed March 15, 2017, www.marxists.org/archive/pannekoe/free7/public-ownership.htm.
24 Cumbers, *Reclaiming Public Ownership*, p. 7.
25 Saul Estrin, 'Yugoslavia: The Case of Self-Managing Market Socialism', *Journal of Economic Perspectives*, vol. 5, no. 4 (1991).
26 Estrin, 'Yugoslavia'.

Chapter 1

1 All the OECD countries, with the exception of Iceland, Luxembourg, and Slovakia, plus Colombia, Latvia, and Lithuania. See: OECD, *The Size and Sectoral Distribution of SOEs in OECD and Partner Countries* (Paris, France: OECD, September 8, 2014), p. 7.
2 OECD, *The Size and Sectoral Distribution of SOEs in OECD and Partner Countries*, p. 7.
3 *Ibid.*, p. 9.
4 Primary sectors are industries responsible for the extraction or production of natural resources. See: OECD, *The Size and Sectoral Distribution of SOEs in OECD and Partner Countries*, p. 11.
5 Max Büge, Matias Egeland, Przemyslaw Kowalski, and Monika Sztajerowska, 'State-Owned Enterprises in the Global Economy: Reason for Concern?' *Vox: CEPR's Policy Platform*, May 2, 2013, accessed March 16, 2017, www.voxeu.org/article/state-owned-enterprises-global-economy-reason-concern.
6 Ian Bremmer, 'The Long Shadow of the Visible Hand', *Wall Street Journal*, May 22, 2010, accessed March 16, 2017, http://online.wsj.com/article/SB10001424052748704852004575258541875590852.html; Steven F. Hayward, 'Energy Fact of the Week: State-Owned Oil Reserves Dwarf Private Companies', *AEI*, November 2, 2011, accessed November 27, 2017, www.aei.org/publication/energy-fact-of-the-week-state-owned-oil-reserves-dwarf-private-companies/.
7 For Gazprom, see: 'Equity Capital Structure', *Gazprom*, 2015, accessed March 16, 2017, www.gazprom.com/investors/stock/structure/. As of April 1, 2017, JSC Rosneftgaz, which is in 100 percent federal government ownership, owned 50.00000001 percent of Rosenft. However, the National Settlement Depository also owns 10.37 percent. The National Settlement Depository is 99.97 percent owned by Moscow Exchange, which, in turn, is 11.7 percent owned by the Russian Central Bank (a publicly owned entity). The Russian Federation (through the Federal Agency for State Property Management) also retains ownership of a single share in Rosneft. See: 'Shareholder Structure', *Rosneft*, accessed April 9, 2017, www.rosneft.com/Investors/Equity/Shareholder_structure/; 'Shareholders', *National Settlement Depository*, accessed April 9, 2017, www.nsd.ru/en/about/structure/shareholders/; 'Shareholder

Structure', *Moscow Exchange*, accessed April 9, 2017, http://moex.com/s1352. As of December 2015, state owned China National Petroleum Corporation owned 97 percent of PetroChina's Class A Shares. See: 'PetroChina Company Limited: Form 20-F', *United States Securities and Exchange Commission*, 2016, accessed April 9, 2017, www.petrochina.com.cn/ptr/ndbg/201604/10cb348e2425464f8a87aeb3881f5722/files/d23992d74dd246ccb389a4b6f64cfca9.pdf. For Statoil, see: 'Our Shareholders', December 2016, *Statoil*, accessed March 16, 2017, www.statoil.com/content/statoil/en/investors/our-dividend/our-shareholders.html.

8 For Air France-KLM, see: 'Capital Structure as of March 31, 2016', *Air France-KLM*, March 31, 2016, accessed March 16, 2017, www.airfranceklm.com/fr/finance/informations-financieres/repartition-du-capital; For SAS, see: 'SAS 20 Largest Shareholder on 31 January 2017', *SAS Group*, January 31, 2017, accessed March 16, 2017, www.sasgroup.net/SASGroup/default.asp; For El-Al, see: 'Shareholders as of October 31, 2014', *El Al*, October 31, 2014, accessed March 16, 2017, www.elal.co.il/ELAL/English/AboutElAl/InvestorRelations/shareholders.htm; For Singapore Airlines, see Temasek Holdings (Pte) Ltd: 'Stock and Shareholding Information', *Singapore Airlines*, December 31, 2016, accessed March 16, 2017, www.singaporeair.com/jsp/cms/en_UK/global_header/shareholdinginfo.jsp.

9 'Capital Structure as of 31 December 2016', *Airbus*, December 31, 2016, accessed March 16, 2017, www.airbusgroup.com/int/en/investors-shareholders/Share-information.html.

10 For France, see: 'EPIC Story', *SNCF*, accessed March 17, 2017, www.sncf.com/en/meet-sncf/epic-status; For Spain, see: 'The Company', *Renfe*, accessed March 17, 2017, www.renfe.com/EN/empresa/index.html; For Belgium, see: 'About Thalys', *Thalys*, accessed March 17, 2017, www.thalys.com/fr/en/about-thalys/presentation; For Germany, see: 'Investor Relations- Deutsche Bahn AG', *DB*, accessed March 17, 2017, www.deutschebahn.com/en/investor_relations/ir_tochtersite_dbag.html; For Italy, see: 'Italy: Trenitalia', *Rail Europe*, accessed March 17, 2017, www.raileurope-world.com/about-us-23/railways/article/italy-trenitalia; For the Netherlands, see: 'About NS – Corporate Governance', *NS*, accessed March 17, 2017, www.ns.nl/en/about-ns/corporate-governance; For China, see: Keith Bradsher, 'High-Speed Rail Poised to Alter China', *New York Times*, June 22, 2011, accessed March 17, 2016, www.nytimes.com/2011/06/23/business/global/23rail.html?pagewanted=all; For South Korea, see: 'Korail Innovation Way', *Korail*, accessed March 17, 2016, http://info.korail.com/2007/eng/ekr/ekr03000/w_ekr03100.jsp.

11 Luciana Pontes, 'Ownership Policy and SOE Autonomy' (Presentation at 2nd Meeting of the OECD Global Network on Privatisation and Corporate Governance of State-Owned Enterprises, Paris, FR,

March 2–3, 2010), accessed March 20, 2017, www.oecd.org/datao-ecd/4/41/44787618.pdf.
12. Organization for Economic Co-Operation and Development, 'Table 2.6. Government Ownership of Public Telecommunication Network Operators', in *OECD Communications Outlook 2013* (Paris, FR: OECD, 2013), p. 61, accessed March 20, 2017, www.oecd.org/sti/broadband/2-6.pdf.
13. Mathias Schmit, Laurent Gheeraert, Thierry Denuit, and Cédric Warny, *Public Financial Institutions in Europe* (Brussels, Belgium: European Association of Public Banks, March 15, 2011).
14. 'Facts & Figures – The Savings Banks Finance Group's Market Position', *Finazgruppe Deutscher Sparkassen-und Giroverband*, 2015, accessed March 17, 2017, www.dsgv.de/en/facts/facts-and-figures.html.
15. 'Old-Fashioned but in Favor: Defending the Three Pillars', *The Economist*, November 10, 2012, accessed March 17, 2017, www.economist.com/news/finance-and-economics/21566013-defending-three-pillars-old-fashioned-favour.
16. Finazgruppe Deutscher Sparkassen-und Giroverband, 'Facts & Figures – The Savings Banks Finance Group's Market Position'.
17. Ellen Brown, 'Japan Post's Stalled Sale a Saving Grace', *Asia Times*, April 1, 2011, accessed March 20, 2017, http://atimes.com/atimes/Japan/MD01Dh01.html.
18. Thomas Marois, 'Costa Rica's Banco Popular Shows How Banks Can Be Democratic, Green – and Financially Sustainable', *The Conversation*, September 5, 2017, accessed October 31, 2017, http://theconversation.com/costa-ricas-banco-popular-shows-how-banks-can-be-democratic-green-and-financially-sustainable-82401.
19. The majority owned listed companies included: 54.4 percent of Aeroports de Paris SA; 84.4 percent of Électricité de France SA; and 55.3 percent of Icade SA, a property investment company. The minority owned listed companies included: 15.88 percent of Air France KLM; 14.33 percent of Areva SA, an energy company; 41.09 percent of CNP Assurances SA, an insurance company; 45.1 percent of Dexia, a financial company; 14.96 percent of EADS, an aerospace manufacturer; 26.95 percent of France Telecom SA [Orange SA]; 38.01 percent of GDF Suez SA, a multinational electric utility; 27.17 percent of Thales SA, an electric systems manufacturer; 15.01 percent of Renault Fr, an automobile manufacturer; 30.2 percent of Safran SA, an aircraft engine manufacturer; and 27.02 percent of Tessenderlo Chemie NV, a multinational consulting company). The majority owned non-listed companies included: SNCF, the national railway company; La Poste, the postal service; DCNS, a naval dockyard and defense company; France Televisions, the national public TV network; Nexter (GIAT), a weapons manufacturer; Francaise des Jeux, the national lottery; Radio France; RATP Group, the public transport operator in the Paris region; Resau Ferre de France, a railroad

infrastructure company; Imprimerie Nationale, the national printer; Le Monnaie de Paris, the national mint; and LFB, a bio-medical laboratory and national blood bank, among many others. See: OECD, *The Size and Sectoral Distribution of SOEs in OECD and Partner Countries*, pp. 18 and 33.

20 The majority owned listed companies included: 50.001 percent of Kongsberg Gruppen ASA, a multinational industrial technology company; 67 percent of Statoil; and 53.97 percent of Telenor ASA, a multinational telecommunications company. The minority owned listed companies included: 43.54 percent of Cermaq ASA, a fish farming company subsequently sold to Mitsubishi in late 2014; 34 percent of DNB ASA, a financial services company; 34.26 percent of Norsk Hydro ASA, an aluminum and renewables company; 36.21 percent of Yara International ASA, a chemical company; and 14.29 percent of SAS, a major international airline. The majority owned non-listed companies included: Argentum Fondsinvesteringer, a venture capital firm; Avinor, operator of most of the country's airports; Baneservice, a railroad infrastructure company; Enova SF, a renewable energy marketing company; Entra Eiendom, a large real estate company; Innovation Norway, a national development bank; Mesta, a road construction company; Norfund, a foreign investment company; Norsk Tipping AS, a gambling company; Norges Statsbaner AS, the passenger railroad company; Husbanken, a state housing bank; Posten Norge, the postal service; Secora, a maritime construction company; Statskraft, the national electricity company; Statskog, a real-estate company responsible for forest and mountain land; Staur Farm, a farm, conference center, and agricultural research center; Vinmonopolet, the state alcohol distributor; and NRK, the public broadcasting company. See: OECD, *The Size and Sectoral Distribution of SOEs in OECD and Partner Countries*, pp. 20 and 47.

21 Sarah Lidé et al., *State-Owned Enterprises: Catalysts for Public Value Creation?* (London, UK: PricewaterhouseCoopers, 2015), accessed April 3, 2016, www.pwc.com/gx/en/psrc/publications/assets/pwc-state-owned-enterprise-psrc.pdf.

22 In its research, TNI used a broad definition of re-municipalization that is similar to some of the more encompassing definitions of public ownership. 'For instance,' the report states, 'citizen co-operatives that have taken over profit-driven commercial energy service providers (e.g. Minnesota and Hawaiian Island Kauai in the US) fall into our research scope.' See: Satoko Kishimoto and Olivier Petitjean, eds., *Reclaiming Public Services: How Cities and Citizens are Turning Back Privatisation* (Amsterdam, NL: Transnational Institute, June 2017), pp. 12 and 20.

23 Kishimoto and Petitjean, eds., *Reclaiming Public Services*, p. 12.

24 Jeevan Vasagar, 'German Grids Restored to Public Ownership', *Financial Times*, November 25, 2013, accessed February 16, 2017, www.ft.com/

content/2f3b0b1e-4dee-11e3-8fa5-00144feabdc0; 'Hamburg Buys Its Energy Grid Back', *New Compass*, April 21, 2014, accessed April 3, 2017, http://new-compass.net/articles/hamburg-buys-its-energy-grid-back.
25 Hardy Graupner, 'What Exactly Is Germany's "Energiewende"?' *DW*, January 22, 2013, accessed April 3, 2017, www.dw.com/en/what-exactly-is-germanys-energiewende/a-16540762; Andrew Cumbers, 'Remunicipalization, the Low-Carbon Transition, and Energy Democracy', in Lisa Mastny, ed., *Can a City Be Sustainable?* (Washington, DC: Worldwatch Institute and Island Press, 2016), p. 281.
26 'The Re-Municipalization of the Hamburg Grid', *Energy Transition*, June 27, 2014, accessed April 3, 2017, https://energytransition.org/2014/06/remunicipalization-of-hamburg-grid/.
27 David Hall, 'Barcelona Reorganises Public Services in the People's Interest', *Transnational Institute*, February 14, 2017, accessed April 3, 2017, www.tni.org/en/article/barcelona-reorganises-public-services-to-serve-public-interest; Míriam Planas, 'A Citizen Wave to Reclaim Public and Democratic Water in Catalan Municipalities', in Satoko Kishimoto and Olivier Petitjean, eds., *Reclaiming Public Services: How Cities and Citizens Are Turning Back Privatisation* (Amsterdam, NL: Transnational Institute, June 2017), p. 146.
28 Planas, 'A Citizen Wave to Reclaim Public and Democratic Water in Catalan Municipalities', p. 147.
29 Hall, 'Barcelona Reorganises Public Services in the People's Interest'.
30 James Meek, 'How We Happened to Sell Off Our Electricity', *London Review of Books*, 34, no. 17 (September 2012), accessed April 3, 2017, www.lrb.co.uk/v34/n17/james-meek/how-we-happened-to-sell-off-our-electricity.
31 Terry Macalister, 'Nuclear Adviser Attacks "Perverse" Idea of Chinese Building UK Reactors', *Guardian*, June 18, 2015, accessed April 3, 2017, www.theguardian.com/business/2015/jun/18/nuclear-adviser-attacks-chinese-uk-reactors-dieter-helm-hinkley.
32 Emily Gosden, 'China to Build Nuclear Reactor in Essex after Hinkley Deal Approves', *Telegraph*, September 15, 2016, accessed April 4, 2017, www.telegraph.co.uk/business/2016/09/15/china-to-build-nuclear-reactor-in-essex-after-hinkley-deal-appro/.
33 Mika Minio-Paluello, *Who Owns the Wind, Owns the Future* (Labour Energy Forum, September 2017), p. 7.
34 'Our Company', *Vattenfall*, accessed April 4, 2017, www.vattenfall.co.uk/en/wind-power.htm.
35 Minio-Paluello, *Who Owns the Wind, Owns the Future*, pp. 15–17.
36 'For the Many Not the Few', *Labour Party*.
37 Adam Vaughan, 'Publicly Owned Energy Minnows Take on Big Six in Troubled UK Market', *Guardian*, October 27, 2017, accessed November 1, 2017, www.theguardian.com/business/2017/oct/27/publicly-owned-energy-minnows-take-on-big-six-in-troubled-uk-market.

Notes: Chapter 1

38 David Hall and Cat Hobbs, 'Public Ownership is Back on the Agenda in the UK,' in Satoko Kishimoto and Olivier Petitjean, eds., *Reclaiming Public Services: How Cities and Citizens are Turning Back Privatisation* (Amsterdam, NL: Transnational Institute, June 2017), p. 137.
39 *APPA Annual Directory and Statistical Report 2015–2016: US Electric Utility Industry Statistics* (Washington, D.C.: American Public Power Association, 2016), accessed April 3, 2017, www.publicpower.org/files/PDFs/USElectricUtilityIndustryStatistics.pdf.
40 Thomas M. Hanna, 'Community-Owned Energy: How Nebraska Became the Only State to Bring Everyone Power from a Public Grid', *Yes! Magazine*, January 30, 2015, accessed April 7, 2017, www.yesmagazine.org/commonomics/nebraskas-community-owned-energy.
41 Mark Jaffe, 'Boulder Mulls Xcel Energy's Future', *Denver Post*, January 6, 2013, accessed April 3, 2017, www.denverpost.com/ci_22314716/boulder-city-mulls-xcels-future.
42 Nathan Rice, 'Boulder, Colo., Votes for Energy Independence – From Its Utility', *High Country News*, December 28, 2011, accessed April 7, 2017, www.hcn.org/issues/43.22/boulder-colo-votes-for-energy-independence-from-its-corporate-utility.
43 David Shaffer, 'Boulder Votes to Keep Going with Xcel Ouster', *Star Tribune*, November 6, 2013, accessed April 3, 2017, www.startribune.com/business/230837811.html; 'Campaign for Local Power', *Indiegogo*, accessed April 3, 2017, www.indiegogo.com/projects/campaign-for-local-power.
44 Robert Walton, 'Five Years in, Boulder's Municipalization Fight Could Be Drawing to a Close', *Utility Dive*, July 5, 2016, accessed April 4, 2017, www.utilitydive.com/news/five-years-in-boulders-municipalization-fight-could-be-drawing-to-a-close/421709/.
45 'An Update on Boulder's Campaign for Local Power', *New Era Colorado Foundation*, April 10, 2017, accessed April 21, 2017, http://neweracolorado.org/2017/04/10/an-update-on-boulders-campaign-for-local-power/#.WPpwYdLyuUk.
46 Jeannine Anderson, 'Boulder City Council Votes to Proceed with Municipalization', *Public Power Daily*, April 18, 2017, accessed April 21, 2017, www.publicpower.org/Media/daily/ArticleDetail.cfm?ItemNumber=47940. Jensen Werley, 'PUC Postpones Boulder's Municipalization Hearing but Does Not Dismiss It', *BizWest*, April 19, 2017, accessed April 21, 2017, http://bizwest.com/2017/04/19/puc-postpones-boulders-municipalization-hearing-not-dismiss/.
47 'City Offers Statement on Public Utilities Commission Written Ruling; Outlines Next Steps in Ongoing Analysis Process', *City of Boulder*, September 14, 2017, accessed October 26, 2017, https://bouldercolorado.gov/newsroom/city-offers-statement-on-public-utilities-commission-written-ruling-outlines-next-steps-in-ongoing-analysis-process; Alex Burness, 'Boulder Municipalization Persists after Surprise Election Comeback', *Daily Camera*, November 8, 2017, accessed

November 20, 2017, www.dailycamera.com/boulder-election-news/ci_31439744/boulder-municipalization-persists-after-surprise-election-comeback?platform=hootsuite.
48. Frank Jossi, 'Minneapolis Utility Fight Ends with Unique Clean-Energy Deal', *Midwest Energy News*, October 17, 2014, accessed April 3, 2017, www.midwestenergynews.com/2014/10/17/minneapolis-utility-fight-ends-with-unique-clean-energy-deal/.
49. 'What Is CCA', *LEAN Energy*, accessed April 10, 2017, www.leanenergyus.org/what-is-cca/.
50. Joshua Emerson Smith, 'Focus: More Cities, Counties Choosing Green Energy Sources', *San Diego Union-Tribune*, August 14, 2016, accessed April 10, 2017, www.sandiegouniontribune.com/news/environment/sdut-cca-california-community-choice-aggregation-2016aug14-story.html.
51. *The State of Public Water in the United States* (Washington, D.C.: Food and Water Watch, February 2016), accessed April 3, 2017, www.foodandwaterwatch.org/sites/default/files/report_state_of_public_water.pdf; For a discussion of the public and private ownership of water in Britain, see: Rachel Graham, 'Water in the UK – Public Versus Private', *openDemocracy*, December 19, 2014, accessed April 12, 2017, www.opendemocracy.net/ourkingdom/rachel-graham/water-in-uk-public-versus-private.
52. Food and Water Watch, *The State of Public Water in the United States*.
53. *Aqua America: A Corporate Profile* (Washington, D.C.: Food and Water Watch, May 2014), accessed April 3, 2017, www.foodandwaterwatch.org/sites/default/files/Aqua%20America%20Profile%20IB%20May%202014.pdf.
54. Maude Barlow and Wenonah Hauter, 'The Dangerous Return of Water Privatization', *Utne Reader*, January/February 2014, accessed April 9, 2017, www.utne.com/politics/water-privatization-zm0z14jfzros?pageid=4#PageContent4.
55. Nina Feldman, 'Atlantic City Activists Scored a Victory for Public Water', *Next City*, July 28, 2017, accessed November 20, 2017, https://nextcity.org/daily/entry/atlantic-city-public-water-privatized-city-council-vote.
56. 'Community Network Map', *Community Broadband Networks*, October 2015, accessed April 3, 2017, www.muninetworks.org/communitymap.
57. The Executive Office of the President, 'Community-Based Broadband Solutions', *The White House*, January 2015, accessed April 3, 2017, https://obamawhitehouse.archives.gov/sites/default/files/docs/community-based_broadband_report_by_executive_office_of_the_president.pdf.
58. Brian Fung, 'Twenty States Bar Cities from Building Their Own Internet. Netflix Wants the FCC to Change That', *Washington Post*, September 3, 2014, accessed April 3, 2017, www.washingtonpost.com/blogs/the-switch/wp/2014/09/03/twenty-states-bar-cities-from-building-their-own-internet-netflix-wants-the-fcc-to-change-that/.
59. All told, it is estimated that around 100 Colorado municipalities have opted out of the state law. See: Nancy Scola, '7 Colorado Communities Just Secured the Right to Build Their Own Broadband', *Washington*

Post, November 5, 2014, accessed April 3, 2017, www.washingtonpost.com/blogs/the-switch/wp/2014/11/05/7-colo; Tamara Chuang, '19 More Colorado Cities and Counties Vote in Favor of City-Owned Internet, While Fort Collins Approves $150 Million to Move Forward', *Denver Post*, November 8, 2017, accessed November 20, 2017, www.denverpost.com/2017/11/08/19-more-colorado-municipalities-vote-for-city-owned-internet-fort-collins-approves-150-million/.

60 Kyle Daly, 'Sixth Circuit Kills FCC's Municipal Broadband State Preemption Order', *Bloomberg BNA*, August 17, 2016, accessed April 3, 2017, www.bna.com/sixth-circuit-kills-n73014446456/.

61 Mark Oswald, 'Public Banking Debate Starts in Santa Fe', *Albuquerque Journal*, October 3, 2014, accessed April 3, 2017, www.abqjournal.com/473239/news/public-banking-debate-starts-in-santa-fe.html.

62 Daniel J. Chacón, 'City Council OKs $50K Contract for Study on Public Bank', *Sante Fe New Mexican*, January 28, 2015, accessed April 3, 2017, www.santafenewmexican.com/news/local_news/city-council-oks-k-contract-for-study-on-public-bank/article_0006287b-36b5-516c-b9e9-bb25ff2ef366.html; T.S. Last, 'Study: Santa Fe Public Bank Is Feasible', *Albuquerque Journal*, January 14, 2016, accessed April 4, 2017, www.abqjournal.com/705662/study-santa-fe-public-bank-is-feasible.html.

63 Katherine L. Updike and Christopher Erickson, 'Public Banking Feasibility Study Final Report for the City of Santa Fe', *Building Solutions LLC and the Arrowhead Center at New Mexico State University*, January 2016, accessed April 7, 2017, www.santafenm.gov/document_center/document/4520.

64 Elaine Sullivan, 'Santa Fe City Council Launches a Task Force to Formally Consider a Public Bank for Santa Fe', *Banking on New Mexico*, April 27, 2017, accessed May 4, 2017, http://bankingonnewmexico.org/wp-content/uploads/2017/05/PublicBank_SantaFeResolution_4.27.17.pdf.

65 Mike Krauss, 'A Public Bank in Philadelphia', *OpEdNews*, February 26, 2016, accessed April 3, 2017, www.opednews.com/articles/1/A-Public-Bank-in-Philadelp-by-Mike-Krauss-Bank-Failure_Bankers_Bankers_Banking-Crisis-160226-373.html.

66 Richard Knee, 'Oakland Public Bank Feasibility Study Delayed by at Least 8 Weeks', *Hoodline*, March 1, 2017, accessed April 7, 2017, http://hoodline.com/2017/03/oakland-public-bank-feasibility-study-delayed-by-at-least-8-weeks.

67 'LA Considers First Ever City-Owned Public Bank in US', *CBS Los Angeles*, October 4, 2017, accessed October 26, 2017, http://losangeles.cbslocal.com/2017/10/04/la-considers-city-owned-bank/.

68 'Motion', *City of Los Angeles*, July 2017, accessed October 26, 2017, http://clkrep.lacity.org/onlinedocs/2017/17-0831_mot_07-26-2017.pdf.

69 John Nichols, 'Vermont Votes for Public Banking', *Nation*, March 9, 2014, accessed April 3, 2017, www.thenation.com/blog/178759/vermont-votes-public-banking.

70 Alexis Goldstein, 'Vermonters Lobby for Public Bank – And Win Millions for Local Investment Instead', *Yes! Magazine*, January 7, 2015, accessed April 3, 2017, www.yesmagazine.org/commonomics/vermonters-lobby-public-bank-win-millions-for-local-investment.

71 John Reitmeyer, 'Phil Murphy Makes State Bank Centerpiece of Gubernatorial Campaign', *New Jersey Spotlight*, September 9, 2016, accessed May 4, 2017, www.njspotlight.com/stories/16/09/09/murphy-makes-state-bank-centerpiece-of-gubernatorial-campaign/.

72 'A Public Bank – Investing in New Jersey Not Wall Street', *Phil Murphy, Democrat for Governor*, accessed May 4, 2017, www.murphy4nj.com/issue/a-public-bank-investing-in-new-jersey-not-wall-street/.

73 James Rufus Koren, 'Should California Start Its Own Bank to Serve Marijuana Companies? It Wouldn't Be Easy', *Los Angeles Times*, July 27, 2017, accessed October 26, 2017, www.latimes.com/business/la-fi-public-bank-marijuana-20170727-htmlstory.html.

74 '2015 Annual Report', *Bank of North Dakota*, April 20, 2016, accessed April 4, 2017, https://bnd.nd.gov/2015-annual-report/.

75 Ellen Brown, 'North Dakota's Economic "Miracle" – It's Not Oil', *Yes! Magazine*, August 31, 2011, accessed April 4, 2017, www.yesmagazine.org/new-economy/the-north-dakota-miracle-not-all-about-oil.

76 Matt Stannard, 'North Dakota's Public Bank Was Built for the People – Now It's Financing Police at Standing Rock', *Yes! Magazine*, December 14, 2016, accessed April 4, 2017, www.yesmagazine.org/people-power/north-dakotas-public-bank-was-built-for-the-people-now-its-financing-police-at-standing-rock-20161214.

77 'About', *North Dakota Mill*, accessed April 4, 2017, www.ndmill.com/index.cfm/about/about-us/.

78 'State Life Insurance Fund', *Wisconsin Office of the Commissioner of Insurance*, February 18, 2016, accessed October 31, 2017, https://oci.wi.gov/Pages/Funds/SLIFOverview.aspx.

79 Joe Chrisman, *State Life Insurance Fund* (Madison, WI: State of Wisconsin, Office of the Commissioner of Insurance, October 2013), accessed October 31, 2017, http://legis.wisconsin.gov/lab/reports/13-16full.pdf. The number of policies is more than double that of 1975, and the amount of insurance coverage is more than triple. See: Martin Carnoy and Derek Shearer, *Economic Democracy: The Challenge of the 1980s* (Armonk, NY: M.E. Sharpe, 1980), p. 69.

80 Carnoy and Shearer, *Economic Democracy*, p. 68.

81 Eugene V. Debs, 'The Socialist Party's Appeal', *The Independent*, vol. LXV, no. 3124, October 15, 1908, accessed April 7, 2017, www.marxists.org/archive/debs/works/1908/appeal.htm.

82 'The Socialist Party's Platform, 1912', *Labor History Links*, accessed April 7, 2017, www.laborhistorylinks.org/PDF%20Files/Socialist%20Party%20Platform%201912.pdf.

83 The Editors of Encyclopedia Britannica, 'The United States Presidential Election of 1912', *Encyclopedia Britannica*, October

10, 2016, accessed April 7, 2017, www.britannica.com/event/United-States-presidential-election-of-1912.
84 Victor Berger, *Broadsides* (Milwaukee, WI: Social-Democratic Publishing Company, 1913), p. 179.
85 Carl D. Thompson, *The Constructive Program of Socialism* (Milwaukee, WI: Social-Democratic Publishing, Co., 1908), p. 28.
86 According to biographer Nick Salvatore, 'Debs applauded the recent 1910 electoral gains but cautioned against an infatuation with municipal Socialism.' See: Nick Salvatore, *Eugene V. Debs: Citizen and Socialist* (Champaign, IL: Illini Books, 1984), p. 246.
87 Richard W. Judd, *Socialist Cities: Municipal Politics and the Grassroots of American Socialism* (Albany, NY: State University of New York Press, 1989), pp. 13–14.
88 Bruce Stave, ed., *Socialism and the Cities* (Port Washington, NY: Kennikat Press, 1975), p. 5.
89 Stave, ed., *Socialism and the Cities*, pp. 5–6.
90 David Paul Nord, 'Minneapolis and the Pragmatic Socialism of Thomas Van Lear', *Minnesota History*, Spring 1976, pp. 2–10, accessed April 3, 2017, http://collections.mnhs.org/MNHistoryMagazine/articles/45/v45i01p002–010.pdf.
91 Sally M. Miller, 'Milwaukee: Of Ethnicity and Labor', in Bruce Stave, ed., *Socialism and the Cities* (Port Washington, NY: Kennikat Press, 1975), pp. 62–63.
92 'Environmental Stewardship: Milorganite', *Milorganite*, accessed April 7, 2017, www.milorganite.com/about-us.
93 Kenneth E. Hendrickson, Jr., 'Tribune of the People: George R. Lunn', in Bruce Stave, ed., *Socialism and the Cities* (Port Washington, NY: Kennikat Press, 1975), pp. 84–85.
94 'Public Ownership', *Public Ownership League of America*, vol. iv, nos. 1–11 (1922).
95 'Minnesota Avenue', *Washington Metropolitan Transit Authority*, accessed April 7, 2017, www.wmata.com/about/business/real-estate/Minnesota-Avenue.cfm.
96 Robert R. Nelson, 'Public Financing of Headquarter Hotels in the United States', in Robert R. Nelson, ed., *Developing a Successful Infrastructure for Convention & Event Tourism* (New York, NY: Routledge, 2013), p. 31; 'Bay City DoubleTree Hotel and Conference Center', *Garfield Public Private*, accessed April 3, 2017, http://garfieldpublicprivate.com/portfolio/doubletree-hotel-and-conference-center/; Erin Golden, 'City-Owned Hilton Omaha Faces a More Challenging Financial Future', *Omaha.com*, March 11, 2014, accessed April 3, 2017, www.omaha.com/news/city-owned-hilton-omaha-faces-a-more-challenging-financial-future/article_61644b44–1826–5cde-be11–572cac9a684f.html.
97 Nelson, ed., *Developing a Successful Infrastructure for Convention & Event Tourism*, p. 35.

Notes: Chapter 1

98 'City Fact Sheet: Vancouver Hilton Hotel/Convention Center 2015 Operations', *City of Vancouver Washington*, June 11, 2015, accessed April 3, 2017, www.cityofvancouver.us/sites/default/files/fileattachments/downtown_redevelopment_authority/page/2892/hilton_hotel_convention_center_-_fact_sheet_-_2015.pdf.

99 'The Economic Impact of Commercial Airports in 2010', *CDM Smith*, January 2012, accessed April 3, 2017, www.aci-na.org/sites/default/files/airport_economic_impact_report_2012.pdf; 'Airport Privatization: Issues Related to the Sale of Lease of Commercial Airports', *United States Subcommittee on Aviation*, November 1996, accessed April 3, 2017, www.gpo.gov/fdsys/pkg/GAOREPORTS-RCED-97–3/html/GAOREPORTS-RCED-97–3.htm. By definition, a commercial airport must be publicly owned, must have regularly scheduled passenger service, and must surpass 2,500 travelers per year. See: 'Airport Categories', *Federal Aviation Administration*, accessed April 3, 2017, www.faa.gov/airports/planning_capacity/passenger_allcargo_stats/categories/. There are around 10 privately owned airports that would meet all the criteria (expect public ownership) of a commercial airport. See: United States Subcommittee on Aviation 'Airport Privatization: Issues Related to the Sale of Lease of Commercial Airports.'

100 CDM Smith, 'The Economic Impact of Commercial Airports in 2010.'

101 'Airport Privatization Pilot Program: Airports', *Federal Aviation Administration*, accessed April 17, 2017, https://www.faa.gov/airports/airport_compliance/privatization/.

102 Reid Wilson, 'How Parking Meters Killed Privatization of Midway', *Washington Post*, September 13, 2013, accessed April 17, 2017, www.washingtonpost.com/blogs/govbeat/wp/2013/09/13/how-parking-meters-killed-privatization-of-midway-airport/?utm_term=.9046a5bbf7db.

103 Marcia Alexander-Adams, 'Fact Sheet – Airport Privatization Pilot Program', *Federal Aviation Administration*, December 2, 2016, accessed April 17, 2017, www.faa.gov/news/fact_sheets/news_story.cfm?newsId=21174.

104 David Smith, 'A Trillion Is Not Enough: Trump's Infrastructure Ambitions Grow', *Guardian*, April 12, 2017, accessed April 17, 2017, www.theguardian.com/us-news/2017/apr/12/donald-trump-infrastructure-bill-cost-private-airports-dams?CMP=share_btn_link. While the details of any such privatization push are currently unknown, as *Mother Jones* columnist Kevin Drum writes, 'the federal government can't privatize airports that are owned by states and cities. And even if it could, states and cities would get the money. So what's the point?' See: Kevin Drum, 'Trump Floats Nonsense Idea of Privatizing Airport and Dams', *Mother Jones*, April 12, 2017, accessed April 17, 2017, www.motherjones.com/kevin-drum/2017/04/trump-floats-nonsense-idea-privatizing-airports-and-dams.

Notes: Chapter 1

105 'Ports', *MARAD*, accessed April 18, 2017, www.marad.dot.gov/ports/; 'U.S. Public Port facts', *American Association of Port Authorities*, July 2008, accessed April 18, 2017, www.aapa-ports.org/files/PDFs/facts.pdf; 'Exports, Jobs & Economic Growth', *American Association of Port Authorities*, accessed April 18, 2017, www.aapa-ports.org/advocating/content.aspx?ItemNumber=21150.

106 'Overview of Facilities and Services', *The Port Authority of New York and New Jersey*, accessed April 7, 2017, www.panynj.gov/about/facilities-services.html.

107 'Fast Facts on US Hospitals: Fast Facts 2017', *American Hospital Association*, January 2017, accessed April 3, 2017, www.aha.org/research/rc/stat-studies/fast-facts.shtml.

108 'Board of Directors', *Denver Health*, 2016, accessed April 9, 2017, www.denverhealth.org/about-us/who-we-are/board-of-directors.

109 'About Us', *Montana Health Center*, accessed January 6, 2017, https://healthcenter.mt.gov/Admin/About-Us.

110 Dan Boyce, 'Montana's State-Run Free Clinic Sees Early Success', *NPR*, July 30, 2013, accessed April 3, 2017, www.npr.org/2013/07/30/206654000/montanas-state-run-free-clinic-sees-early-success.

111 Justin Horwath, 'Governor Announces Healthcare Clinic for State Workers', *Santa Fe New Mexican*, October 21, 2015, accessed April 4, 2017, www.santafenewmexican.com/news/health_and_science/governor-announces-health-care-clinic-for-state-workers/article_2ff62cc1-83fd-5644-a17d-c6c2f467e0d8.html.

112 'Fast Facts: Back to School Statistics', *National Center for Education Statistics*, accessed April 8, 2017, https://nces.ed.gov/fastfacts/display.asp?id=372.

113 Jonathan D. Weiss, *Public Schools and Economic Development: What the Research Shows* (Cincinnati, Ohio: KnowledgeWorks Foundation, 2004).

114 'Table 314.20: Employees in degree-granting postsecondary institutions, by sex, employment status, control and level of institution, and primary occupation: Selected years, fall 1991 through fall 2013', and 'Table 105.50: Number of educational institutions, by level and control of institution: Selected years, 1980–81 through 2013–14', *Digest of Education Statistics 2015*, *National Center for Education Statistics*, accessed April 8, 2017, https://nces.ed.gov/programs/digest/d15/tables/dt15_314.20.asp?referrer=report.

115 'Expenditure of public and private colleges and universities in the U.S. from 1970 to 2014 (in billion U.S. dollars)', *Statista*, accessed April 8, 2017, www.statista.com/statistics/184231/expenditure-of-public-and-private-colleges-and-universities/.

116 'Annual Report: 2016', *Virginia Department of Alcoholic Beverage Control*, accessed April 4, 2017, www.abc.virginia.gov/library/about/pdfs/2016ar.pdf?la=en.

117 Derek Thompson, 'Lotteries: America's $70 Billion Shame', *Atlantic*, May 11, 2015, accessed April 4, 2017, www.theatlantic.com/business/archive/2015/05/lotteries-americas-70-billion-shame/392870/.
118 Todd C. Frankel, 'In Wash. State, a 10-Person Team Toils for the Government – Selling Pot', *Washington Post*, March 16, 2015, accessed April 4, 2017, www.washingtonpost.com/business/economy/a-local-government-in-wash-state-tries-to-corner-the-market-on-marijuana/2015/03/16/fccb8216-c9b7-11e4-b2a1-bed1aaea2816_story.html?utm_term=.ad707ff3a638.
119 'About Us', *The Cannabis Corner*, accessed April 4, 2017, http://thecannabiscorner.org/about/.
120 Robert Benzie, 'LCBO to Run 150 Marijuana Stores', *The Star*, September 8, 2017, accessed October 26, 2017, www.thestar.com/news/queenspark/2017/09/08/lcbo-will-run-150-standalone-marijuana-stores-when-weed-is-legalized.html.
121 'What Is the Alaska Permanent Fund?' *Alaska Permanent Fund Corporation*, accessed April 8, 2017, www.apfc.org/home/Content/aboutFund/aboutPermFund.cfm.
122 'Texas Permanent School Fund', *Texas Education Agency*, accessed April 8, 2017, http://tea.texas.gov/psf/.
123 As of August 31, 2016, the Fund's balance was $37.3 billion. See: Texas Permanent School Fund, *Comprehensive Annual Financial Report: Fiscal Year Ending August 31, 2016* (Austin, Texas: Texas Permanent School Fund, December 2016).
124 'Permanent University Fund – PUF', *University of Texas Investment Management Company*, accessed April 8, 2017, www.utimco.org/scripts/internet/fundsdetail.asp?fnd=2.
125 'Sovereign Wealth Funds', *SWFI*, accessed April 8, 2017, www.swfinstitute.org/sovereign-wealth-fund-profiles/. Similar sovereign wealth funds exist around the world. In 2014, it was reported that every Norwegian was a 'millionaire' (in the local currency) due to the country's massive $828.66 billion sovereign wealth fund (now up to $885 billion). See: Alister Doyle, 'All Norwegians Become Crown Millionaires, in Oil Saving Landmark', *Reuters*, January 8, 2014, accessed April 4, 2017, www.reuters.com/article/us-norway-millionaires-idUSBREA0710U20140108. The fund is held out as a model of how to ensure that the exploitation of natural resources (in this case oil) benefits society over the long-term. It is often compared to Britain, which hit oil in the North Sea at about the same time as Norway, but did not establish a public fund. 'The result is that Norway has amassed ... enough to cope with the cost of looking after a population of 5 million as it ages,' *Guardian* economics editor Larry Elliot wrote in early 2017. 'In Britain, by contrast, the NHS is at breaking point, the social care system is struggling to cope and there is no pot of gold to pay for the healthcare and nursing fees of the baby boomer generation as it advances

into old age.' See: Larry Elliot, 'Norway's $885bn–Nil Advantage in Britain's Sea of Social Troubles', *Guardian*, January 15, 2017, accessed April 4, 2017, www.theguardian.com/business/2017/jan/15/land-reforms-and-a-sovereign-fund-could-secure-uks-long-term-future. The fund is also taking proactive steps to combat climate change, announcing in 2015 that they would be divesting from coal, selling off over $8 billion worth of investments in 122 companies across the world. See: Damian Carrington, 'Norway Confirms $900bn Sovereign Wealth Fund's Major Coal Divestment', *Guardian*, June 5, 2015, accessed April 4, 2017, www.theguardian.com/environment/2015/jun/05/norways-pension-fund-to-divest-8bn-from-coal-a-new-analysis-shows.

126 For instance, Oxford University political theorist Angela Cummine states that 'sovereign funds are the closest real-world approximation of a community fund since Meade first articulated this idea in the 1960s. Yet, the current design and operation of sovereign funds offers little basis for their characterisation as such. With some isolated exceptions, citizens are largely quarantined from exerting any direct influence over or enjoying any direct benefit from the management, investment and distribution of "their" sovereign wealth. Yet, as more states move toward establishing these funds with forecasts predicting the establishment of a further 20 SWFs in the next five years, there is real potential to reform these institutions so they not only better resemble the original community fund vision, but also help to more generally democratize the ownership and control of assets within domestic economies.' See: Angela Cummine, 'Sovereign Wealth Funds: Can They Be Community Funds?' *open Democracy*, November 6, 2013, accessed April 17, 2017, www.opendemocracy.net/ourkingdom/angela-cummine/sovereign-wealth-funds-can-they-be-community-funds. In another variant, Peter Barnes has articulated a vision for 'common wealth trusts.' 'Outwardly,' he writes, 'the shells would be not-for-profit corporations with state charters, self-governance, perpetual life, and legal personhood. Inwardly, the managers of these not-for-profit corporations would be required to protect their assets for future generations and to share current income (if any) equally… The trust form of organization need not be applied to all forms of common wealth. However, at the very minimum, it should be applied to ecosystems that are approaching irreversible tipping points.' See: Peter Barnes, 'Common Wealth Trusts: Structures of Transition', *Great Transition Initiative*, August 2015, accessed April 17, 2017, www.greattransition.org/publication/common-wealth-trusts.

127 'Comparing the Costs of the Veterans' Health System with Private Sector Costs', *Congressional Budget Office*, December 2014, accessed April 4, 2017, www.cbo.gov/sites/default/files/113th-congress-2013-2014/reports/49763-VA_Healthcare_Costs.pdf. In 2012, then presidential candidate Mitt Romney proposed privatizing parts of the VA, only to be roundly criticized by veterans and quickly dropping the idea. See: Steve Benan, 'Trump's Efforts to Privatize Veterans' Care

Causes Alarm', *MSNBC*, November 22, 2017, accessed November 27, 2017, www.msnbc.com/rachel-maddow-show/trumps-efforts-privatize-veterans-care-causes-alarm. Many veterans believe that the VA is being intentionally sabotaged by Congress and that, rather than be privatized, it should be adequately funded. See: Kristofer Goldsmith, 'It's Time to End the Decades-Long Sabotage of Veterans Healthcare', *The Hill*, November 26, 2017, accessed November 27, 2017, http://thehill.com/opinion/healthcare/361829-its-time-to-end-the-decades-long-sabotage-of-veterans-healthcare.

128 'Organizational Structure of the Social Security Administration', *Social Security Administration*, accessed April 4, 2017, www.ssa.gov/org/.

129 Carol Hardy Vincent, Laura A. Hanson, and Carla N. Argueta, *Federal Land Ownership: Overview and Data* (Washington, D.C.: Congressional Research Service, March 3, 2017), accessed April 8, 2017, https://fas.org/sgp/crs/misc/R42346.pdf.

130 Heather Hansman, 'Congress Moves to Give Away National Lands, Discounting Billions in Revenue', *Guardian*, January 19, 2017, accessed April 8, 2017, www.theguardian.com/environment/2017/jan/19/bureau-land-management-federal-lease. Public ownership of land – especially at the federal level – is a contentious issue that cuts across party lines (especially in western states where such ownership is concentrated). Many Republican politicians envision transferring federally owned land to the states, with an eye to either selling it outright to private interests or increasing the exploitation of natural resources (and royalty income to state coffers) through leases. On the other hand, many environmentalists and conservationists see the management and leasing of public lands as a large-scale subsidy to timber and mining corporations. See: Kimberly Lisagor, 'Missing the Forest for the Trees', *Mother Jones*, September 12, 2000, accessed April 8, 2017, www.motherjones.com/politics/2000/09/missing-forest-fees.

131 Robert Pollin, 'Tools for a New Economy: Proposals for a Financial Regulatory System', *Boston Review*, January–February 2009, accessed April 4, 2017, http://bostonreview.net/BR34.1/pollin.php.

132 Gary Childs, 'Vilsack Promotes USDA Rural Housing Program', *Journal Star*, June 2, 2009, accessed April 8, 2017, www.pjstar.com/x124609769/Vilsack-promotes-USDA-rural-housing-program.

133 'About Us', EXIM, accessed April 4, 2017, http://www.exim.gov/about.

134 Lisa Mascaro, 'Export–Import Bank's Expiration a Victory for Billionaire Koch Brothers', *Los Angeles Times*, July 2, 2015, accessed April 4, 2017, www.latimes.com/business/la-fi-export-import-bank-20150701-story.html.

135 Andrew Taylor, 'Momentum Builds for Reviving Export–Import Bank Months after Charter Expired', *Associated Press*, November 5, 2015, accessed April 4, 2017, www.usnews.com/news/business/articles/2015/11/05/momentum-builds-for-reviving-export-import-bank.

Notes: Chapter 1

136 'About TVA', *TVA*, accessed April 8, 2017, www.tva.gov/About-TVA.
137 'Board of Directors', *TVA*, accessed April 8, 2017, www.tva.gov/About-TVA/Our-Leadership/Board-of-Directors.
138 Erwin Hargrove, *Prisoners of Myth: The Leadership of the Tennessee Valley Authority, 1933–1990* (Princeton, NJ: Princeton University Press, 1994), p. 20.
139 Jim Snyder, 'Parties Switch Roles over Possible U.S. Sale of New Deal TVA', *Bloomberg*, April 12, 2013, accessed April 4, 2017, www.bloomberg.com/news/articles/2013-04-12/parties-switch-roles-over-possible-u-s-sale-of-new-deal-era-tva; Sue Sturgis, 'The Strange Politics of TVA Privatization', *Facing South*, April 16, 2013, accessed April 4, 2017, www.southernstudies.org/2013/04/the-strange-politics-of-tva-privatization.html.
140 'About: Size and Scope', *United States Postal Service*, accessed April 4, 2017, https://about.usps.com/who-we-are/postal-facts/size-scope.htm.
141 Ralph Nader, 'The Manufactured "Financial Crisis" of the U.S. Postal Service', *Monthly Review Zine*, September 21, 2011, accessed April 4, 2017, http://mrzine.monthlyreview.org/2011/nader230911.html.
142 Rick Newman, 'Why the U.K. Can Privatize Its Postal Service, but the U.S. Can't', *Yahoo! Finance*, October 14, 2013, accessed April 4, 2017, http://finance.yahoo.com/blogs/the-exchange/why-u-k-privatize-postal-u-t-195031232.html.
143 'Amtrak National Facts', *Amtrak*, accessed April 4, 2017, www.amtrak.com/servlet/ContentServer?c=Page&pagename=am%2FLayout&cid=1246041980246.
144 Phillip Longman, 'Washington's Turnaround Artists', *Washington Monthly*, March/April 2009, accessed April 4, 2017, www.unz.org/Pub/WashingtonMonthly-2009mar-00014.
145 Selima Sultana and Joe Weber, eds., *Minicars, Maglevs, and Mopeds: Modern Modes of Transportation Around the World* (Santa Barbara, CA: ABC-CLIO, LLC, 2016), p. 13.
146 'The Northeast Corridor: Critical Infrastructure for the Northeast', *Amtrak*, accessed April 8, 2017, https://nec.amtrak.com/sites/default/files/NEC%20Fact%20Sheet%202017_Final.pdf.
147 Lauren Gardner, 'Republicans Embrace Amtrak's Gulf Coast Rebirth', *Politico*, January 1, 2017, accessed April 4, 2017, www.politico.com/story/2017/01/amtrak-gulf-coast-republicans-katrina-233080.
148 Gardner, 'Republicans Embrace Amtrak's Gulf Coast Rebirth'.
149 Richard D. Bingham, *Industrial Policy American Style: From Hamilton to HDTV* (Armonk, NY: M.E. Sharpe, 2009), p. 44.
150 Longman, 'Washington's Turnaround Artists'.
151 Henry Kirby, 'Privatisation: The Good, the Bad, and the Ugly', *Guardian*, April 12, 2013, accessed April 4, 2017, www.theguardian.com/politics/2013/apr/12/privatisation-good-bad-ugly.

152 Lucy Tobin, 'Nationalised East Coast Rail Line Returns £209m to Taxpayers', *Independent*, October 8, 2013, accessed April 4, 2017, www.independent.co.uk/news/uk/politics/nationalised-east-coast-rail-line-returns-209m-to-taxpayers-8866157.html.

153 Gwyn Topham, 'East Coast Rail Line Returns to Private Hands', *Guardian*, March 1, 2015, accessed April 4, 2017, www.theguardian.com/uk-news/2015/mar/01/east-coast-rail-line-returns-to-private-hands. *Guardian* columnist Owen Jones was even more direct. 'No wonder they're flogging off the publicly owned east coast rail franchise,' he wrote, 'its very existence is a stubborn rejection of 'the market does best' dogma. Public ownership has routinely been caricatured as a wasteful, subsidy-guzzling failure. How infuriating it must be, then, for free-market ideologues that east coast depended on less public subsidies than any of the 15 privately run rail franchises ... East coast is an embarrassing success story for public ownership. Instead, it must be run by a tax exile and a Scottish businessman perhaps best known for campaigning against gay equality.' See: Owen Jones, 'East Coast Rail Has Been Too Successful – Quick, Privatise It', *Guardian*, November 27, 2014, accessed April 4, 2017, www.theguardian.com/commentisfree/2014/nov/27/privatising-east-coast-rail-rip-off.

154 Food and Water Watch and the Cornell University Global Labor Institute, *Public–Public Partnerships: An Alternative Model to Leverage the Capacity of Municipal Water Utilities* (Washington, D.C. and New York: Food and Water Watch and the Global Labor Institute, January 2012), accessed April 8, 2017, www.foodandwaterwatch.org/sites/default/files/Public%20Public%20Partnerships%20Report%20Feb%202012.pdf.

155 Food and Water Watch and the Cornell University Global Labor Institute, *Public–Public Partnerships: An Alternative Model to Leverage the Capacity of Municipal Water Utilities*.

156 *Ibid.*

157 Hanna, 'Community-Owned Energy'.

158 'Weingarten Announces $10 Billion Investment in Infrastructure and Workforce', *American Federation of Teachers*, June 24, 2014, accessed April 8, 2017, www.aft.org/press-release/weingarten-announces-10-billion-investment-infrastructure-and-workforce.

159 'The Burlington Waterfront', *City of Burlington*, accessed April 4, 2017, www.burlingtonvt.gov/CEDO/The-Burlington-Waterfront; Peter Dreier and Pierre Clavel, 'Bernie's Burlington: What Kind of Mayor Was Bernie Sanders?' *Huffington Post*, June 4, 2015, accessed April 4, 2017, www.huffingtonpost.com/peter-dreier/bernies-burlington-what-k_b_7510704.html; 'Burlington Waterfront Revitalization Plan', *City of Burlington*, December 7, 1998, accessed April 4, 2017, www.burlingtonvt.gov/sites/default/files/CEDO/Waterfront/Waterfront%20Revitalization%20Plan.pdf.

160 Ari Phillips, 'Largest City in Vermont Now Gets All Its Power from Wind, Water and Biomass', *Climate Progress*, September 15, 2014, accessed April 4, 2017, http://thinkprogress.org/climate/2014/09/15/3567307/vermont-renewable-power/; 'How Did Burlington Achieve 100 percent renewable energy?' *Burlington Electric Department*, January 31, 2015, accessed April 4, 2017, www.burlingtonelectric.com/about-us/our-mission/news/how-did-burlington-achieve-100-percent-renewable-energy.

161 'City of Burlington, Vermont: Annual Financial Report, Year Ended June 30, 2014', *City of Burlington*, 2015, accessed April 4, 2017, https://www.burlingtonvt.gov/sites/default/files/Mayor/AnnualReports/AR-2014.pdf.

Chapter 2

1 In the United States, this era arguably began during the presidency of Jimmy Carter (1977–1981) with the start of deregulation in the airline, trucking, and oil industries. See: W. Carl Biven, *Jimmy Carter's Economy: Policy in an Age of Limits* (Chapel Hill, NC: University of North Carolina Press, 2002), pp. 218–222.

2 Michael Hudson, 'Failed Privatizations – The Thatcher Legacy', *Michael-Hudson.com*, April 8, 2013, accessed December 15, 2016, http://michael-hudson.com/2013/04/failed-privatizations-the-thatcher-legacy/.

3 Johan Willner, 'Social Objectives, Market Rule and Public Policy: The Case of Ownership', in Pat Devine *et al.*, eds., *Competitiveness, Subsidiarity and Industrial Policy* (Oxford, UK: Taylor and Francis e-Library, 2005), p. 28.

4 'The present tendency to privatise and deregulate is largely explained by the widespread view that public ownership is inefficient,' Willner wrote. 'The empirical and theoretical research is however fairly inconclusive, which raises questions about policies that favor, unequivocally, either nationalisation or privatisation.' See: Johan Willner and David Parker, 'The Performance of Public and Private Enterprise under Conditions of Active and Passive Ownership and Competition and Monopoly', *Journal of Economics*, vol. 90, no. 3 (2007).

5 Yair Aharoni, 'The Performance of State-Owned Enterprise', in Pier Angelo Toninelli, ed., *The Rise and Fall of State-Owned Enterprise in the Western World* (Cambridge, UK: Cambridge University Press, 2000), p. 50.

6 Cumbers, *Reclaiming Public Ownership*, pp. 33–35.

7 'There is little evidence the privatized entities have yielded better long-term performance than their nationalized predecessors,' Cumbers states. 'A detailed study in the late 1990s found that: "evidence does not support any notion of the inferiority of public ownership, a conclusion reached even without regarding the wider objectives of public ownership with

private ownership"' (Sawyer and O'Donnell, 1999: 1). See: Cumbers, *Reclaiming Public Ownership*, p. 94.
8   Stacey R. Kole and J. Harold Mulherin, 'The Government as a Shareholder: A Case from the United States', *Journal of Law and Economics*, vol. 40, no. 1 (April 1997).
9   Colin Kirkpatrick, David Parker, and Yin-Fang Zhang, 'An Empirical Analysis of State and Private-Sector Provision of Water Services in Africa', *World Bank Economic Review*, vol. 20, no. 1 (2006).
10 Chang also states that some of the issues (such as agency and principal-agent problems) faced by state owned enterprises are the same as those faced by large for-profit businesses. 'When discussing the problems of SOEs, many people often implicitly assume that private-sector firms are perfectly controlled by their owners, thus assuming away their agency problems,' he writes. 'If we compare idealized private-sector firms with real-life SOEs, it is not surprising that the former come out on top.' See: Ha-Joon Chang, *State-Owned Enterprise Reform* (New York: United Nations DESA, 2007), pp. 6–7.
11 'While a few studies from the 1970s find cost savings with privatization,' they wrote, 'these results do not persist over time. For water, only three studies found cost savings with privatization.' See: Germá Bel and Mildred Warner, 'Does Privatization of Solid Waste and Water Services Reduce Costs? A Review of Empirical Studies', *Resources, Conservation and Recycling*, no. 52 (2008).
12 Francisco Flores-Macias and Aldo Musacchio, 'The Return of State-Owned Enterprises', *Harvard International Review*, April 4, 2009.
13 *OECD Economic Surveys: Germany 2014* (Paris, France: OECD, May 2014), p. 22, accessed January 9, 2017, www.oecd.org/eco/Germany-Overview-2014.pdf.
14 Robert Millward, 'State Enterprise in Britain in the Twentieth Century', in Pier Angelo Toninelli, ed., *The Rise and Fall of State-Owned Enterprise in the Western World* (Cambridge, UK: Cambridge University Press, 2000), pp. 170–173. See also: Cumbers, *Reclaiming Public Ownership*, p. 94.
15 Michael Oliver, 'The Retreat of the State in the 1980s and 1990s', in Francesca Carnevali and Julie Marie Strange, eds., *Twentieth-Century Britain: Economic, Cultural and Social Change*, 2nd ed. (Harlow, UK: Pearson, 2007), p. 271.
16 Peter Robinson and Marcus Rubin, 'The Future of the Post Office', *Institute for Public Policy Research* (1998), p. 17.
17 Hudson, 'Failed Privatizations'.
18 William Megginson and Jeffry Netter, 'From State to Market: A Survey of Empirical Studies on Privatization', *Journal of Economic Literature*, vol. 39, no. 2 (2001).
19 Rhys Andrews and Tom Entwistle, *Public Service Efficiency: Reframing the Debate* (New York, NY: Routledge, 2014), p. 1.
20 'It is not enough to measure performance in strict economic terms,' Aharoni writes. 'One has to measure the stimulus provided to other

socioeconomic activities and other externalities ... Financial measures are misleading for those who see [a public enterprise] as a government instrument that should strive to achieve objectives such as a more egalitarian distribution of income, regional development, technological self-sufficiency, poverty reduction, or development.' See: Yair Aharoni, 'The Performance of State-Owned Enterprise', pp. 52–53.

21. Holger Muehlenkamp, 'From State to Market Revisited: A Reassessment of the Empirical Evidence on the Efficiency of Public (and Privately-Owned) Enterprises', *Annals of Public and Cooperative Economics*, vol. 86, no. 4 (2015).

22. See, for instance: Michael I. Obadan, *The Economic and Social Impact of Privatisation of State-Owned Enterprises in Africa* (Dakar, Senegal: Council for the Development of Social Science Research in Africa, 2008), p. 60.

23. Tatyana P. Soubbotina, *Beyond Economic Growth: An Introduction to Sustainable Development, Second Edition* (Washington, D.C.: The World Bank, 2004), p. 78.

24. Mary S. Elcano and Anthony Alverno, 'Reform in the Universal Postal Union and the World Trade Organization', in Michael A. Crew and Paul R. Kleindorfer, eds., *Future Directions in Postal Reform* (New York, NY: Springer Science + Business Media, 2001), p. 297.

25. Mark R. Rutgers and Hendriekje van der Meer, 'The Origins and Restriction of Efficiency in Public Administration: Regaining Efficiency as the Core Value of Public Administration', *Administration & Society*, vol. 42, no. 7 (2010).

26. Megginson and Netter, 'From State to Market'.

27. Douglas W. Caves and Laurits R. Christensen, 'The Relative Efficiency of Public and Private Firms in a Competitive Environment: The Case of Canadian Railroads', *Journal of Political Economy*, vol. 88, no. 5 (October 1980).

28. Aharoni, 'The Performance of State-Owned Enterprise', p. 57; John D. Donahue, *The Privatization Decision: Public Ends, Private Means* (New York, NY: Basic Books, 1989), p. 76.

29. American Public Power Association, *Payments and Contributions by Public Power Distribution Systems to State and Local Governments, 2012 Data* (Washington, D.C.: APPA, March 2014), www.publicpower.org/files/PDFs/PaymentsandContributionsbyPublicPowerDistributionSystems.pdf.

30. Ann P. Bartel and Ann E. Harrison, 'Ownership Versus Environment: Disentangling the Sources of Public-Sector Inefficiency', *Review of Economics and Statistics*, vol. 87, no. 1 (2005), pp. 135–147.

31. Bartel and Harrison, 'Ownership Versus Environment'.

32. Joshua Greene, 'State-Owned Enterprises: Justifications, Risks, and Reform', *IMF Institute for Capacity Development*, Fiscal Analysis and Forecasting Workshop, Bangkok, Thailand, June 16–27, 2014, accessed January 9, 2017, www.imf.org/external/region/tlm/rr/pdf/aug5.pdf.

33 Willner and Parker, 'The Performance of Public and Private Enterprise under Conditions of Active and Passive Ownership and Competition and Monopoly.'
34 Mary Shirley and Patrick Walsh, 'Public versus Private Ownership: The Current State of the Debate', *World Bank*, 2000, p. 5.
35 John Vickers and George Yarrow, *Privatization: An Economic Analysis* (Cambridge, MA: MIT University Press, 1989), reviewed in Shirley and Walsh, 'Public versus Private Ownership', p. 6.
36 John Kay and D.J. Thompson, 'Privatisation: A Policy in Search of a Rationale', *Economic Journal*, vol. 96, no. 381 (1986), reviewed in Shirley and Walsh, 'Public versus Private Ownership', p. 8.
37 George Yarrow, 'Privatization in Theory and Practice,' *Economic Policy*, vol. 2 (1986), reviewed in Shirley and Walsh, 'Public versus Private Ownership', p. 9.
38 Paul Cook and Colin Kirkpatrick, *Privatisation in Less Developed Countries* (New York, NY: St. Martin's Press, 1988), reviewed in Shirley and Walsh, 'Public versus Private Ownership', p. 9.
39 'Privatization by itself,' Wallsten found, 'does not appear to generate many benefits and is negatively correlated with main line penetration ... competition appears to be the most successful agent of change.' See: Scott Wallsten, 'An Econometric Analysis of Telecom Competition, Privatization, and Regulation in Africa and Latin America', *Journal of Industrial Economics*, vol. 49, no. 1 (2001).
40 'On their own,' they wrote, 'privatization and regulation do not lead to obvious gains in economic performance, though there are some positive interaction effects. By contrast, introducing competition does seem to be effective in stimulation performance improvements.' See: Yin-Fang Zhang, David Parker, and Colin Kirkpatrick, 'Electricity Sector Reform in Developing Countries: An Econometric Assessment of the Effects of Privatization, Competition, and Regulation', *Journal of Regulatory Economics*, vol. 33, no. 2 (April 2008). Earlier studies from the same authors came to similar conclusions. In 2006, the authors wrote that 'studies of privatization have found that competition is generally more important than ownership itself in explaining improvements in performance in developing countries.' See: Kirkpatrick, Parker, and Zhang, 'An Empirical Analysis of State and Private-Sector Provision of Water Services in Africa'.
41 Albert O. Hirschman, *Exit, Voice, and Loyalty: Responses to Decline in Firms, Organizations, and States* (Cambridge, MA: Harvard University Press, 1970), p. 45.
42 Anthony Boardman and Aidan Vining, 'Ownership and Performance in Competitive Environments: A Comparison of the Performance of Private, Mixed, and State-Owned Enterprises', *Journal of Law and Economics*, vol. 32, no. 1 (1989).
43 Boardman and Vining, 'Ownership and Performance in Competitive Environments'.

44 Interestingly, Vining and Boardman's 1989 study does not investigate the degree of internal competition a public enterprise may or may not be subjected to. In other words, while these companies may compete with each other in a global market places, they may also face little to no domestic competition for capital, labor, natural resources, or other factors that may impact efficiency and performance. See: Boardman and Vining, 'Ownership and Performance in Competitive Environments'.

45 Aidan Vining and Anthony Boardman, 'Ownership versus Competition: Efficiency in Public Enterprise', *Public Choice*, vol. 73, no. 2 (1992).

46 Willner and Parker, 'The Performance of Public and Private Enterprise under Conditions of Active and Passive Ownership and Competition and Monopoly'.

47 Muehlenkamp, 'From State to Market Revisited'.

48 Shirley and Walsh went on to discuss the literature concerning which is more effective in such situations, state owned enterprises or regulated private monopolies, and found that a host of other factors – including, among others, complete or incomplete contracts, operational autonomy, the efficiency of political markets, and the regulatory capacity of the state – impact results. See: Shirley and Walsh, 'Public versus Private Ownership', p. 11.

49 Megginson and Netter, From State to Market'.

50 Chang, *State-Owned Enterprise Reform*, p. 23.

51 William J. Baumol and Allan S. Blinder, *Microeconomics: Principles and Policy, Eleventh Edition* (Mason, OH: South-Western Cengage Learning, 2009), p. 198.

52 Chang writes that 'even SOEs in natural monopolies can be given some competitive stimulus because all products and services are at least partially substitutable.' See: Chang, *State-Owned Enterprise Reform*, p. 24.

53 Koen Verhoest *et al.*, 'The Study of Organisational Autonomy: A Conceptual Review', *Public Administration and Development*, no. 24 (2004). In 1990, University of California business professor Carl Shapiro and Princeton University economist (emeritus) Robert Willig theorized that public enterprises with a high degree of operational autonomy might perform as well as, if not better than, regulated private enterprises. 'If those who operate the enterprise are likely to have significant private information about the cost and demand conditions under which the enterprise will operate, and if there is a deadweight-loss burden associated with raising funds in the public sector,' they wrote, 'then public enterprise is the preferred form of ownership and control.' On the other hand, 'a pronounced private agenda on the part of the public official or a poorly functioning political system favor privatization.' See: Carl Shapiro and Robert D. Willig, 'Economic Rationales for the Scope of Privatization', in George Yarrow and Piotr Jasiński, eds., *Privatization: Critical Perspectives on the World Economy*, vol. 2 (New York, NY: Routledge, 1996), p. 115. Empirically, one 2014 study by Sangeetha

Gunasekar and Jayati Sarkar of the effects of enterprise autonomy on state owned enterprises in India over 30 years found that 'enterprise autonomy through performance contracts matter in SOE performance.' 'Specifically,' they write, 'enhanced autonomy has a statistically positive effect on SOE profitability. Further, when the impact of partial privatization is estimated after controlling for the impact of autonomy, in most cases, partial privatization has no independent impact on profitability while autonomy continues to have a positive impact.' See: Sangeetha Gunasekar and Jayati Sarkar, 'Does Autonomy Matter in State Owned Enterprises? – Evidence from Performance Contracts in India', *Indira Gandhi Institute of Development Research*, August 2014.

54 Verhoest *et al.*, 'The Study of Organisational Autonomy'.
55 Parkash Chander *et al.*, eds., *Public Goods, Environmental Externalities and Fiscal Competition: Essays by Henry Tulkens* (New York, NY: Springer Science + Business Media, 2006), p. 366.
56 *OECD Guidelines on Corporate Governance of State-Owned Enterprises: 2015 Edition* (Paris, France: OECD, 2015), accessed December 11, 2016, www.oecd.org/daf/ca/OECD-Guidelines-Corporate-Governance-SOEs-2015.pdf.
57 The performance of public enterprises, the report states at the outset, 'is of great importance to broad segments of the population and to other parts of the business sector. Consequently, good governance of SOEs is critical to ensure their positive contribution to economic efficiency and competitiveness.' OECD, *OECD Guidelines on Corporate Governance of State-Owned Enterprises: 2015 Edition*.
58 OECD, *OECD Guidelines on Corporate Governance of State-Owned Enterprises: 2015 Edition*.
59 PWCs' 'Agenda for Action' offers several standards for SOE owners, SOE boards, and SOE managers. See: Lidé *et al.*, *State-Owned Enterprises*.
60 Chang suggests five important organizational principles for publicly owned enterprises: 1) Carefully reviewing and streamlining the goals of publicly owned enterprises; 2) Enhancing the quality of information the agencies supervising publicly owned enterprises have and increasing their capacity to use it; 3) Improving the incentive system for the managers of publicly owned enterprises; 4) Consolidating the supervision and monitoring of publicly owned enterprises to a singular agency; and 5) Potentially reducing the number of publicly owned enterprises that need supervision through consolidation, liquidation, or even privatization.' See: Chang, *State-Owned Enterprise Reform*, pp. 22–23.
61 OECD, *OECD Guidelines on Corporate Governance of State-Owned Enterprises: 2015 Edition*.
62 *Ibid.*
63 *Federal Tax Provisions Affecting the Electric Power Industry* (Washington, D.C.: Joint Committee on Taxation, June 11, 2001), accessed December 11, 2016, www.jct.gov/x-54-01.pdf.

64 Steven M. Davidoff, 'Uncomfortable Embrace: Federal Corporate Ownership in the Midst of the Financial Crisis', *Minnesota Law Review*, vol. 95 (2011).
65 Davidoff, 'Uncomfortable Embrace', p. 1761.
66 *Ibid.*
67 *Ibid.*, p. 1735.
68 *Ibid.*, p. 1740.

Chapter 3

1 Lidé *et al.*, *State-Owned Enterprises*.
2 Joe Wallis and Brian Dollery, *Market Failure, Government Failure, Leadership and Public Policy* (New York, NY: St. Martin's Press, Inc., 1999), p. 16.
3 Ingo Vogelsang, *Public Enterprise in Monopolistic and Oligopolistic Enterprises* (Abingdon, UK: Routledge, 2001), p. 16.
4 Shirley and Walsh, 'Public versus Private Ownership', p. 15.
5 With regards to market failure, Peng *et al.* also noted that 'mature economies in which severe problems arise can also give rise to SOEs. The 2009 US efforts to rescue GM and Chrysler illustrate this argument.' See: Mike Peng *et al.*, 'Theories of the (State-Owned) Firm', *Asia Pacific Journal of Management*, May 3, 2016, accessed January 17, 2017, https://www.utdallas.edu/~mikepeng/documents/Peng16_APJM_BrutonStanHuang.pdf.
6 Shirley and Walsh, 'Public versus Private Ownership', p. 16. The 1979 World Bank report by Armeane Choksi concludes that 'there is a role to be played both by the forces of the state and those of the market in the process of industrialization.' See: Armeane Choksi, 'State Intervention in the Industrialization of Developing Countries: Selected Issues', *World Bank Staff Working Paper No. 341* (1979). Several other studies support components from Choksi's list, including Emilio Sacristan (1980) and Armando Labra (1980) who, in the words of Shirley and Walsh, maintain that public ownership can 'contribute to capital formation, technology transfer, and income redistribution.' See: Emilio, Sacristan, 'Some Considerations on the Role of Public Enterprise', and Armando Labra, 'Public Enterprise in an Underdeveloped Economy', in Baumol, William, ed., *Public and Private Enterprise in a Mixed Economy: Proceedings of a Conference Held by the International Economic Association* (New York, NY: St. Martin's Press, 1980).
7 Shirley and Walsh, 'Public versus Private Ownership', p. 16.
8 Chang gives the example of the publicly owned Korean steelmaker POSCO. 'If the venture subsequently proved so successful, why did the private sector fail to finance it?' Chang asks. 'This is because capital markets have an inherent bias towards short-term gains and do not like risky, large-scale projects with long gestation periods.' See: Chang, *State-Owned Enterprise Reform*, p. 12.

9 Chang, *State-Owned Enterprise Reform*, p. 12.
10 *Ibid.*
11 Bob Beck, 'The Importance of Wyoming's Permanent Mineral Trust Fund', *Wyoming Public Media*, February 15, 2013, accessed April 10, 2017, http://wyomingpublicmedia.org/post/importance-wyomings-permanent-mineral-trust-fund.
12 'Budget & Financial Plan, Fiscal Year 2013–2014', *City of Edmond*, accessed April 10, 2017, http://edmondok.com/DocumentCenter/View/2105.
13 'Commitment', *Stadtwerke München*, accessed November 1, 2017, www.swm.de/english/company/commitment.html.
14 Vogelsang, *Public Enterprise in Monopolistic and Oligopolistic Enterprises*, p. 17.
15 Thomas Piketty, *Capital in the Twenty-First Century* (Cambridge, MA: The Belknap Press of Harvard University Press, 2014), p. 298.
16 Lawrence Mishel and Alyssa Davis, 'Top CEOs Make 300 Times More than Typical Workers', *EPI*, June 21, 2015, accessed January 19, 2016, www.epi.org/publication/top-ceos-make-300-times-more-than-workers-pay-growth-surpasses-market-gains-and-the-rest-of-the-0-1-percent/. Both Piketty and Mishel and Davis reference a study by Jon Bakija (Williams College), Adam Cole (US Department of Treasury), and Bradley Haim (Indiana University) that shows corporate executives accounting for around 40 percent of the growth in incomes for the top 1 percent and 0.1 percent (with financial sector employees accounting for another 23 percent). See: Jon Bakija *et al.*, *Jobs and Income Growth of Top Earners and the Causes of Changing Income Inequality: Evidence from U.S. Tax Return Data* (Washington, D.C.: US Department of Treasury, April 2012), accessed February 26, 2017, https://web.williams.edu/Economics/wp/BakijaColeHeimJobsIncomeGrowthTopEarners.pdf.
17 'Form 10-K: Annual Report for the Fiscal Year Ended September 30, 2016', *TVA*, accessed April 10, 2017, www.snl.com/Cache/37234822.PDF?O=PDF&T=&Y=&D=&FID=37234822&iid=4063363; Dave Flessner, 'Outgoing TVA Directors Give CEO Bill Johnson Boost in Pay, Bigger Golden Parachute', *Times Free Press*, December 20, 2016, accessed April 10, 2017, www.timesfreepress.com/news/business/aroundregion/story/2016/dec/20/tvboard-shakeup-ceo-pay-raise/403794/.
18 TVA, 'Form 10-K: Annual Report for the Fiscal Year Ended September 30, 2016'.
19 For Xcel, see: 'Form 10-K: Annual Report for the Fiscal Year Ended December 31, 2016', *Xcel Energy*, accessed April 10, 2017, http://investors.xcelenergy.com/Cache/1500096310.PDF?O=PDF&T=&Y=&D=&FID=1500096310&iid=4025308; For Sempra, see: 'Form 10-K: Annual Report for the Fiscal Year Ended December 31, 2016', *Sempra Energy*, accessed April 10, 2017, http://files.shareholder.com/downloads/SRE/4251407853x0xS86521-17-17/1032208/filing.pdf; For PPL, see:

'Form 10-K: Annual Report for the Fiscal Year Ended December 31, 2016', *PPL*, accessed April 10, 2017, http://pplweb.investorroom.com/financial-highlights.

20 For Xcel, see: '2017 Notice of Annual Meeting and Proxy Statement', *Xcel Energy*, April 14, 2017, accessed April 10, 2017, http://investors.xcelenergy.com/interactive/newlookandfeel/4025308/Xcel_Energy_Inc_ClientDL/proxy/images/Xcel_Energy-Proxy2017.pdf; For Sempra, see: '2017 Notice of Annual Shareholders Meeting and Proxy Statement', *Sempra Energy*, March 24, 2017, accessed April 10, 2017, http://files.shareholder.com/downloads/SRE/425140785 3x0xS1193125-17-94064/1032208/filing.pdf; For PPL, see: '2017 Notice of Annual Meeting and Proxy Statement', *PPL*, April 5, 2017, accessed April 10, 2017, http://www.pplweb.com/wp-content/uploads/2017/04/2017-Proxy-Statement-334463_002_web_bmk.pdf.

21 Dave Flessner, 'TVA Pays Out an Average Bonus of $11,400 to Each Worker', *Times Free Press*, November 18, 2014, accessed February 15, 2016, www.timesfreepress.com/news/local/story/2014/nov/18/tva-pays-out-11400-bonus-to-each-worker/273591/; Dave Flessner, 'With No Employee Pay Cap TVA Boosts Base Salary for Top Managers', *Times Free Press*, March 25, 2012, accessed February 15, 2016, www.timesfreepress.com/news/news/story/2012/mar/25/tva-boosts-top-salaries/73855/; 'Utilities: NAICS 22', *Bureau of Labor Statistics*, accessed February 15, 2016, www.bls.gov/iag/tgs/iag22.htm.

22 'Amtrak National Facts', *Amtrak*, accessed February 26, 2016, www.amtrak.com/servlet/ContentServer?c=Page&pagename=am%2FLayout&cid=1246041980246. In August 2016, Boardman retired and was replaced by Charles Moorman, former Chairman of the freight rail company Norfolk Southern. Moorman has taken a symbolic salary of $1, with the potential of a yearly bonus of up to $500,000. His annual salary at Norfolk Southern had been more than $13 million. See: Patrick McGeehan, 'Amtrak Picks Freight Rail Veteran as New Leader at a Critical Time', *New York Times*, August 19, 2016, accessed April 10, 2017, www.nytimes.com/2016/08/20/nyregion/amtrak-ceo-charles-w-moorman.html.

23 '2015 Annual Report', *Kansas City Southern*, accessed March 29, 2017 http://investors.kcsouthern.com/~/media/Files/K/KC-Southern-IR-V2/annual-report-2015.pdf; 'Notice of 2016 Annual Meeting of Stockholders and Proxy Statement', *Kansas City Southern*, May 5, 2016, accessed March 29, 2017, www.envisionreports.com/ksu/2016/01B29FE16E/a21604e0bfd84c42869148e573222e82/Kansas_City_Southern_PS_4-4-16_SECURED.pdf.

24 Les Leopold, 'Runaway Inequality: Presentation', accessed March 29, 2017, http://files.cwa-union.org/teletech/FinancilizationPresentation.pdf.

25 'Northwest Bancshares, Inc.: Schedule 14A', *United States Securities and Exchange Commission*, March 9, 2016, accessed January 5, 2017, www.sec.gov/Archives/edgar/data/1471265/000119312516497492/d40181ddef14a.htm; 'BerkshireHills Bancorp: Proxy Statement', March 24, 2016, accessed January 5, 2017, http://ir.berkshirebank.com/Cache/1500082938.PDF?Y=&O=PDF&D=&FID=1500082938&T=&IID=4054645.

26 Piketty, *Capital in the Twenty-First Century*, p. 569.

27 Thomas Piketty et al., 'Juncture Interview: Thomas Piketty on Capital, Labour, Growth and Inequality', *IPPR*, May 14, 2014, accessed February 22, 2016, www.ippr.org/juncture/juncture-interview-thomas-piketty-on-capital-in-the-twenty-first-century.

28 Martin O'Neill, 'Piketty, Meade and Predistribution', *Crooked Timber*, December 17, 2015, accessed February 22, 2016, http://crookedtimber.org/2015/12/17/piketty-meade-and-predistribution/.

29 Noel Thompson, *Political Economy and the Labour Party: The Economics of Democratic Socialism, 1884–2005* (New York, NY: Routledge, 2006), p. 117.

30 William A. Edmundson, *John Rawls: Reticent Socialist* (New York, NY: Cambridge University Press, 2017), p. 46.

31 Bruce Western and Jake Rosenfeld, 'Unions, Norms, and the Rise in U.S. Inequality', *American Sociological Review*, vol. 76, no. 4 (2011).

32 Matthew Walters and Lawrence Mishel, 'How Unions Help All Workers', *EPI*, August 26, 2003, accessed April 11, 2017, www.epi.org/publication/briefingpapers_bp143/.

33 George I. Long, 'Differences between Union and Nonunion Compensation, 2001–2011', *Monthly Labor Review*, April 2013, accessed February 11, 2016, www.bls.gov/opub/mlr/2013/04/art2full.pdf.

34 Walters and Mishel, 'How Unions Help All Workers.'

35 William J. Wiatrowski, 'The Last Private Pension Plans: A Visual Essay', *Monthly Labor Review*, December 2012, accessed February 11, 2016, www.bls.gov/opub/mlr/2012/12/art1full.pdf.

36 Monique Morrissey, 'Private-Sector Pension Coverage Fell by Half Over Two Decades', *EPI*, January 11, 2013, accessed February 11, 2016, www.epi.org/blog/private-sector-pension-coverage-decline/.

37 Robin Blackburn, *Banking on Death or, Investing in Life: The History and Future of Pensions* (New York, NY: Verso, 2002).

38 Gerald Mayer, *Union Membership Trends in the United States* (Washington, D.C.: Congressional Research Service, 2004), accessed April 11, 2017, http://digitalcommons.ilr.cornell.edu/cgi/viewcontent.cgi?article=1176&context=key_workplace; 'Union Members Summary -2016', *Bureau of Labor Statistics*, January 26, 2017, accessed April 11, 2017, https://www.bls.gov/news.release/union2.nr0.htm.

39 BLS, 'Union Members Summary -2016'.

40 Barry T. Hirsch, *An Anatomy of Public Sector Unions* (Bonn, Germany: Institute for the Study of Labor, March 2013), accessed April 11, 2017, http://ftp.iza.org/dp7313.pdf.
41 'Table 4. Median Weekly Earnings of Full-Time Wage and Salary Workers by Union Affiliation, Occupation, and Industry, 2014–2014 Annual Averages', *Bureau of Labor Statistics*, accessed January 19, 2017, www.bls.gov/news.release/union2.t04.htm.
42 Barbara A. Butrica, Howard M. Iams, Karen E. Smith, and Eric J. Toder, 'The Disappearing Defined Benefit Pension and Its Potential Impact on the Retirement Incomes of Baby Boomers', *Social Security Bulletin*, vol. 69, no. 3 (2009).
43 David Cooper, Mary Gable, and Algernon Austin, 'The Public-Sector Jobs Crisis', *EPI Briefing Paper #339*, May 2012, accessed January 19, 2017, www.epi.org/publication/bp339-public-sector-jobs-crisis/.
44 Cooper *et al.*, 'The Public-Sector Jobs Crisis.' A subsequent report from the Congressional Research Service using data from 2013 came to similar conclusions. It found that 'women held almost three-fifths (57.7 percent) of full-time jobs in state and local governments). By contrast women held approximately two-fifths of full-time jobs in the federal government and in the private sector (42 percent and 41.7 percent) respectively.' See: Gerald Mayer, *Selected Characteristics of Private and Public Sector Workers* (Washington, D.C. Congressional Research Service, March 21, 2014), accessed April 11, 2017, https://fas.org/sgp/crs/misc/R41897.pdf.
45 David Cooper *et al.*, 'The Public-Sector Jobs Crisis'.
46 Gar Alperovitz and Lew Daly, *Unjust Deserts: How the Rich Are Taking Our Common Inheritance* (New York, NY: The New Press, 2008).
47 Robert M. Solow, 'Technical Change and the Aggregate Production Function', *The Review of Economics and Statistics*, vol. 39, no. 3 (1957).
48 Thomas Paine, *Collected Writings* (New York, NY: Library of America, 1995), p. 408.
49 Alperovitz and Daly, *Unjust Deserts*, p. 110.
50 Guido Erreygers, 'Views on Inheritance in the History of Economic Thought', in Guido Erreygers and Toon Vandevelde, eds., *Is Inheritance Legitimate?: Ethical and Economic Aspects of Wealth Transfers* (New York, NY: Springer, 1997).
51 Robert B. Ekelund, Jr. and Douglas M. Walker, 'J.S. Mill on the Income Tax Exemption and Inheritance Taxes: The Evidence Reconsidered', *History of Political Economy*, vol. 28, no. 4 (1996).
52 Joseph Persky, *The Political Economy of Progress: John Stuart Mill and Modern Radicalism* (New York, NY: Oxford University Press, 2016), p. 95.
53 Karl Marx, 'The Right of Inheritance', in *Report of the Fourth Annual Congress of the International Working Men's Association*, 1869, accessed February 2, 2017, www.marxists.org/history/international/iwma/documents/1869/inheritance-report.htm.

54 Karl Marx, 'The Right of Inheritance'.
55 Theodore Roosevelt, 'New Nationalism Speech', Teaching-AmericanHistory.org, accessed April 17, 2017, http://teachingamericanhistory.org/library/document/new-nationalism-speech/.
56 The Tax Policy Center estimates that of the 2.7 million people that will die in 2017, only 11,000 estate tax returns will be filed. And of those, only 5,200 will be eligible for taxation. See: 'Tax Policy Center Briefing Book; Key Elements of the U.S. Tax System; How Many People Pay the Estate Tax?' *Tax Policy Center*, accessed April 17, 2017, http://www.taxpolicycenter.org/briefing-book/how-many-people-pay-estate-tax.
57 Piketty, *Capital in the Twenty-First Century*, pp. 377–378.
58 G.D.H. Cole, *The Next Ten Years: In British Social and Economic Policy* (Abingdon-on-Thames, UK: Routledge, 2010).
59 On the former, Meade wrote that 'state beneficial ownership [of capital wealth] without State management [of business concerns] could occur if the State owned (directly or indirectly through investment trusts and similar financial intermediaries) shares in various companies on just the same terms as many private rentiers now invest directly or indirectly in privately managed companies.' See James Meade, *Liberty, Equality and Efficiency* (London, UK: Macmillan, 1993), p. 12. 'As usual,' Alan Thomas observes, 'the source of this gradually accumulated state capital asset is Meade's capital tax, and the output of the scheme is the unconditional basic income component of his overall scheme (which is not, recall, intended to be free-standing as this would damage incentives to work).' Alan Thomas, *Republic of Equals: Predistribution and Property-Owning Democracy* (New York, NY: Oxford University Press, 2017), p. 160.
60 James Manyika, Michael Chui, Mehdi Miremadi, Jacque Bughin, Katy George, Paul Willmott, and Martin Dewhurst, 'Harnessing Automation for a Future That Works', *McKinsey Global Institute*, January 2017, accessed November 2, 2017, www.mckinsey.com/global-themes/digital-disruption/harnessing-automation-for-a-future-that-works.
61 Guy Standing, 'The Precariat, Populism and Robots: Is Basic Income a Political Imperative?' *World Economic Forum*, December 20, 2016, accessed November 3, 2017, www.weforum.org/agenda/2016/12/the-precariat-populism-and-robots-is-basic-income-a-political-imperative/.
62 Derek Thompson, 'A World Without Work', *The Atlantic*, July/August 2015, accessed November 24, 2017, www.theatlantic.com/magazine/archive/2015/07/world-without-work/395294/.
63 'For the first time since his creation man will be faced with his real, his permanent problem – how to use his freedom from pressing economic cares, how to occupy the leisure, which science and compound interest will have won for him, to live wisely and agreeably and well,' Keynes wrote. See: John Maynard Keynes, 'Economic Possibilities for Our Grandchildren,' in John Maynard Keynes, *Essays in Persuasion* (New York, NY: W.W. Norton & Company, 1963), p. 367.

64 Peter Frase, 'Four Futures', *Jacobin*, December 13, 2011, accessed November 3, 2017, www.jacobinmag.com/2011/12/four-futures/.
65 Richard B. Freeman, 'Who Owns the Robots Rules the World', *Harvard Magazine*, May–June 2016, accessed November 2, 2017, https://harvardmagazine.com/2016/05/who-owns-the-robots-rules-the-world.
66 Labour Party, 'Alternative Models of Ownership'.
67 David A. Anderson, *Environmental Economics and Natural Resource Management, 4th Edition* (New York, NY: Routledge, 2014), p. 175.
68 'Electricity: What's the Issue?' *Opensecrets*, accessed January 19, 2017, www.opensecrets.org/news/issues/electricity/.
69 'The Public Utility Holding Company Act', *Public Citizen*, accessed January 19, 2017, www.citizen.org/Page.aspx?pid=2303.
70 'Energy Policy Act of 2005 Fact Sheet', *Federal Energy Regulatory Commission*, August 8, 2006, accessed January 19, 2017, www.ferc.gov/legal/fed-sta/epact-fact-sheet.pdf.
71 'Lobbying Spending Database Electric Utilities, 2014', *Opensecrets*, accessed January 19, 2017, www.opensecrets.org/lobby/indusclient.php?id=E08&year=2014; 'Lobbying Spending Database, Federal Energy Regulatory Commission, 2014', *Opensecrets*, accessed January 19, 2017, www.opensecrets.org/lobby/agencysum.php?id=197&year=2014.
72 Opensecrets, 'Lobbying Spending Database Electric Utilities, 2014'.
73 For the purpose of this analysis, trade associations in which publicly owned utilities, cooperatives, and/or employee owned companies participate alongside private companies are counted as 'publicly owned,' ensuring that the figures presented here are the most expansive possible. Generally, advocacy organizations have been excluded. Author's calculations based on: 'U.S. Electric Utility Industry Statistics', *American Public Power Association, 2015–2016 Annual Directory and Statistical Report*, accessed January 19, 2017, www.publicpower.org/files/PDFs/USElectricUtilityIndustryStatistics.pdf; Opensecrets, 'Lobbying Spending Database Electric Utilities, 2014'.
74 'Public Power Annual Directory and Statistical Report', *American Public Power Association*, accessed March 28, 2017, www.publicpower.org/Programs/Landing.cfm?ItemNumber=38710&navItemNumber=37577.
75 'Electricity: What's the Issue?' *Opensecrets*, accessed January 19, 2017, www.opensecrets.org/news/issues/electricity/.
76 'The Laws That Govern the Securities Industry', *US Securities and Exchange Commission*, accessed April 28, 2017, www.sec.gov/answers/about-lawsshtml.html.
77 'Disclosure and Transparency in the State-Owned Sector', *9th meeting of the OECD-Asia Network on Corporate Governance of State-Owned Enterprises*, December 6–7, 2016, accessed April 28, 2017, www.oecd.org/daf/ca/Dec2016_PresentationsDay1_AsiaSOENetwork.pdf; Michael Penfold, Andrés Oneto, and Guillermo Rodríguez Guzmán, 'Transparency in the Corporate Governance of State-Owned Enterprises

in Latin America', *Public Policy and Productive Transformation Series, Development Bank of Latin America*, no. 20 (2015), accessed April 28, 2017, http://scioteca.caf.com/bitstream/handle/123456789/845/CAF%20N20%20ENGLISH%20VFINAL.pdf?sequence=1&isAllowed=y.
78 Timothy Cama, 'Trump Signs Repeal of Transparency Rule for Oil Companies', *The Hill*, February 14, 2017, accessed April 28, 2017, http://thehill.com/policy/energy-environment/319488-trump-signs-repeal-of-transparency-rule-for-oil-companies.
79 'Reports & Documents', *Amtrak*, accessed April 28, 2017, www.amtrak.com/servlet/ContentServer?c=Page&pagename=am%2FLayout&cid=1241245669222.
80 Under most open meetings laws, an executive session can be called when discussing certain, clearly delineated topics, and the public excluded. See, for instance, the open meetings law that the Port Authority of New York and New Jersey is subject to. 'Port of New York Authority', *The New York State Senate*, accessed April 28, 2017, www.nysenate.gov/legislation/laws/PNY/1.
81 Scott Green, 'A Look at the Causes, Impact and Future of the Sarbanes-Oxley Act', *Journal of International Business and Law*, vol. 3, no. 1 (2004); Rosemary Peavler, 'Sarbanes-Oxley Act and the Enron Scandal – Why Are They Important?' *The Balance*, October 18, 2016, accessed May 1, 2017, www.thebalance.com/sarbanes-oxley-act-and-the-enron-scandal-393497.
82 Paul Lanois, 'The Legacy of the Sarbanes-Oxley Act, 15 Years On', *Columbia Law School's Blog on Corporations and the Capital Markets*, February 9, 2017, accessed May 1, 2017, http://clsbluesky.law.columbia.edu/2017/02/09/the-legacy-of-the-sarbanes-oxley-act-15-years-on/; William A. Niskanen, 'Repeal Sarbanes-Oxley – Lock, Stock and Barrel', *Forbes*, December 17, 2008, accessed May 1, 2017, www.forbes.com/2008/12/16/sarbanes-oxley-reform-oped-cx_wn_1217niskanen.html.
83 Steven Mufson, 'Trump Signs Law Rolling Back Disclosure Rule for Energy and Mining Companies', *Washington Post*, February 14, 2017, accessed November 28, 2017, www.washingtonpost.com/business/economy/trump-signs-law-rolling-back-disclosure-rule-for-energy-and-mining-companies/2017/02/14/ccd93e90-f2cd-11e6-b9c9-e83fce42fb61_story.html?utm_term=.da6cd78df2cb.
84 The Act subsequently died in the Senate, and components were incorporated into the Fixing America's Surface Transportation (FAST) Act, which was signed by President Obama in December 2015. See: 'House Passes Amtrak Reform Bill', *House Transportation and Infrastructure Committee*, March 4, 2015, accessed May 1, 2017, http://transportation.house.gov/news/documentsingle.aspx?DocumentID=398713; 'H.R. 749 (114th): Passenger Rail Reform and Investment Act of 2015',

GovTrack, accessed May 1, 2017, https://www.govtrack.us/congress/bills/114/hr749; 'H.R. 22 (114th): FAST Act', *GovTrack*, accessed May 1, 2017, https://www.govtrack.us/congress/bills/114/hr22.
85 Burness, 'Boulder Municipalization Persists After Surprise Election Comeback'.
86 Shirley and Walsh, 'Public versus Private Ownership', p. 22.
87 Citing Jones and others, Megginson writes that 'SOEs are especially attractive for transferring wealth between groups precisely because their operations are nontransparent.' See: William Megginson, *The Financial Economics of Privatization* (New York: Oxford University Press, 2005), p. 41; Leroy P. Jones, 'Public Enterprise for Whom? Perverse Distributional Consequences of Public Operational Decisions', *Economic Development and Cultural Change*, vol. 33, no. 2 (1985). Without commenting on the potential benefits of using SOEs to transfer wealth from *more* to *less* affluent groups, the issue of public enterprise transparency is, indeed, important and will be discussed further in the context of democratizing public ownership.
88 Peng et al., 'Theories of the (State-Owned) Firm'.
89 For instance, Peng et al. write that 'in deregulated or liberalized "open" industries (such as consumer goods), SOEs' political ties may be less critical.' See: Peng et al., 'Theories of the (State-Owned) Firm'.
90 'Hayek and the Welfare State', *Crooked Timber*, May 13, 2012, accessed February 3, 2017, http://crookedtimber.org/2012/05/13/hayek-and-the-welfare-state/.
91 Milton Friedman, *Capitalism and Freedom: Fortieth Anniversary Edition* (Chicago, IL: University of Chicago Press, 2002), p. 29.
92 Douglas A. Irwin, 'The Aftermath of Hamilton's "Report on Manufactures"', *Journal of Economic History*, vol. 64, no. 3 (2004); Bruce Katz and Jessica Lee, 'Alexander Hamilton's Manufacturing Message', *Brookings*, December 5, 2011, accessed April 14, 2017, www.brookings.edu/articles/alexander-hamiltons-manufacturing-message/.
93 The bank was capitalized with both private and public funds, and while the government was the largest shareholder, it was prevented from having any participation in governance or management of the bank. See: David Cowen, 'The First Bank of the United States', *EH.Net Encyclopedia*, March 16, 2008, accessed April 14, 2017, http://eh.net/encyclopedia/the-first-bank-of-the-united-states/; Francis G. Walett, *Economic History of the United States: Summary of all Phases of Economic Growth* (Oxon, UK: Routledge, 2006), p. 102.
94 Erik Reinert, *How Rich Countries Got Rich and Why Poor Countries Stay Poor* (London, UK: Constable, 2007). Quoted in Mariana Mazzucato, *The Entrepreneurial State: Debunking Public vs. Private Sector Myths* (New York, NY: PublicAffairs, 2015), p. 79.
95 Mazzucato, *The Entrepreneurial State*, p. 1.

96   Martin Wolf, 'A Much-Maligned Engine of Innovation', *Financial Times*, August 4, 2013, accessed April 4, 2017, www.ft.com/content/32ba9b92-efd4–11e2-a237–00144feabdc0.

97   Andrew Cline, 'What "You Didn't Build That" Really Means – and Why Romney Can't Explain It', *Atlantic*, August 10, 2012, accessed May 1, 2017, www.theatlantic.com/politics/archive/2012/08/what-you-didnt-build-that-really-means-and-why-romney-cant-explain-it/260984/. In his 2011 State of the Union address, President Obama made similar comments, stating 'but because it's not always profitable for companies to invest in basic research, throughout our history, our government has provided cutting-edge scientists and inventors with the support that they need. That's what planted the seeds for the Internet. That's what helped make possible things like computer chips and GPS. Just think of all the good jobs – from manufacturing to retail – that have come from these breakthroughs.' See: Eugene Kiely, '"You Didn't Build That," Uncut and Unedited', *FactCheck.org*, July 23, 2012, accessed May 1, 2017, www.factcheck.org/2012/07/you-didnt-build-that-uncut-and-unedited/.

98   Peter Walker, 'John McDonnell: Labour Will Be an Interventionist Government', *Guardian*, September 26, 2016, accessed April 4, 2017, www.theguardian.com/politics/2016/sep/26/labour-will-offer-interventionist-government-john-mcdonnell.

99   John McDonnell, 'Building an Entrepreneurial State at a Local Level – John McDonnell', *Labour Press*, April 20, 2016, accessed April 4, 2017, http://press.labour.org.uk/post/143115086454/building-an-entrepreneurial-state-at-a-local-level.

100   Hans A. Baer, *Global Capitalism and Climate Change: The Need for an Alternative World System* (Lanham, MD: AltaMira Press, 2012), p. 220.

101   Most analyses of the carbon bubble are predicated on staying at or below 2°C change in temperature. However, even this would prove catastrophic for many communities, especially those in low-lying areas vulnerable to sea level rise and those reliant on fishing and agriculture. See: Alissa Scheller, '2 Degrees Will Change the World', *Mother Jones*, December 3, 2015, accessed May 3, 2017, www.motherjones.com/environment/2015/11/2-degrees-will-change-world-paris-climate-change.

102   Donella Meadows, Jorgen Randers, and Dennis Meadows, 'A Synopsis: Limits to Growth: The 30-Year Update', *The Donella Meadows Project*, accessed May 1, 2017, www.donellameadows.org/archives/a-synopsis-limits-to-growth-the-30-year-update/.

103   Graham Turner and Cathy Alexander, 'Limits to Growth Was Right. New Research Shows We're Nearing Collapse', *Guardian*, September 1, 2014, accessed May 1, 2017, www.theguardian.com/

commentisfree/2014/sep/02/limits-to-growth-was-right-new-research-shows-were-nearing-collapse.
104   Alana Semuels, 'How to Stop Short-Term Thinking at America's Companies', *Atlantic*, December 30, 2016, accessed May 2, 2017, www.theatlantic.com/business/archive/2016/12/short-term-thinking/511874/.
105   Walter K. Dodds, *Humanity's Footprint: Momentum, Impact, and Our Global Environment* (New York, NY: Columbia University Press, 2008), p. 164.
106   *Natural Capital at Risk: The Top 100 Externalities of Business* (London, UK: Trucost, 2013), accessed May 2, 2017, http://natural-capitalcoalition.org/wp-content/uploads/2016/07/Trucost-Nat-Cap-at-Risk-Final-Report-web.pdf.
107   David Hall, 'The West's Throwaway Culture Has Spread Waste Worldwide', *Guardian*, March 13, 2017, accessed May 2, 2017, www.theguardian.com/environment/2017/mar/13/waste-plastic-food-packaging-recycling-throwaway-culture-dave-hall.
108   Gabor Zovanyi, *The No-Growth Imperative: Creating Sustainable Communities under Ecological Limits to Growth* (New York, NY: Routledge, 2013), p. 149.
109   Zovanyi, *The No-Growth Imperative*, p. 149.

Chapter 4

1   A January 2016 YouGov poll, for instance, found that 43 percent of Americans under 30 had a positive opinion of socialism (compared with 32 percent who had a positive view of capitalism). See: 'Favorability of Socialism', *YouGov*, January 25–26, 2016.
2   These theories and models have a long pre-history, especially with regards to the various efforts in eastern Europe throughout the twenty-first century to find an alternative to Soviet-style central planning. See: Johanna Bockman, 'The Long Road to 1989: Neoclassical Economics, Alternative Socialisms, and the Advent of Neoliberalism', *Radical History Review*, no. 112 (winter 2012).
3   How much of an actual 'debate' this was is questionable. 'The fact that Lange first responded sixteen years after Mises made his initial salvo raises some questions about the nature of this "debate"', Bockman writes. See: Johanna Bockman, *Markets in the Name of Socialism: The Left-Wing Origins of Neoliberalism* (Stanford, CA: Stanford University Press, 2011), p. 18.
4   For a summary of the socialist calculation debate, see: Theodore Burczak, *Socialism After Hayek: Advances in Heterodox Economics* (Ann Arbor, MI: University of Michigan Press, 2006), pp. 29–36; John Roemer, *A Future for Socialism* (Cambridge, MA: Harvard University Press, 1994), pp. 28–32. See also: Oskar Lange, 'On the Economic Theory of Socialism, Part One', *Review of Economic Studies*, vol. 4, no. 1 (1936);

Oskar Lange, 'On the Economic Theory of Socialism, Part Two', *Review of Economic Studies*, vol. 4, no. 2 (1937).
5   Theodore Burczak, *Socialism After Hayek*, p. 31.
6   Theodore Burczak, *Socialism After Hayek*, p. 32; Bruce Caldwell, 'Hayek and Socialism', *Journal of Economic Literature*, vol. xxxv (December 1997).
7   Geoffrey M. Hodgson, 'Socialism Against Markets? A Critique of Two Recent Proposals', *Economy and Society*, vol. 27, no. 4 (1998).
8   Some of the most notable include by: Alec Nove, Jaroslav Vaněk, John Roemer, Leland Stauber, David Ellerman, Christopher Pierson, James Yunker, Theodore Burczak, Radoslav Selucký, and Robin Archer. See: Nove *et al.*, *The Economics of Feasible Socialism* (London, UK: George Allen & Unwin, 1983); Jarolsav Vanek, *The General Theory of Labor-Managed Market Economies* (Ithaca, NY: Cornell University Press, 1970); Jaroslav Vanek, *The Labor-Managed Economy: Essays* (Ithaca, NY: Cornell University Press, 1977); John Roemer, *A Future for Socialism*; Leland Stauber, 'A Proposal for a Democratic Market Economy', *Journal of Comparative Economics*, no. 1, no. 3 (1977); David Ellerman, *The Democratic Worker-Owned Firm: A New Model for the East and West* (London, UK: Unwin Hyman, 1990); David Ellerman, *Property and Contract in Economics: The Case for Economic Democracy* (Cambridge, MA: Basil Blackwell, Inc., 1992); Christopher Pierson, *Socialism After Communism: The New Market Socialism* (University Park, PA: Pennsylvania State University Press, 1995); James A. Yunker, *Capitalism versus Pragmatic Market Socialism: A General Equilibrium Evaluation* (New York, NY: Springer Science + Business Media, 1993); Radoslav Selucký, *Marxism, Socialism, Freedom: Towards a General Democratic Theory of Labour-Managed Systems* (London, UK: MacMillan Press Ltd., 1979); and Robin Archer, *Economic Democracy: The Politics of Feasible Socialism* (Oxford, UK: Clarendon Press, 1995).
9   David Schweickart, *After Capitalism* (Lanham, MD: Rowman & Littlefield Publishers, Inc., 2011), p. 49.
10 'Although workers control the workplace,' Schweickart writes, 'they do not "own" the means of production. These are regarded as the collective property of society.' See: Schweickart, *After Capitalism*, p. 50.
11 Schweickart, *After Capitalism*, p. 50.
12 David Schweickart, 'Economic Democracy,' *Next System Project*, March 1, 2016, accessed April 11, 2017, www.thenextsystem.org/economic-democracy/.
13 Schweickart, *After Capitalism*, p. 103.
14 Tom Malleson, *After Occupy: Economic Democracy for the 21st Century* (New York, NY: Oxford University Press, 2014).
15 Malleson, *After Occupy*, p. 43.
16 'These kinds of industries,' Malleson writes, 'are inhospitable for cooperative governance because it is basically impossible for average-income

workers to acquire ownership of firms like this.' See: Malleson, *After Occupy*, p. 44.
17 Malleson, *After Occupy*, p. 44.
18 Ibid.
19 Nove et al., *The Economics of Feasible Socialism*, p. 200.
20 'The big state-owned units,' Nove wrote, 'could be described as constituting the "commanding heights" of large-scale industry and public utilities, plus finance.' See: Nove et al., *The Economics of Feasible Socialism*, pp. 201–202.
21 Nove et al., *The Economics of Feasible Socialism*, p. 203.
22 In Nove's words, 'the means of production would not belong to the workers, and the state would have a residual responsibility for their use or misuse, or for debts incurred.' See: Nove et al., *The Economics of Feasible Socialism*, p. 206.
23 Gar Alperovitz, *America Beyond Capitalism: Reclaiming Our Wealth, Our Liberty, and Our Democracy* (Takoma Park, MD: Democracy Collaborative Press, 2011), p. xxvii.
24 'Home', *The Pluralist Commonwealth*, accessed January 9, 2017, www.pluralistcommonwealth.org/.
25 'Democratized Ownership', *The Pluralist Commonwealth*, accessed January 9, 2017, www.pluralistcommonwealth.org/democratized-ownership-forms.html.
26 Cumbers, *Reclaiming Public Ownership*, p. 162.
27 'Although the economy would be primarily organized into forms of public ownership,' Cumbers writes, 'some limited forms of private ownership should continue to exist. The self-employed would remain as a category, and even small firms up to a certain size (perhaps fifteen to twenty employees), after which conversion into forms of cooperative or mutual ownership would be required by law.' See: Cumbers, *Reclaiming Public Ownership*, p. 163. 'Inevitably,' Cumbers maintains, 'a socialist economy will have elements of both market and non-market exchange.' See: Cumbers, *Reclaiming Public Ownership*, p. 163.
28 Cumbers, *Reclaiming Public Ownership*, p. 163.
29 Ibid., pp. 162–171.
30 Ibid., p. 167.
31 Ibid., p. 168.
32 Ibid., pp. 170–171.
33 Bertell Ollman, 'Market Mystification in Capitalist and Market Societies', in Bertell Ollman and David Schweickart, eds., *Market Socialism: The Debate Among Socialists* (New York, NY: Routledge, 1998), p. 106.
34 'In a market economy – any form of a market economy, no matter how "mixed", including the economy of "market socialism" – ... decisions cannot be taken freely by the producers,' he argued. See: Ernest Mandel, 'In Defence of Socialist Planning', *New Left Review*, no. 159 (September–October 1986).

35 '"Market socialism" by contrast,' he continued, 'is no solution for the evils of either the capitalist legend of a free market or the bureaucratic travesty of a free socialism. The mixed economy it proposes is merely mixed misery. The real economics of a feasible and desirable socialism would supersede either alternative.' See: Mandel, 'In Defence of Socialist Planning'.

36 Michael Albert, *Parecon: Life After Capitalism* (New York, NY: Verso, 2004), p. 79.

37 'Everything needed to produce our way of life belongs to everyone, no more to one person than any other. While individuals own personal property, everything we need to produce goods and services is owned in common,' Hahnel writes. See: Robin Hahnel, 'Participatory Economics and the Next System', *Next System Project*, October 2015, accessed April 20, 2017, http://thenextsystem.org/wp-content/uploads/2016/03/NewSystems_RobinHahnel.pdf.

38 Albert, *Parecon*, p. 90.

39 The 1963 Yugoslav Constitution stated that 'no one can have a right of ownership of the social means of production – neither the sociopolitical community, nor the work organization, nor the worker, taken individually; no one can appropriate, in virtue of any legal deed of ownership whatever, the product of social labor,' See: Roger Garaudy, 'The Possibility of Other Models of Socialism', in Branko Horvat, Mihailo Marković, and Rudi Supek, eds., *Self-Governing Socialism, Volume Two: A Reader* (New York, NY: Routledge, 2015), p. 33.

40 Marjolein Benschop, ed., *Housing and Property Rights in Bosnia and Herzegovina, Croatia, and Serbia and Montenegro* (Nairobi, Kenya: United Nations Human Settlements Programme, 2005).

41 Robert Dahl, *A Preface to Economic Democracy* (Berkeley, CA: University of California Press, 1985), p. 145.

42 Pat Devine, 'Participatory Planning through Negotiated Coordination', *Science & Society*, vol. 66, no. 1 (Spring 2002).

43 Devine, 'Participatory Planning through Negotiated Coordination'.

44 Archon Fung, 'The Principle of Affected Interests: An Interpretation and Defense', in Jack Nagel and Rogers Smith, eds., *Representation: Elections and Beyond* (Philadelphia, PA: University of Pennsylvania Press, 2013), p. 237. 'I define social ownership as ownership by those who are affected by, who have an interest in, the use of the assets involved,' Devine writes. 'Social ownership is not only, in my view, a fundamental socialist principle, it is also more efficient than private, state or workforce ownership.' See: Devine, 'Participatory Planning through Negotiated Coordination'.

45 Devine, 'Participatory Planning through Negotiated Coordination'.

46 Even Adam Smith envisioned a strong state sector in his classic work *The Wealth of Nations* – seen by many modern conservatives as one of the foundational texts of capitalism – particularly with respect to public education. See: Mark Thoma, 'Adam Smith and the Role of Government',

Economist's View, March 4, 2010, accessed April 11, 2010, http://economistsview.typepad.com/economistsview/2010/03/adam-smith-and-the-role-of-government.html.

47 In recent years the Next System Project (an initiative of The Democracy Collaborative) has collected and published dozens of these alternative system models, designs, and approaches as part of its *New Systems: Possibilities and Proposals* Series. Contributors include: John Restakis, Michael T. Lewis, Andrew Cumbers, Gus Speth, Christian Felber, Gus Hagelberg, Paul Raskin, Michael Shuman, J. K. Gibson-Graham, Jenny Cameron, Kelly Dombroski, Stephen Healy, Ethan Miller, Michael Albert, Richard Smith, Peter A. Victor, Tim Jackson, Lorenzo Fioramonti, David Korten, Henning Meyer, Richard D. Wolff, Ed Whitfield, David Bollier, Jessica Gordon Nembhard, Hans A. Baer, Marvin T. Brown, Robin Hahnel, David Schweickart, Riane Eisler, and Lane Kenworthy. See: 'New Systems: Possibilities and Proposals', Next System Project, June 28, 2017, accessed November 28, 2017, https://thenextsystem.org/learn/collections/new-systems-possibilities-and-proposals.

Chapter 5

1 Karl Polanyi, *The Great Transformation: The Political and Economic Origins of Our Time* (Boston, MA: Beacon Press, 2001), p. 147.
2 Karl Marx and Frederick Engels, 'Manifesto of the Communist Party', *Marxists.org*, February 1848, accessed January 19, 2017, www.marxists.org/archive/marx/works/download/pdf/Manifesto.pdf.
3 'After attainment of a wholly socialist economy markets could continue to regulate all production, together with a private sector of consumption, within a framework of planning,' Moore continued. See: Stanley Moore, *Marx Versus Markets* (University Park, PA: University of Pennsylvania Press, 1993), p. 67.
4 'North American Industry Classification System, 2017 NAICS', *United States Census Bureau*, accessed April 24, 2017, www.census.gov/cgi-bin/sssd/naics/naicsrch?chart=2017.
5 Carnoy and Shearer, *Economic Democracy*, p. 79.
6 In addition to calling for a public energy company and expanded public involvement in the media industry, Carnoy and Shearer do begin to identify some industries where their form of public ownership would be appropriate ('the automobile, drug, chemical, and computer industries, as well as others'). See: Carnoy and Shearer, *Economic Democracy*, pp. 79–80.
7 While Schumacher left open what this 'minimum size' would actually be, he stated that 'since every business loses its private and personal character and becomes, in fact, a public enterprise once the number of its employees rises above a certain limit, minimum size is probably best defined in terms of persons employed. In special cases it may be necessary to define size in terms of capital employed or turnover.' See: E.F.

Schumacher, *Small Is Beautiful: Economics as if People Mattered* (New York, NY: Harper & Row, 1989), pp. 304–305.
8   Paul Krugman and Robin Wells, *Microeconomics* (New York, NY: Worth Publishers, 2013), p. 378.
9   As a result of the Energy Policy Act of 1992 and associated regulatory actions, wholesale electric markets were opened to competition. Subsequently, 22 states and the District of Columbia began to pursue so-called 'retail choice.' Essentially, this allows consumers to choose among competing suppliers that will transmit energy via the local utilities' infrastructure. According to the American Coalition of Competitive Energy Suppliers, the bottom line is that the supplier 'obtains sources of energy for you,' and the utility 'delivers your energy to you.' In other words, the utility does not compete with other utilities to deliver energy within its service area, although multiple suppliers might compete to source and sell the energy. In the early 2000s, this process ran into serious trouble, and eight of the 22 states subsequently reversed course and banned retail choice. According to a 2016 report, the energy crisis of the early 2000s made 'it clear that there were fundamental problems with the manner in which electricity sector restructuring had been implemented in some regions. The suspensions were also motivated by the bankruptcies of several merchant generating and trading companies; shrinking retail supply options; fraudulent trading, price reporting, and accounting practices by merchant firms; unanticipated high wholesale market price volatility; and rising retail electricity prices.' The process is beset by other problems as well, including an increase in utility mergers in retail choice states and very low uptake among individual consumers as opposed to industry and commercial clients. See: Mathew J. Morey, Laurence D. Kirsch, and Christensen Associates Energy Consulting LLC, *Retail Choice in Electricity: What Have We Learned in 20 Years?* (Madison, WI: Christensen Associates Energy Consulting), February 11, 2016, accessed February 3, 2017, www.hks.harvard.edu/hepg/Papers/2016/Retail%20Choice%20in%20Electricity%20for%20EMRF%20Final.pdf; 'What is Energy Choice?' *American Coalition of Competitive Energy Suppliers*, accessed February 3, 2017, http://competitiveenergy.org/what-is-choice/.
10 'The Public Utility Holding Company Act': Its Protections Are Needed Today More Than Ever, *American Public Power Association*, February 2003, accessed January 9, 2017, www.publicpower.org/files/PDFs/PUHCA0203.pdf.
11 APPA, 'The Public Utility Holding Company Act'. Upon PUHCA's repeal, the consumer advocacy group Public Citizen lamented that 'today, we go backwards to the 1920s prior to the Great Depression. … Now, oil companies, investment banks, foreign companies can own our utilities and engage in all the abuses of the Power Trusts in the 1920s.' See: 'We Mourn the Death Today, February 8, 2006, of the Public Utility

Holding Company Act of 1935 (PUHCA)', *Public Citizen*, February 8, 2006, accessed January 19, 2017, www.citizen.org/documents/Dead%20 PUHCA.pdf.
12. Robert Kuttner, *The Squandering of America: How the Failure of Our Politics Undermines Our Prosperity* (New York, NY: Vintage Books, 2008), p. 58.
13. Gerry Anderson, 'Electric Market Deregulation Has Failed to Deliver On the Promise of Lower Rates', *Utility Dive*, July 12, 2016, accessed January 19, 2017, www.utilitydive.com/news/electric-market-deregulation-has-failed-to-deliver-on-the-promise-of-lower/422398/.
14. John Farrell, 'Electricity's Un-Natural Monopoly', *Institute for Local Self-Reliance*, January 9, 2015, accessed January 19, 2017, https://ilsr.org/electricitys-unnatural-monopoly/.
15. *Ibid*.
16. 'Wind Generation', *Nebraska Public Power District*, accessed November 20, 2017, www.nppd.com/about-us/power-plants-facilities/wind-generation/.
17. Minio-Paluello, *Who Owns the Wind, Owns the Future*, p. 10.
18. Cécile L. Blanchet, 'R&C04 – Remunicipalisation of energy systems – Part 1', *Energy, Commons, and the Rest*, January 30, 2017, accessed November 21, 2017, https://energycommonsblog.wordpress.com/2017/01/30/rc04-remunicipalisation-of-energy-systems/.
19. Gerald A. Epstein, 'Introduction: Financialization and the World Economy', in Gerald A. Epstein, ed., *Financialization and the World Economy* (Northampton, MA: Edward Elgar Publishing, 2005), p. 3.
20. See, for instance: Roy Kwon and Anthony Roberts, 'Financialization and Income Inequality in the New Economy', *Sociology of Development*, vol. 1, no. 4 (2015); Ken-Hou Lin and Donald Tomaskovic-Devey, 'Financialization and U.S. Income Inequality: 1970–2008', *American Journal of Sociology*, vol. 118, no. 5 (2013); and Bradford Van Arnum and Michele Naples, 'Financialization and Income Inequality in the United States, 1967–2010', *American Journal of Economics*, vol. 72, no. 5 (2013).
21. 'Senators Warren, McCain, Cantwell and King Introduce 21st Century Glass-Steagall Act', *Elizabeth Warren US Senator for Massachusetts*, July 7, 2015, accessed March 27, 2017, www.warren.senate.gov/?p=press_release&id=872.
22. 'Brown, Kaufman File Amendment on Too Big to Fail Legislation', *Office of Senator Sherrod Brown*, April 29, 2010, accessed April 16, 2017, www.brown.senate.gov/newsroom/press/release/brown-kaufman-file-amendment-on-too-big-to-fail-legislation.
23. Simon Johnson, 'Breaking Up the Banks', *New York Times*, April 22, 2010, accessed March 27, 2017, http://economix.blogs.nytimes.com/2010/04/22/breaking-up-the-banks/.
24. Willem Buiter, 'The End of Capitalism as We Knew It', *Financial Times Blog*, September 17, 2008, accessed March 27, 2017, http://blogs.ft.com/maverecon/2008/09/the-end-of-american-capitalism-as-we-knew-it/.

25 Alexandre Berthaud and Gisela Davico, *Global Panorama on Postal Financial Inclusion: Key Issues and Business Models* (Berne, Switzerland: Universal Postal Union, March 2013), p. 9.
26 Steve Benen, 'Bernie Sanders Makes the Case for Banking at Post Offices', *MSNBC*, January 5, 2016, accessed January 19, 2017, www.msnbc.com/rachel-maddow-show/bernie-sanders-makes-the-case-banking-post-offices.
27 Jesse Nankin and Krista Kjellman Schmidt, 'History of U.S. Gov't Bailouts', *ProPublica*, April 15, 2009, accessed March 27, 2017, www.propublica.org/special/government-bailouts.
28 Carter Dougherty, 'Sweden's Fix for Banks: Nationalize Them', *New York Times*, January 22, 2009, accessed October 30, 2017, www.nytimes.com/2009/01/23/business/worldbusiness/23sweden.html.
29 David Leonhardt, 'More Than One Way to Take Over a Bank', *New York Times*, February 25, 2009, accessed October 30, 2017, www.nytimes.com/2009/03/01/magazine/01wwln-lede-t.html.
30 Carnoy and Shearer, *Economic Democracy*, pp. 71–72.
31 Neel Kashkari, 'Lessons from the Crisis: Ending Too Big to Fail: Speech to the Brookings Institution', *Federal Reserve Bank of Minneapolis*, February 16, 2016, accessed January 19, 2017, www.minneapolisfed.org/news-and-events/presidents-speeches/lessons-from-the-crisis-ending-too-big-to-fail.
32 Nuno Teles, 'Socialize the Banks', *Jacobin*, April 27, 2016, accessed October 30, 2017, www.jacobinmag.com/2016/04/banks-credit-recession-finance-socialism/.
33 Teles, 'Socialize the Banks'.
34 Marois, 'Costa Rica's Banco Popular Shows How Banks Can Be Democratic, Green – and Financially Sustainable.'
35 David Squires and Chloe Anderson, *U.S. Health Care from a Global Perspective: Spending, Use of Services, Prices, and Health in 13 Countries* (New York: The Commonwealth Fund, October 2015), accessed January 19, 2017, www.commonwealthfund.org/publications/issue-briefs/2015/oct/us-health-care-from-a-global-perspective.
36 'Despite its heavy investment,' the report found, 'the U.S. sees poorer results on several key health outcome measures such as life expectancy and the prevalence of chronic conditions.' See: Squires and Anderson, *U.S. Health Care from a Global Perspective*.
37 'National Health Expenditure Projections 2015–2025', *Centers for Medicare and Medicaid Services*, accessed January 19, 2017, www.cms.gov/Research-Statistics-Data-and-Systems/Statistics-Trends-and-Reports/NationalHealthExpendData/Downloads/Proj2015.pdf.
38 'Fast Facts on US Hospitals: Fast Facts 2017', *American Hospital Association*, January 2017, accessed January 19, 2017, www.aha.org/research/rc/stat-studies/fast-facts.shtml.
39 Jill R. Horwitz, 'Making Profits and Providing Care: Comparing Nonprofit, For-Profit, and Government Hospitals', *Health Affairs*, vol. 24, no. 3 (May 2005).

40 Sabrina Tavernise, 'Disparity in Life Spans of the Rich and the Poor Is Growing', *New York Times*, February 12, 2016, accessed January 19, 2017, www.nytimes.com/2016/02/13/health/disparity-in-life-spans-of-the-rich-and-the-poor-is-growing.html?_r=0.
41 Patrick Jeurissen, *For-Profit Hospitals: A Comparative and Longitudinal Study of the For-Profit Hospital Sector in Four Western Countries* (Doctoral Thesis, Erasmus University Rotterdam, 2010).
42 'For-Profit Hospitals Cost More and Have Higher Death Rates', *Physicians for a National Health Program*, accessed January 19, 2017, www.pnhp.org/resources/for-profit-hospitals-cost-more-and-have-higher-death-rates.
43 Jesse Geneson, 'Nonprofit Obamacare Insurers Have Lower Premiums Than For-Profit Insurers in Most Counties That Use Healthcare.gov', *HealthPocket*, July 14, 2015, accessed January 19, 2017, www.healthpocket.com/healthcare-research/infostat/nonprofit-obamacare-insurers-have-lower-premiums-than-for-profit-insurers#.WAfM6eArKUk.
44 'Health Insurance Coverage of the Total Population: 2015', *Kasier Family Foundation*, accessed January 19, 2017, http://kff.org/other/state-indicator/total-population/?currentTimeframe=0.
45 'Key Facts about the Uninsured Population', *Kaiser Family Foundation*, September 29, 2016, accessed January 25, 2017, http://kff.org/uninsured/fact-sheet/key-facts-about-the-uninsured-population.
46 Sara R. Collins, David C. Radley, Munira Z. Gunja, and Sophie Beutel, *The Slowdown in Employer Insurance Cost Growth: Why Many Workers Still Feel the Pinch* (New York: The Commonwealth Fund, October 2016), accessed January 19, 2017, www.commonwealthfund.org/publications/issue-briefs/2016/oct/slowdown-in-employer-insurance-cost-growth.
47 Robert Reich, 'Why a Single-Payer Healthcare System Is Inevitable', *Robertreich.org*, August 22, 2016, accessed January 19, 2017, http://robertreich.org/post/149326712440.
48 Helen Halpin and Peter Harbage, 'The Origins and Demise of the Public Option', *Health Affairs*, vol. 29, no. 6 (2010).
49 Jacob S. Hacker, 'A Public Option Would Greatly Improve Obamacare', *New York Times*, August 24, 2016, accessed January 19, 2017, www.nytimes.com/roomfordebate/2016/08/24/is-obamacare-sustainable/a-public-option-would-greatly-improve-obamacare. At the time of writing, the Affordable Care Act (ACA) has avoided repeal by the Republican-controlled Congress and newly elected President Donald Trump. However, President Trump has indicated a willingness to possibly neglect or undermine the ACA, stating that 'the best thing we can do, politically speaking, is let Obamacare explode.' Without any alternative strategy in place, this may accelerate the arguably inevitable transition to some form of a public option or single-payer system. For Trump's statement, see: Danielle Kurtzleben, 'FACT CHECK: Trump Says Obamacare Is "Exploding." It's Not,' *National Public Radio*, March 27th, 2017, accessed March 27, 2017, www.npr.org/2017/03/27/521441490/fact-check-trump-says-obamacare-is-exploding-its-not.

50 Patricia Murphy, 'Bernie Sanders's Single-Payer Health Care Plan Failed in Vermont', *Daily Beast*, January 25, 2016, accessed January 19, 2017, www.thedailybeast.com/articles/2016/01/25/bernie-sanders-s-single-payer-health-care-plan-failed-in-vermont.html.

51 Jay Makarenko, 'Canada's Health Care System: An Overview of Public and Private Participation', *Mapleleafweb*, October 22, 2010, accessed January 19, 2017, www.mapleleafweb.com/features/canada-s-health-care-system-overview-public-and-private-participation.html.

52 A third model, sometimes called the Bismarck model, is prevalent in a number of countries in Europe, Asia, and South America. The classic example is Germany, where health insurance is largely publicly financed (with a small percentage of the population paying for alternative or supplemental private insurance) and provided by highly regulated, competing nonprofit companies. Hospitals are mainly nonprofit or publicly owned (although there is a growing sector of for-profit hospitals), and general physicians often operate sole practices. See: Reinhard Busse, 'The German Healthcare System', *The Commonwealth Fund*, 2008, accessed February 3, 2017, www.commonwealthfund.org/~/media/files/resources/2008/health-care-system-profiles/germany_country_profile_2008_2-pdf.pdf.

53 It should be noted that the 'federal government' was also particularly reviled (scoring the same favorability rating, 28 percent, as the pharmaceutical industry). However, it is unlikely that respondents were fully able to differentiate between the federal government as a 'business sector' and their general distaste for national-level politics and politicians. See: Lydia Saad, 'Restaurants Again Voted Most Popular U.S. Industry', *Gallup*, August 15, 2016, accessed January 19, 2017, www.gallup.com/poll/194570/restaurants-again-voted-popular-industry.aspx.

54 Joanne Kenen, 'POLITICO–Harvard Poll: Americans Blame Drug Companies for Rising Health Costs', *Politico*, September 28, 2016, accessed January 19, 2017, www.politico.com/story/2016/09/americans-blame-drug-companies-for-rising-health-cost-poll-228866.

55 Dan Mangan, 'Accused Fraudster Martin Shkreli Pleads Not Guilty to Indictment Filed Last Week', *CNBC*, June 6, 2016, accessed January 19, 2017, www.cnbc.com/2016/06/06/accused-fraudster-martin-shkreli-pleads-not-guilty-to-indictment-filed-last-week.html.

56 Travis Gettys, 'Mylan Pushed for Law to Make EpiPens Mandatory in US Schools – Then Fled Overseas to Avoid Taxes', *RawStory*, August 25, 2016, accessed January 19, 2017, www.rawstory.com/2016/08/mylan-pushed-for-law-to-make-epipens-mandatory-in-us-schools-then-fled-overseas-to-avoid-taxes/.

57 Andrew Pollack and Sabrina Tavernise, 'Valeant's Drug Price Strategy Enriches It, but Infuriates Patients and Lawmakers', *New York Times*, October 4, 2015, accessed January 19, 2017, www.nytimes.com/2015/10/05/business/valeants-drug-price-strategy-enriches-it-but-infuriates-patients-and-lawmakers.html?_r=0.

58 Sanjay Gupta, 'Doctors Must Lead Us Out of Our Opioid Abuse Epidemic', *CNN*, June 2, 2016, accessed January 19, 2017, www.cnn.com/2016/05/11/health/sanjay-gupta-prescription-addiction-doctors-must-lead/.
59 Nora D. Volkow, 'America's Addiction to Opioids: Heroin and Prescription Drug Abuse: Testimony to the Senate Caucus on International Narcotics Control', *National Institute on Drug Abuse*, May 14, 2014, accessed January 19, 2017, www.drugabuse.gov/about-nida/legislative-activities/testimony-to-congress/2016/americas-addiction-to-opioids-heroin-prescription-drug-abuse.
60 Alex Lawson, 'Bottomless Big Pharma Greed Drives Heroin and Opiate Addiction Across America', *Alternet*, January 21, 2016, accessed January 19, 2017, www.alternet.org/economy/bottomless-big-pharma-greed-drives-heroin-and-opiate-addiction-across-america.
61 Uwe Reinhardt, 'Perspectives on the Pharmaceutical Industry', *Health Affairs*, vol. 20, no. 5 (2001).
62 'Research Reveals Role of Government Funding in Pharmaceutical R&D', *Medical Life Sciences News*, December 16, 2011, accessed January 19, 2017, www.news-medical.net/news/20111216/Research-reveals-role-of-government-funding-in-pharmaceutical-RD.aspx.
63 Mariana Mazzucato, *The Entrepreneurial State* (London, UK: Demos, 2011), accessed January 19, 2017, www.demos.co.uk/files/Entrepreneurial_State_-_web.pdf.
64 'Government Establishes Pharmaceutical Company', *South African Government News Agency*, February 11, 2016, accessed January 19, 2017, www.sanews.gov.za/south-africa/government-establishes-pharmaceutical-company.
65 The problems of the for-profit pharmaceutical industry in the United States are already driving interest in the development of new, nonprofit drug companies. 'We want to create a competitor to stabilize the prices,' Deborah J. Drew, founder and chief executive of a non-profit startup called Drew Quality Group, told reporters in 2015. 'When you end up with a single-source manufacturer, they can charge any price they want.' See: Robert Weisman, 'Nonprofit Vows to Lower Generic Drug Cost', *Boston Globe*, December 14, 2015, accessed February 3, 2017, www.bostonglobe.com/business/2015/12/13/nonprofit-aims-make-affordable-generic-drugs/u0kd8MHfZmawSzAh0pRnKI/story.html.
66 'Gross-Domestic-Product-(GDP)-by-Industry Data', *Bureau of Economic Analysis*, accessed March 28, 2017, www.bea.gov/industry/gdpbyind_data.htm.
67 'Jobs and Impact: Overview', *American Chemistry Council*, accessed January 19, 2017, www.americanchemistry.com/Industry-Impact/Jobs-Economy/Overview/.
68 Centers for Disease Control and Prevention, *Fourth National Report on Human Exposure to Environmental Chemicals* (Washington, D.C.: Department of Health and Human Services, 2009).

69 'Understanding Toxic Substances', *State of California*, 2008, accessed April 11, 2017, www.cdph.ca.gov/programs/hesis/Documents/introtoxsubstances.pdf.
70 Safer Chemicals, Healthy Families, '*Toxic Chemicals: The Cost to Our Health*', January 2012, accessed April 16, 2017, http://protectcalifornia.org/wordpress/wp-content/uploads/2012/01/toxichealth.pdf; Margaret Sears and Stephen J. Genuis, 'Environmental Determinants of Chronic Disease and Medical Approaches: Recognition, Avoidance, Supportive Therapy, and Detoxification', *Journal of Environmental and Public Health*, vol. 2012 (2012).
71 Rachel Carson, *Silent Spring* (New York, NY: Mariner Books, 2002), p. 8.
72 Monica Bruckner, 'The Gulf of Mexico Dead Zone', *Microbial Life Educational Resources*, accessed January 19, 2017, http://serc.carleton.edu/microbelife/topics/deadzone/index.html.
73 For chemicals in Americans, see: National Center for Environmental Health, *Fourth National Report on Human Exposure to Environmental Chemicals* (Atlanta, GA: Centers for Disease Control and Prevention, 2009), accessed March 28, 2017, www.cdc.gov/exposurereport/pdf/FourthReport.pdf; Jonathan Benson, 'CDC Analysis Shows Americans Are Loaded with Toxic Chemicals', *Natural News*, October 13, 2010, accessed March 28, 2017, www.naturalnews.com/030033_chemicals_toxins.html; For TSCA, see: US Environmental Protection Agency, *Summary of the Toxic Substances Control Act* (Washington, D.C.: EPA, October 21, 2010), accessed March 28, 2017, www.epa.gov/lawsregs/laws/tsca.html; Bryan Walsh, 'Regulation of Toxic Chemicals Faces Tightening', *Time*, April 16, 2010, accessed March 28, 2017, www.time.com/time/health/article/0,8599,1982489,00.html; 'Take Out Toxics', *Natural Resources Defense Council*, accessed March 28, 2017, www.nrdc.org/health/toxics.asp.
74 Allison Hyeyeon In and Robert B. McKinstry, Jr., 'Amendments Strengthen Toxic Substances Control Act', *Ballard Spahr*, June 22, 2016, accessed January 19, 2017, www.ballardspahr.com/alertspublications/legalalerts/2016-06-22-amendments-strengthen-toxic-substances-control-act.aspx.
75 'What the EPA Should Do Under the Amended TSCA', *NRDC*, September 2, 2016, accessed January 19, 2017, www.nrdc.org/resources/what-epa-should-do-under-amended-tsca.
76 Brad Johnson, 'Dow's Toxic Legacy of EPA Corruption', *ThinkProgress*, May 2, 2008, accessed January 19, 2017, https://thinkprogress.org/dows-toxic-legacy-of-epa-corruption-6f4b70e54f76#.pl6lvnm8d.
77 Michael Hawthorne, 'EPA Official Ousted While Fighting Dow', *Chicago Tribune*, May 2, 2008, accessed January 19, 2017, http://articles.chicagotribune.com/2008-05-02/news/0805020086_1_dioxin-mary-gade-dow-chemical.

Notes: Chapter 5

78 Bill McGee, 'How Much Do Taxpayers Support Airlines?' *USA Today*, September 2, 2015, accessed January 19, 2017, www.usatoday.com/story/travel/columnist/mcgee/2015/09/02/how-much-do-taxpayers-support-airlines/71568226/.

79 'Table 1–4: Public Road and Street Mileage in the United States by Type of Surface,' *Bureau of Transportation Statistics*, accessed January 19, 2017, www.rita.dot.gov/bts/sites/rita.dot.gov.bts/files/publications/national_transportation_statistics/html/table_01_04.html.

80 *2015 Report on Tolling in the United States* (Washington, D.C.: International Bridge, Tunnel and Turnpike Association, 2015), accessed January 19, 2017, http://ibtta.org/sites/default/files/documents/MAF/2015_FactsInBrief_Final.pdf.

81 Steven J. Markovich, 'Transportation Infrastructure: Moving America', *Council on Foreign Relations*, October 14, 2014, accessed January 19, 2017, www.cfr.org/infrastructure/transportation-infrastructure-moving-america/p18611.

82 Eduardo Engel, Ronald Fischer, and Alexander Galetovic, 'Public–Private Partnerships to Revamp U.S. Infrastructure', *Brookings*, February 25, 2011, accessed January 19, 2017, www.brookings.edu/research/public-private-partnerships-to-revamp-u-s-infrastructure/.

83 Michael Laris, 'State Control of I-66 Expansion Could Net Virginia Substantial Revenue', *Washington Post*, May 19, 2015, accessed January 19, 2017, www.washingtonpost.com/local/trafficandcommuting/state-control-of-i-66-expansion-could-net-virginia-substantial-revenue/2015/05/18/a3629d58-fd7f-11e4–805c-c3f407e5a9e9_story.html. Despite this, Virginia subsequently did decide to use a public–private partnership for the I-66 project. Upon selecting a consortium led by Spanish conglomerate Ferrovial, its subsidiary Cintra, the global investment firm Meridiam, and the construction company Allan Myers, Virginia officials assured the public that 'new rules' were in place to 'protect taxpayers from the risks and costs the state was saddled with under previous agreements.' See: Michael Martz and Robert Zullo, 'Virginia Awards Contract for I-66 Under New Approach That Saves State $2.5 billion', *Richmond Times Dispatch*, November 2, 2016, accessed November 15, 2016, www.richmond.com/news/virginia/government-politics/general-assembly/article_5f76e8e6–4871–57dd-9c4d-49f091f8a787.html.

84 Trevor Baratko, 'Loudon County to Spend $95k Appealing Dulles Greenway Ruling', *Loudon Times-Mirror*, November 5, 2015, accessed January 19, 2017, www.loudountimes.com/news/article/loudoun_supervisors_to_spend_95k_appealing_dulles_greenway_ruling432.

85 Liz Essley, 'Debt Raises Doubt About Virginia Buying Dulles Greenway Toll Road', *Washington Examiner*, January 27, 2013, accessed January 19, 2017, www.washingtonexaminer.com/debt-raises-doubt-about-virginia-buying-dulles-greenway-toll-road/article/2519749?rel=author.

86 'Amtrak National Facts', *Amtrak*, accessed January 19, 2017, www.amtrak.com/national-facts.

87 Christie Aschwanden, 'Every Time You Fly, You Trash the Planet – And There Is No Easy Fix', *FiveThirtyEight*, January 2, 2015, accessed January 19, 2017, http://fivethirtyeight.com/features/every-time-you-fly-you-trash-the-planet-and-theres-no-easy-fix/.

88 Amtrak has proposed a series of improvements that will greatly increase the speed and reliability of regular and high-speed trains along the NEC. These include building a new 427-mile two-track system from Washington, D.C. to Boston, Massachusetts and spending tens of billions of dollars to repair and improve existing track infrastructure that is 80 to 100 years old. However, in one of the densest and most expensive regions in the country, there has thus far been little political appetite to approve the expense. 'The Amtrak Vision for the Northeast Corridor: 2012 Update Report', *Amtrak*, accessed February 3, 2017, www.amtrak.com/ccurl/453/325/Amtrak-Vision-for-the-Northeast-Corridor.pdf.

89 Matthew Yglesias, 'Amtrak Turns 45 Today. Here's Why American Passenger Trains Are So Bad', *Vox*, May 1, 2016, accessed January 19, 2017, www.vox.com/2016/5/1/11539966/amtrak-45-anniversary.

90 'About the MBTA: MBTA Leadership', *Massachusetts Bay Transportation Authority*, accessed January 19, 2017, www.mbta.com/about_the_mbta/leadership/.

91 'Board of Directors', *Bay Area Rapid Transit*, accessed January 19, 2017, www.bart.gov/about/bod.

92 'The MTA Network', *Metropolitan Transportation Authority*, accessed January 19, 2017, http://web.mta.info/mta/network.htm.

93 'MTA Leadership', *Metropolitan Transportation Authority*, accessed January 19, 2017, http://web.mta.info/mta/leadership/.

94 'MTA Board Members', *Metropolitan Transportation Authority*, accessed January 19, 2017, http://web.mta.info/mta/leadership/board.htm.

95 Nicole Dungca, 'T Considering Privatizing Bus Maintenance', *Boston Globe*, February 13, 2017, accessed May 2, 2017, www.bostonglobe.com/metro/2017/02/13/considering-privatizing-bus-maintenance-save-jobs-impacted/VnFD75ekIc0z6ZZjborkMM/story.html.

96 Martine Powers, 'As Metro Eyes Privatization, Inspiration Comes from Boston's Subway', *Washington Post*, April 29, 2017, accessed May 2, 2017, www.washingtonpost.com/local/trafficandcommuting/as-metro-eyes-privatization-inspiration-comes-from-bostons-subway/2017/04/29/f7c7d386-2ac8-11e7-b605-33413c691853_story.html?utm_term=.6de07ccb99e6.

97 In Boston, Craig Hughes, a representative of the union responsible for bus mechanics, has presented data showing that MBTA buses are among the best maintained in the country and has been quoted as saying that instead of privatization, 'if the agency works with the union to be more efficient, the possibilities are "endless."' See: Dungca, 'T Considering Privatizing Bus Maintenance'.

98   Essley, 'Debt Raises Doubt about Virginia Buying Dulles Greenway Toll Road'.
99   'CalPERS Makes First U.S. Transportation Investment, Purchases Share of Toll Road in State of Indiana', *CalPERS*, May 4, 2016, accessed January 19, 2017, www.calpers.ca.gov/page/newsroom/calpers-news/2016/infrastructure-investment-indiana-toll-road.
100 'Investment Committee: Agenda Item 6a', *CalPERS*, June 13, 2016, accessed January 19, 2017, www.calpers.ca.gov/docs/board-agendas/201606/invest/item06a-00.pdf .
101 Tom Finn, 'Qatar Plans to Invest $10 Billion in U.S. Infrastructure', *Business Insider*, December 13, 2016, accessed January 19, 2017, www.businessinsider.com/qatar-to-invest-10-billion-in-us-infrastructure-2016-12.
102 Jim Garrison, 'From Climate Change to Climate Shock: The Result of a Perfect Eco-Political Storm', *Huffington Post*, August 31, 2010, accessed November 29, 2017, www.huffingtonpost.com/jim-garrison/from-climate-change-to-cl_b_701126.html; Daniel J. Weiss, 'Anatomy of a Senate Climate Bill Death', *Center for American Progress*, October 12, 2010, accessed November 29, 2017, www.americanprogress.org/issues/2010/10/senate_climate_bill.html.
103 Weiss, 'Anatomy of a Senate Climate Bill Death'; 'NPRA Says New Senate Climate Bill Should be Rejected', *PR Newswire*, May 12, 2010, accessed March 28, 2017, www.prnewswire.com/news-releases/npra-says-new-senate-climate-bill-should-be-rejected-93597544.html.
104 'Ads', *American Petroleum Institute*, accessed March 28, 2017, www.api.org/aboutapi/ads/.
105 Evan Mackinder, 'Pro-Environment Groups Outmatched, Outspent in Battle Over Climate Change Legislation', *Open Secrets*, August 23, 2010, accessed March 28, 2017, www.opensecrets.org/news/2010/08/pro-environment-groups-were-outmatc/.
106 *Ibid.*
107 *Ibid.*
108 *Ibid.*
109 Neela Banerjee, Lisa Song, and David Hasemyer, 'Exxon's Own Research Confirmed Fossil Fuels' Role in Global Warming Decades Ago', *Inside Climate News*, September 16, 2015, accessed March 28, 2017, https://insideclimatenews.org/news/15092015/Exxons-own-research-confirmed-fossil-fuels-role-in-global-warming.
110 Bill McKibben, 'Exxon Knew Everything There Was to Know About Climate Change by the Mid-1980s – and Denied It', *Nation*, October 20, 2015, accessed March 28, 2017, www.thenation.com/article/exxon-knew-everything-there-was-to-know-about-climate-change-by-the-mid-1980s-and-denied-it/.
111 George Monbiot, *Heat: How to Stop the Planet from Burning* (Cambridge, MA: South End Press, 2009), pp. 27–28.
112 Monbiot, *Heat*, p. 28.

Notes: Chapter 5   201

113 Jason Breslow, 'Steve Coll: How Exxon Shaped the Climate Debate', *Frontline*, October 23, 2012, accessed November 29, 2017, www.pbs.org/wgbh/pages/frontline/environment/climate-of-doubt/steve-coll-how-exxon-shaped-the-climate-debate/.
114 Andrew C. Revkin, 'Industry Ignored Its Scientists on Climate', *New York Times*, April 23, 2009, accessed March 28, 2017, www.nytimes.com/2009/04/24/science/earth/24deny.html.
115 Dan Bacher, 'Western States Petroleum Association Spent $8.9M Lobbying Against Climate and Fracking Efforts in California Last Year', *Desmog*, February 5, 2015, accessed January 19, 2017, www.desmogblog.com/2015/02/05/western-states-petroleum-association-spent-8-9m-lobbying-against-climate-and-fracking-efforts-california-last-year.
116 'Unburnable Carbon – Are the World's Financial Markets Carrying a Carbon Bubble?' *Carbon Tracker Initiative*, November, 2011, accessed September 26, 2016, www.carbontracker.org/wp-content/uploads/2014/09/Unburnable-Carbon-Full-rev2-1.pdf; John Fullerton, 'The Big Choice', *The Capital Institute*, http://capitalinstitute.org/blog/big-choice-0/#_ednref3, accessed September 26, 2016; Bill McKibben, 'Global Warming's Terrifying New Math', *Rolling Stone*, July 19, 2012, accessed January 19, 2017, www.rollingstone.com/politics/news/global-warmings-terrifying-new-math-20120719?page=3.
117 'Bank of England Warns Stranded Assets Pose Threat to Financial Stability', *Carbon Tracker Initiative*, accessed January 19, 2017, www.carbontracker.org/news/bank-of-england-warns-stranded-assets-pose-threat-to-financial-stability/.
118 Chris Mooney and Steven Mufson, 'How Coal Titan Peabody, the World's Largest, Fell into Bankruptcy', *Washington Post*, April 13, 2016, accessed March 29, 2017, www.washingtonpost.com/news/energy-environment/wp/2016/04/13/coal-titan-peabody-energy-files-for-bankruptcy/?utm_term=.e73fddd1eea8.
119 John Brinkley, 'The Coal Industry Is Bankrupt', *Sierra*, April 6, 2016, accessed January 25, 2017, www.sierraclub.org/sierra/2016-3-may-june/feature/coal-industry-bankrupt.
120 Stephen L. Kass, 'The Federal Government Should Buy Coal Plants, Shut Them Down and Pay to Retrain Their Employees', *Washington Post*, June 3, 2016, accessed January 19, 2017, www.washingtonpost.com/opinions/the-federal-government-should-buy-coal-plants-shut-them-down-and-pay-to-retrain-their-employees/2016/06/03/eb08ebf4-0bdd-11e6-8ab8-9ad050f76d7d_story.html?utm_term=.3f01d87679ce.
121 *Ibid.*
122 Anne-Britt Dullforce, 'FT 500 2015 Introduction and Methodology', *Financial Times*, June 19, 2015, accessed January 20, 2017, www.ft.com/content/1fda5794-169f-11e5-b07f-00144feabdc0; Christopher Coats, 'Market Cap of U.S. Coal Companies Continues

to Fall', *Institute for Energy Economics and Financial Analysis*, March 23, 2016, accessed January 20, 2017, http://ieefa.org/market-cap-u-s-coal-companies-continues-fall/.
123. Leo Shane III, 'Report: Wars in Iraq, Afghanistan Cost Almost $5 Trillion So Far', *Military Times*, September 12, 2016, accessed January 20, 2017, www.militarytimes.com/articles/war-costs-report-brown-university.
124. Brad Plummer, 'A Not-So-Modest Climate Proposal: Why Not Just Buy Out the US Coal Industry?' *Vox*, June 7, 2016, accessed May 3, 2017, www.vox.com/2016/6/7/11875978/coal-industry-buyout.
125. 'Credit and Liquidity Programs and the Balance Sheet: Recent Balance Sheet Trends: Total Assets of the Federal Reserve', *Board of Governors of the Federal Reserve System*, accessed May 3, 2017, www.federalreserve.gov/monetarypolicy/bst_recenttrends.htm.
126. For more on this proposal, including a discussion of the effect it may have on inflation, see: Gar Alperovitz, Joe Guinan, and Thomas M. Hanna, 'The Policy Weapon Climate Activists Need', *Nation*, April 26, 2017, accessed May 3, 2017, www.thenation.com/article/the-policy-weapon-climate-activists-need/.
127. Carnoy and Shearer, *Economic Democracy*, pp. 73–74.
128. 'Resource Governance Index: State-Owned Companies', *Natural Resource Governance Institute*, accessed January 20, 2017, www.resourcegovernance.org/resource-governance-index/report/state-owned-companies.
129. Dwight D. Eisenhower, 'Military–Industrial Complex Speech, 1961', *Public Papers of the Presidents*, accessed January 20, 2017, http://coursesa.matrix.msu.edu/~hst306/documents/indust.html.
130. 'SIPRI Arms Industry Database', *SIPRI*, accessed January 20, 2017, www.sipri.org/databases/armsindustry.
131. In 2015–2016, these seven companies alone spent more than $14.5 million on lobbying. See: 'Defense, Top Contributors, 2015–2016', *OpenSecrets.org*, accessed March 31, 2017, www.opensecrets.org/industries/indus.php?Ind=D.
132. *Ibid.*
133. Eugene Gholz and Harvey M. Sapolsky, 'Restructuring the U.S. Defense Industry', *International Security*, vol. 24, no. 3 (Winter 1999/2000).
134. 'Army Says No to More Tanks, but Congress Insists', *Associated Press*, April 28, 2013, accessed March 31, 2017, http://www.foxnews.com/politics/2013/04/28/army-says-no-to-more-tanks-but-congress-insists/.
135. Ernesto Londoño, 'Armed Services Committees Reject White House Blueprint for Military Budget Cuts', *Washington Post*, May 24, 2014, accessed March 31, 2017, www.washingtonpost.com/world/national-security/armed-services-committees-reject-white-house-blueprint-for-military-budget-cuts/2014/05/24/c4b40024-e2bd-11e3-810f-764fe508b82d_story.html.
136. '2015 Annual Report', *Lockheed Martin Corporation*, 2016, accessed January 20, 2017, www.lockheedmartin.com/content/dam/lockheed/

data/corporate/documents/2015-Annual-Report.pdf; Aaron Mehta, 'Lockheed Martin Biggest US Government Contractor in 2015', *Defense News*, May 9, 2016, accessed January 20, 2017, www.defensenews.com/story/defense/policy-budget/industry/2016/05/09/lockheed-biggest-government-contractor-2015-defense-industry/83961520/.

137 'Subsidy Tracker Parent Company Summary: Lockheed Martin', *Good Jobs First*, accessed January 20, 2017, http://subsidytracker.goodjobsfirst.org/prog.php?parent=lockheed-martin&company=Lockheed.

138 Nankin and Schmidt, 'History of U.S. Gov't Bailouts'.

139 Michael Parenti, *Democracy for the Few* (Boston, MA: Wadsworth, 2011), p. 60.

140 Stuart D. Brandes, *Warhogs: A History of War Profits in America* (Lexington, KY: University Press of Kentucky, 1997), p. 205.

141 John Kenneth Galbraith, 'The Big Defense Firms Are Really Public Firms and Should Be Nationalized', *New York Times*, November 16, 1969.

142 Charlie Cray and Lee Drutman, 'Corporations and the Public Purpose: Restoring the Balance', *Seattle Journal for Social Justice*, vol. 4, no. 1 (2005).

143 Phil Asquith, 'Bang on Target: A Brief Union History of Arms Conversion', *Red Pepper*, September 11, 2015, accessed January 20, 2017, www.redpepper.org.uk/bang-on-target-a-brief-union-history-of-arms-conversion/.

144 Mary Beth Sullivan, 'Moving from a War Economy to a Peace Economy', in David Swanson, ed., *The Military Industrial Complex at 50* (Charlottesville, VA: MIC50.org, 2011).

145 Ann Markusen, 'How We Lost the Peace Dividend', *American Prospect*, July–August 1997, accessed January 20, 2017, http://prospect.org/article/how-we-lost-peace-dividend.

146 'U.S. Defense Spending Compared to Other Countries', *Peter G. Peterson Foundation*, June 1, 2017, accessed November 30, 2017, www.pgpf.org/chart-archive/0053_defense-comparison.

147 Asquith, 'Bang on Target'.

148 Adrian Smith, 'The Lucas Plan: What Can It Tell Us about Democratising Technology Today?' *Guardian*, January 22, 2014, accessed November 30, 2017, www.theguardian.com/science/political-science/2014/jan/22/remembering-the-lucas-plan-what-can-it-tell-us-about-democratising-technology-today.

149 Tom Risen, 'Study: The U.S. Internet Is Worth $966 Billion', *U.S. News and World Report*, December 11, 2015, accessed January 20, 2017, www.usnews.com/news/blogs/data-mine/2015/12/11/the-internet-is-6-percent-of-the-us-economy-study-says.

150 Susan Crawford, *Captive Audience: The Telecom Industry and Monopoly Power in the New Gilded Age* (New Haven, CT: Yale University Press, 2013), p. 5.

151 *Ibid*, p. 17.

Notes: Chapter 5

152 Tim Wu, 'The Oligopoly Problem', *New Yorker*, April 15, 2013, accessed January 20, 2017, www.newyorker.com/tech/elements/the-oligopoly-problem.
153 The Executive Office of the President, 'Community-Based Broadband Solutions', January 2015, accessed April 2, 2017, https://obamawhitehouse.archives.gov/sites/default/files/docs/community-based_broadband_report_by_executive_office_of_the_president.pdf.
154 *Ibid.*
155 Victor Pickard, *America's Battle for Media Democracy: The Triumph of Corporate Libertarianism and the Future of Media Reform* (New York, NY: Cambridge University Press, 2015), p. 221.
156 *Ibid.*
157 Crawford, *Captive Audience*, p. 265.
158 *Ibid.*
159 Jeremy Rifkin, *The Zero Marginal Cost Society: The Society of Things, The Collaborative Commons, and the Eclipse of Capitalism* (New York, NY: St. Martin's Press, 2014), p. 65.
160 Michel Bauwens, 'Beyond Jeremy Rifkin: How Will the Phase Transition to a Commons Economy Actually Occur?', *Huffington Post*, June 23, 2014, accessed November 5, 2017, www.huffingtonpost.com/entry/beyond-jeremy-rifkin-how-_b_5185948.html.
161 David Bollier, *Think Like a Commoner: A Short Introduction to the Life of the Commons* (Gabriola Island, Canada: New Society Publishers, 2014), p. 60.
162 Gar Alperovitz and Thomas M. Hanna, 'These Cities Built Cheap, Fast, Community-Owned Broadband. Here's What Net Neutrality Means for Them', *Yes! Magazine*, February 23, 2015, accessed November 5, 2017, www.yesmagazine.org/new-economy/these-cities-built-cheap-fast-community-owned-broadband.
163 Jacob Kastrenakes, 'Trump's New FCC Chief is Ajit Pai, and He Wants To Destroy Net Neutrality', *The Verge*, January 23, 2017, accessed November 5, 2017, www.theverge.com/2017/1/23/14338522/fcc-chairman-ajit-pai-donald-trump-appointment.
164 David Morris, 'How To Save Equal Access on the Internet', *On the Commons*, May 4, 2014, accessed November 5, 2017, www.onthecommons.org/magazine/how-save-equal-access-internet#sthash.XT65DoJC.dpbs.
165 In January 1979, manufacturing accounted for 19.38 million jobs out of a total civilian labor force of 104.05 million. In January 2017, manufacturing accounted for 12.37 million jobs out of a total civilian labor force of 159.7 million. See 'Databases, Tables, and Calculators by Subject: Civilian Labor Force Level' and 'Employment, Hours, and Earnings from the Current Employment Statistics survey (Manufacturing)', *Bureau of Labor Statistics*, accessed April 16, 2017.
166 Justin R. Pierce and Peter K. Schott, *The Surprisingly Swift Decline of U.S. Manufacturing Employment* (Cambridge, MA: National

Bureau of Economic Research, December 2012), https://www.usitc.gov/research_and_analysis/documents/Pierce%20and%20Schott%20-%20The%20Surprisingly%20Swift%20Decline%20of%20U.S.%20Manufacturing%20Employment_0.pdf.

167 Lavea Brachman and Torey Hollingsworth, 'Revitalizing America's Small and Medium-Sized Legacy Cities', *Federal Reserve Bank of Boston*, Summer 2016, accessed April 14, 2017, www.bostonfed.org/publications/communities-and-banking/2016/summer/revitalizing-americas-small-and-medium-sized-legacy-cities.aspx.

168 'Profile of General Demographic Characteristics: 2000', *American Fact Finder, United States Census Bureau*, accessed January 31, 2017; '2011–2015 American Community Survey 5-Year Estimates', *American Fact Finder, United States Census Bureau*, accessed January 31, 2017.

169 Matt Woolsey, 'America's Fastest-Dying Towns', *Forbes*, December 9, 2008, accessed January 31, 2017, www.forbes.com/2008/12/08/towns-ten-economy-forbeslife-cx_mw_1209dying.html.

170 'Profile of General Demographic Characteristics: 2000', *American Fact Finder, United States Census Bureau*, accessed January 31, 2017; '2011–2015 American Community Survey 5-Year Estimates', *American Fact Finder, United States Census Bureau*, accessed January 31, 2017.

171 'Rural US Disappearing? Population Share Hits Low', *Associated Press*, July 27, 2011, accessed January 31, 2017, http://www.foxnews.com/us/2011/07/28/rural-us-disappearing-population-share-hits-low/.

172 'Facts about Manufacturing', *Manufacturing Institute, MAP, and the National Association of Manufacturers*, November 2012, accessed January 31, 2017, www.themanufacturinginstitute.org/Research/Facts-About-Manufacturing/~/media/A9EEE900EAF04B2892177207D9FF23C9.ashx.

173 'Top 20 Facts about Manufacturing', *National Association of Manufacturers*, accessed January 31, 2017, www.nam.org/Newsroom/Top-20-Facts-About-Manufacturing/.

174 Ben Casselman, 'Manufacturing Jobs Are Never Coming Back', *FiveThirtyEight*, March 18, 2016, accessed January 31, 2017, http://fivethirtyeight.com/features/manufacturing-jobs-are-never-coming-back/.

175 'Top 20 Facts about Manufacturing', *National Association of Manufacturers*.

176 Barbara Taylor, 'Are Baby Boomers Ready To Exit Their Businesses?' *New York Times*, February 10, 2011, accessed January 31, 2017, http://boss.blogs.nytimes.com/2011/02/10/are-baby-boomers-ready-to-exit-their-businesses/; Stacy Cowley, 'Baby Boomers Ready To Sell Businesses to the Next Generation', *New York Times*, August 19, 2015, accessed April 14, 2017, www.nytimes.com/2015/08/20/business/smallbusiness/baby-boomers-ready-to-sell-businesses-to-the-next-generation.html.

177 'Good Jobs First Submits Comments to SEC on Disclosure Rules', *Good Jobs First*, July 21, 2016, accessed January 31, 2017, www.goodjobsfirst.org/news/releases/good-jobs-first-submits-comments-sec-disclosure-rules; Sarah Kavage, 'Today's Company Town: Seattle's Boeing Fixation', *Next American City*, February 2005.

178 Susan E. Clarke and Gary L. Gaile, *The Work of Cities* (Minneapolis, MN: University of Minnesota, 1998), p. 84.

179 Henry C. Simons, *Economic Policy for a Free Society* (Chicago, IL: University of Chicago Press, 1948), p. 59.

180 Jacob Viner, 'The Economics of Customs Unions', in Miroslav Jovanovic, ed., *International Economic Integration: Critical Perspectives on the World Economy* (New York, NY: Routledge, 1998), p. 172.

181 Thomas H. Naylor and William H. Willimon, *Downsizing the U.S.A* (Grand Rapids, MI: William B. Eerdmans Publishing Company), p. 9.

182 In *The Visible Hand*, the late Harvard business historian Alfred Chandler, Jr. wrote that the 'modern multiunit business enterprise replaced small traditional enterprise when administrative coordination permitted greater productivity, lower costs, and higher profits than coordination by market mechanisms. … Such an enterprise came into being and continued to grow by setting up or purchasing business units that were theoretically able to operate as independent enterprises – in other words, by internalizing the activities that had been or could be carried on by several business units and the transactions that had been or could be carried on between them.' See: Alfred D. Chandler, Jr., *The Visible Hand: The Managerial Revolution in American Business* (Cambridge, MA: Harvard University Press, 1977), pp. 6–7.

183 Vera Negri Zamagni, 'Learning from Emilia Romagna's Cooperative Economy', *Next System Project*, February 18, 2016, accessed February 2, 2017, http://thenextsystem.org/learning-from-emilia-romagna/.

184 Carlo Pietrobelli and Roberta Rabelloti, *Business Development Service Centres in Italy. An Empirical Analysis of Three Regional Experiences: Emilia Romagna, Lombardia and Veneto* (Santiago, Chile: United Nations, 2002), p. 21.

185 Andy Pike, Andrés Rodriguez-Pose, and John Tomaney, *Local and Regional Development* (New York, NY: Routledge, 2006), pp. 136–137; Pietrobelli and Rabelloti, *Business Development Service Centres in Italy*, p. 21.

186 Schumacher, *Small Is Beautiful*, p. 283.

187 NAM, 'Top 20 Facts About Manufacturing'.

188 Pavlina R. Tcherneva, *Beyond Full Employment: The Employer of Last Resort as an Institution for Change* (Annandale-on-Hudson, NY: Levy Economics Institute, September 2012), accessed April 20, 2017, www.levyinstitute.org/pubs/wp_732.pdf.

189 Ruth N. Bolton, Venkatesh Shankar, and Detra Y. Montoya, 'Recent Trends and Emerging Practices in Retailer Pricing', in Manfred Krafft

and Murali K. Mantrala (eds.), *Retailing in the 21st century: Current and Future Trends*, 2nd edition (New York, NY: Springer, 2010), p. 302.
190 'U.S. Largest Employers List', *Statistic Brain*, February 25, 2016, accessed April 20, 2017, www.statisticbrain.com/u-s-largest-employers/.
191 Timothy M. Laseter and Elliot Rabinovich, *Internet Retail Operations: Integrating Theory and Practice for Managers* (Boca Raton, FL: CRC Press, 2012), p. 28.
192 Stacy Mitchell, *Big-Box Swindle: The True Cost of Mega-Retailers and the Fight for America's Independent Businesses* (Boston, MA: Beacon Press, 2006), p. 164.
193 Jay Yarrow, 'Here's How Amazon Can Get Away with Never Earning a Profit', *Business Insider*, December 2, 2014, accessed November 21, 2017, www.businessinsider.com/jeff-bezos-on-profits-2014-12.
194 Spencer Soper, Matthew Townsend, and Lynnley Browning, 'Trump's Bruising Tweet Highlights Amazon's Lingering Tax Fight', *Bloomberg*, August 17, 2017, accessed November 21, 2017, https://www.bloomberg.com/news/articles/2017-08-17/trump-s-bruising-tweet-highlights-amazon-s-lingering-tax-fight.
195 Kirk Victor, 'Who's Winning the Amazon Tax Battles?', *Governing*, November 2011, accessed November 21, 2017, www.governing.com/topics/finance/whos-winning-amazon-tax-battles.html.
196 'Agribusinesses Consolidate Power', *Worldwatch Institute*, accessed February 2, 2017, www.worldwatch.org/node/5468.
197 'Corporate Consolidation in Agriculture Fact Sheet', *Taxpayers for Common Sense*, April 2014, accessed February 2, 2017, www.taxpayer.net/library/article/corporate-consolidation-in-agriculture-fact-sheet.
198 Elanor Starmer, 'Leveling the Field – Issue Brief #4: Hogging the Market', *The Agribusiness Accountability Initiative*, accessed February 2, 2017, www.ase.tufts.edu/gdae/Pubs/rp/AAI_Issue_Brief_4.pdf.
199 *Ibid.*
200 'Mill and Elevator Association', *State Historical Society of North Dakota*, accessed February 2, 2017, http://history.nd.gov/archives/stateagencies/millandelevator.html.
201 Olivia LaVecchia and Stacy Mitchell, *Affordable Space: How Rising Commercial Rents Are Threatening Independent Businesses, and What Cities Are Doing About It* (Minneapolis, MN: Institute for Local Self-Reliance, April 2016), accessed April 14, 2017, https://ilsr.org/wp-content/uploads/downloads/2016/04/ILSR-AffordableSpace-FullReport.pdf.
202 Mitchell, *Big-Box Swindle*, p. 241.
203 Linda Darling-Hammond, 'Educational Quality and Equality', in David Cay Johnston (ed.), *Divided: The Perils of Our Growing Inequality* (New York, NY: New Press, 2014), p. 154.
204 Milton Friedman, 'Public Schools: Make Them Private', *Washington Post*, February 19, 1995, accessed November 15, 2017, www.edchoice.

208   Notes: Conclusion

org/who-we-are/our-founders/the-friedmans-on-school-choice/article/public-schools-make-them-private/.

205 Mark Binelli, 'Michigan Gambled on Charter Schools. Its Children Lost', *New York Times*, September 5, 2017, accessed November 24, 2017, www.nytimes.com/2017/09/05/magazine/michigan-gambled-on-charter-schools-its-children-lost.html; Valerie Strauss, 'A Dozen Problems with Charter Schools', *Washington Post*, May 20, 2014, accessed November 24, 2017, https://www.washingtonpost.com/news/answer-sheet/wp/2014/05/20/a-dozen-problems-with-charter-schools/?utm_term=.f1201adeea0e; Diane Ravitch, 'The Math of Charter Schools', *New York Review of Books*, November 11, 2010, accessed November 24, 2017, www.nybooks.com/articles/2010/11/11/myth-charter-schools/.

206 Alia Wong, 'The Downfall of For-Profit Colleges', *Atlantic*, February 23, 2015, accessed November 24, 2017, www.theatlantic.com/education/archive/2015/02/the-downfall-of-for-profit-colleges/385810/; Paul Fain, 'GAO Takes Another Crack', *Insider Higher Ed*, November 23, 2011, accessed November 24, 2017, https://www.insidehighered.com/news/2011/11/23/gao-releases-new-investigation-profit-colleges; Susan Dynarski, 'A Conveyor Belt of Dropouts and Debt at For-Profit Colleges', *New York Times*, October 28, 2016, accessed November 24, 2017, https://www.nytimes.com/2016/10/30/upshot/a-conveyor-belt-of-dropouts-and-debt-at-for-profit-colleges.html.

207 The rules also expanded a system to wipe out the debts of students who had been defrauded by for-profit universities. See: Stacy Cowley and Patricia Cohen, 'U.S. Halts New Rules Aimed at Abuses by For-Profit Colleges', *New York Times*, June 14, 2017, accessed November 24, 2017, www.nytimes.com/2017/06/14/business/student-loans-for-profit-schools-colleges.html.

208 Michael Stratford, 'Trump and DeVos Fuel a For-Profit College Comeback', *Politico*, August 31, 2017, accessed November 24, 2017, www.politico.com/story/2017/08/31/devos-trump-forprofit-college-education-242193.

209 Corinne Jurney, 'For-Profit College Stocks: How Long Will the Trump Bump Last?' *Forbes*, February 24, 2017, accessed November 24, 2017, www.forbes.com/sites/corinnejurney/2017/02/24/for-profit-college-stocks-how-long-will-the-trump-bump-last/#718c123f75b4.

Conclusion

1 Carnoy and Shearer, *Economic Democracy*, p. 35.
2 Martha Derthick, *Between State and Nation* (Washington, D.C.: The Brookings Institution, 1974), pp. 35–39.
3 'Selznick asserts that TVA's grass roots policy is an ideological weapon enabling it to selectively harness segments of the Valley's population to support its programs and organizational autonomy,' Monmouth College

political scientist Marvin Maurer wrote in a 1986 review. 'He is concerned that the ideology enabled the TVA to accommodate itself to powerful, vested interests in the Valley.' See: Marvin Maurer, 'Review', *Journal of Politics*, vol. 48, no. 1 (1986).
4   Cumbers, *Reclaiming Public Ownership*, p. 5.
5   'The socialization of the means of production,' he writes, 'is a process, with state, or public, ownership constituting a crucial stage and subsequent progress in the direction of fully social ownership consisting of political and economic democratization.' See: Pat Devine, *Democracy and Economic Planning: The Political Economy of a Self-Governing Society* (Cambridge, UK: Polity Press, 1988), p. 129.
6   Although this by itself is not sufficient for Devine. 'Unless that use is integrated into a framework determined by society-level decisions about the broad disposition of the means of production as a whole, such ownership is in effect sectional private ownership, whatever its legal form,' he writes. See: Pat Devine, *Democracy and Economic Planning*, p. 133.
7   Schumacher, *Small Is Beautiful*, pp. 276–277.
8   'The central argument,' Cumbers states, 'is that past and existing forms of public ownership have done little to deliver genuine economic democracy and public participation because they were, on the whole, over-centralized, bureaucratic, and lacking democratic participation.' See: Cumbers, *Reclaiming Public Ownership*, p. 5.
9   Devine, *Democracy and Economic Planning*, p. 4.
10 As Erik Olin Wright and Archon Fung write, 'in the past, the political Left in capitalist democracies vigorously defended the affirmative state … . In its most radical form, revolutionary socialists argued that public ownership of the principle means of production combined with centralized state planning offered the best hope for a just, humane, and egalitarian society.' However, these arguments are fading and no longer sufficient. Now, 'a fundamental challenge for the Left is to develop transformative democratic strategies that can advance our traditional values – egalitarian social justice, individual liberty combined with popular control over collective decisions, community and solidarity, and the flourishing of individuals in ways that enable them to realize their potentials.' See: Archon Fung and Erik Olin Wright, 'Deepening Democracy: Innovations in Empowered Participatory Governance', *Politics & Society*, vol. 29, no. 1 (March 2001).
11 'Labour Is Interested in How We Earn Money Not Just How to Spend It', *Labour Press*, February 16, 2016, accessed December 1, 2017, http://press.labour.org.uk/post/139440665429/labour-is-interested-in-how-we-earn-money-not-just.
12 Decentralized Thematic Team, 'What Is Decentralization?' *World Bank*, accessed February 2, 2017, www.ciesin.org/decentralization/English/General/Different_forms.html.
13 This concept can sometimes also be called 'administrative decentralization,' which, according to the World Bank, 'seeks to redistribute

authority, responsibility and financial resources for providing public services among different levels of government.' See: Decentralized Thematic Team, 'What Is Decentralization?'
14 Schumacher, *Small Is Beautiful*, p. 258.
15 'There will remain the need for planning and ownership at higher geographical scales,' Cumbers writes, 'but these in turn need not necessarily be overwhelmingly concentrated within particular places, organizations or social groups.' See: Cumbers, *Reclaiming Public Ownership*, p. 150.
16 Schumacher, *Small Is Beautiful*, p. 259–261.
17 Dahl, *A Preface to Economic Democracy*, p. 111.
18 Dahl wrote that they have been claimed to 'foster human development, enhance the sense of political efficacy, reduce alienation, create a solidary community based on work, strengthen attachments to the general good of the community, weaken the pull of self-interest, produce a body of active and concerned public-spirited citizens within the enterprises, and stimulate greater participation and better citizenship in the government of the state itself.' He later notes, however, that 'the evidence [that worker self-management will increase civic virtue] although incomplete, is mixed.' See: Dahl, *A Preface to Economic Democracy*, pp. 95–96.
19 Dahl, *A Preface to Economic Democracy*, p. 98. Of course, Yugoslavia's 40-odd-year experiment with self-management did not prevent the violent breakup of the country in the early 1990s along ethnic lines. In fact, some scholars explicitly link deficiencies within the regime of self-management and overall economic management to the breakup. See, for instance, Yoji Koyama, 'Self-management in the Former Yugoslavia: From a Viewpoint of Corporate Governance', *Zarzadzanie I Finanse*, vol. 2, no. 6 (2013).
20 Carnoy and Shearer, *Economic Democracy*, p. 126–127.
21 'Board-Level Representation', *worker-participation.eu*, accessed November 24, 2017, www.worker-participation.eu/National-Industrial-Relations/Across-Europe/Board-level-Representation2.
22 Philip Resnick, 'Trade Unions, Workers' Control, and Democracy', in Lyman Howard Legters, John P. Burke, and Arthur DiQuattro, eds., *Critical Perspectives on Democracy* (Lanham, MD: Rowman & Littlefield Publishers, Inc., 1994), p. 124.
23 Philip Resnick, 'Trade Unions, Workers' Control, and Democracy.'
24 Joseph R. Blasi, Richard B. Freeman, and Douglas L. Kruse, *The Citizen's Share: Putting Ownership Back in Democracy* (New Haven, CT: Yale University Press, 2013), p. 10.
25 Dahl, *A Preface to Economic Democracy*, p. 140. Dahl came down in favor of cooperative ownership, by which he meant that the workers *as a group* would own the enterprise (rather than each worker owning a share). 'Just as citizenship in a democratic country entitles one to full and equal rights as a member of the polity, but does not entitle one to claim ownership of an individual share of the country's wealth,' Dahl

wrote, 'so too in a cooperatively owned enterprise members have full and equal rights but cannot lay claim to a share in the assets or net worth of the firm to dispose of as they choose.' In Dahl's formulation 'cooperative ownership avoids the problems arising from the need to dispose of individually owned shares, as in the plywood co-ops; yet like individual ownership it provides more protection for the autonomy of the firm against bureaucratic control by the state than would state or, in all likelihood, "social" ownership.' See: Dahl, *A Preface to Economic Democracy*, pp. 141–142, and 148.

26 Richard Wolff, *Democracy at Work: A Cure for Capitalism* (Chicago, IL: Haymarket Books, 2012), p. 141.
27 Dahl, *A Preface to Economic Democracy*, p. 143.
28 Wolff, *Democracy at Work*, p. 141.
29 Dahl, *A Preface to Economic Democracy*, p. 143.
30 Nove, *The Economics of Feasible Socialism*, p. 201.
31 George Ciccariello-Maher, *Building the Commune: Radical Democracy in Venezuela* (London, UK: Verso, 2016), pp. 20–21.
32 Peter Gowan and Mio Tastas Viktorsson, 'Revisiting the Meidner Plan', *Jacobin*, August 22, 2017, accessed November 10, 2017, https://jacobinmag.com/2017/08/sweden-social-democracy-meidner-plan-capital.
33 'What is not in question,' they argue, 'is that elected worker representatives in each company should have *immensely* more control over their businesses than they do at present – through French-style councils as well as worker representation on boards, employee ombudsmen, strengthened collective bargaining, and representation in the structures of wage-earner funds and having legal rights over how the shares are used. See: Gowan and Viktorsson, 'Revisiting the Meidner Plan'.
34 'David Graeber and David Harvey in Conversation', *CUNY Graduate Center*, April 25, 2012, accessed November 30, 2017, http://vimeo.com/41997338#t=4369.
35 'At one pole, we might conclude that only these direct producers should enjoy appropriation rights,' DeMartino explains, 'at the other, we might follow the lead of radical institutionalist economists and conclude that insofar as the entire community is responsible for the production of social wealth (and since it is impossible in any event to ascertain the particular contributions of specific individuals or groups), the entire community ought to participate democratically in appropriation.' See: George DeMartino, 'Realizing Class Justice'.
36 'If that is the case,' Burczak contends, 'Marxian socialism would once again fail to confront the Hayekian knowledge problems inherent in economic administration by a central government.' See: Burczak, *Socialism After Hayek*, pp. 10–11.
37 'There is also a tendency in some accounts to dismiss engagement and contestation of capitalist and state structures for perspectives that seek to work outside of capitalist social relations,' Cumbers writes. 'This leads to a rejection of the state and traditional forms of public ownership as a

suitable terrain for constructing alternatives.' See: Cumbers, *Reclaiming Public Ownership*, p. 217.
38 Stuart White, 'The Left After Social Democracy: Towards State-Society Partnerships', in Peter Ackers and Alastair J. Reid, eds., *Alternatives to State-Socialism in Britain: Other Worlds of Labor in the Twentieth Century* (Cham, Switzerland: Palgrave Macmillan, 2016), p. 317.
39 Hilary Wainwright, *Reclaim the State: Experiments in Popular Democracy* (New York, NY: Verso, 2003), pp. 19–26.
40 Maureen M. Donaghy, *Civil Society and Participatory Governance: Municipal Councils and Social Housing Programs in Brazil* (New York, NY: Routledge, 2013), p. 14.
41 'PB Map & Process List', *Participatory Budgeting Project*, accessed November 17, 2017, www.participatorybudgeting.org/pb-map/.
42 Ciccariello-Maher, *Building the Commune*, p. 23.
43 Ibid., pp. 107–108.
44 A. M. Honoré, 'Ownership,' in A.G. Guest, ed., *Oxford Essays in Jurisprudence* (Oxford, UK: Clarendon Press, 1961), accessed February 3, 2017, http://fs2.american.edu/dfagel/www/OwnershipSmaller.pdf. Honoré actually developed his list to 'analyse the concept of ownership, by which I mean the "liberal" concept of "full" individual ownership.' However, as Griffith University professor Hugh Breakey writes, 'Honoré's comprehensive listing of these incidents does not in itself confute Bundle Theory. Indeed, as it turned out, Honoré's list proved a helpful resource for Bundle Theorists; it usefully described the types of sticks that may or may not be present in a proprietor's bundle.' See: Hugh Breakey, 'Property', *Internet Encyclopedia of Philosophy*, accessed February 3, 2017, www.iep.utm.edu/prop-con/.
45 Schumacher, *Small Is Beautiful*, p. 286.
46 David Ellerman, 'On the Labor Theory of Property: Is the Problem Distribution or Predistribution?' *Challenge*, vol. 60 (2017).
47 Ellerman, 'On the Labor Theory of Property'.
48 Theodore Burczak explains: 'Whether or not Marx accepted the fundamental myth of capitalist property rights, Ellerman demonstrates that the myth is clearly false. The right to appropriate is determined by the direction of the hiring contract, not the ownership of property per se.' Burczak summarizes Ellerman's position thus: 'If labor hired capital – rather than capital hiring labor, as in the case in the conventional capitalist firm – workers would be the last owners of their labor time and the first owners of newly created goods and services.' See: Burczak, *Socialism After Hayek*, pp. 110 and 114.
49 Ellerman, 'On the Labor Theory of Property'.
50 Marjorie Kelly, *The Divine Right of Capital: Dethroning the Corporate Aristocracy* (San Francisco, CA: Berrett-Koehler Publishers, Inc., 2001), p. 41.
51 Kelly, *The Divine Right of Capital*, p. 43.

52 Marjorie Kelly, *Owning Our Future: The Emerging Ownership Revolution* (San Francisco, CA: Berrett-Koehler Publishers, Inc., 2012), p. 106
53 In the introduction to the 1991 revised edition, the late Murray Weidenbaum and economist Mark Jensen wrote that 'the most enduring theme of *The Modern Corporation and Private Property* is the divorce of ownership from the control of the modern corporation.' See: Murray Weidenbaum and Mark Jensen, 'Introduction', in Adolf A. Berle and Gardiner C. Means, *The Modern Corporation and Private Property* (New Brunswick, NJ: Transaction Publishers, 1991), p. ix.
54 Seth Ackerman, 'The Red and the Black', *Jacobin*, 2012, accessed February 2, 2017, www.jacobinmag.com/2012/12/the-red-and-the-black/.
55 Sharryn Kasmir, 'The Mondragon Cooperatives: Successes and Challenges', *Global Dialogue*, vol. 6, no. 1 (March 2016).
56 A 'capital-assets tax,' Schweickart explains, is 'a flat-rate property tax on all businesses. (In effect, this tax replaces the interest and dividend payments to shareholders and creditors in a capitalist economy.)' See: Schweickart, 'Economic Democracy'.
57 Giovanni Arrighi, *The Long Twentieth Century: Money, Power and the Origins of Our Times* (London, UK: Verso, 1994), p. 1.
58 Joe Guinan and Thomas M. Hanna, 'Polanyi Against the Whirlwind', *Renewal*, vol. 25, no. 1 (2017).
59 Heather Hansman, 'Congress Moves to Give Away National Lands, Discounting Billions in Value', *Guardian*, January 19, 2017, accessed February 1, 2017, www.theguardian.com/environment/2017/jan/19/bureau-land-management-federal-lease; Caty Enders, 'Republicans Move to Sell Off 3.3m Acres of National Land, Sparking Rallies', *Guardian*, January 31, 2017, accessed February 1, 2017, www.theguardian.com/environment/2017/jan/31/public-lands-sell-congress-bureau-management-chaffetz; 'Step Two in Congressional Push to Steal America's Public Lands', *The Wilderness Society*, January 26, 2017, accessed February 1, 2017, http://wilderness.org/press-release/step-two-congressional-push-steal-america%E2%80%99s-public-lands; Courtney Tanner, 'Utah's Chaffetz Backs Off on Plan to Sell Off "Excess" Public Lands', *Salt Lake Tribune*, February 2, 2017, accessed April 14, 2017, www.sltrib.com/news/4895033-155/utahs-chaffetz-backs-off-on-plan.
60 Cumbers, *Reclaiming Public Ownership*, p. 211.

Index

Page numbers in **bold** refer to tables; "n." after a page reference indicates the number of a note on that page.

Ackerman, Seth 142
Affordable Care Act 95, 96, 194n.49
agriculture sector
  beef-packing industry 127–8
  centralization of 127
  consolidation in 125
  idea of collective ownership 128
  number of farms 127
  production and distribution 127–8
Aharoni, Yair 36, 39, 40
Ainsworth 87
airports 25, 26, 163n.99, 163n.104
air transportation 107
Alaska Permanent Fund 29
Albert, Michael
  Parecon 80
alcohol distribution 27–8
Alexander, Cathy 69
Alperovitz, Gar 77, 123, 148
Alternative Models of Ownership (report) 3, 61
alternative political-economic system models
  cooperative ownership 75–6
  economic democracy 75
  market socialism 72–5, 76
  nation-states' role in 83
  participatory economics 80, 81
  pluralist 77–8
  public ownership and 8, 47, 72, 82

  social ownership 80–1
  theories of 82
  utopian visions of 72
Amazon 126–7
American Coalition of Competitive Energy Suppliers 191n.9
American Electric Power 62
American Federation of Teachers 34
American International Group (AIG) 49
American Petroleum Institute 109
American Public Power Association (APPA) 41, 62, 86
Amtrak (National Railroad Passenger Corporation) 31–2, 54, 63, 104, 199n.88
Anderson, Gerry 86
Andrews, Rhys
  Public Service Efficiency: Reframing the Debate 39
Angell, Marcia 99
Antillano, Andrés 141
appropriative justice 5, 139
appropriative rights 139, 211n.35
Aqua America 18
Aquarion 18
arms companies 113–15
Arrighi, Giovanni
  The Long Twentieth Century 144
Asquith, Phil 116

Index

automation 59–61
autonomy
  impact on efficiency 45–6

Bacon, Francis
  New Atlantis 72
Baer, Hans
  Global Capitalism and Climate Change 68
Banco Popular (BPDC) 11, 93
banking sector *see* financial sector
Bank of America 49
Bank of North Dakota (BND) 21, 54, 91
Barnes, Peter 166n.126
Bartel, Ann 41
Bauwens, Michel 119
Bay Area Rapid Transit (BART) District's board 105
Bel, Germá 37
Bellamy, Edward
  Looking Backward 72
Bentham, Jeremy 57
Berger, Victor L. 22
BerkshireHills Bancorp 54
Berle, Adolph
  The Modern Corporation and Private Property 142, 213n.53
biopharmaceutical industry 99
Blackburn, Robin 4
Blasi, Joseph 137
Boardman, Anthony 43–4
Boardman, Joseph 54, 178n.22
Bollier, David 120
Bolton, Ruth 125
Boston's transit system 105, 199n.97
Boulder, CO
  municipalization of local utilities 16–17, 64, 68, 85
Brazil
  participatory budgeting program 140
  state owned companies 11

Breakey, Hugh 212n.44
Bresch, Heather 97
Brexit 1, 144–5
Brinkley, John 109–10
British Petroleum (BP) 109
British Rail 33
Brown, Jerry 106
Brown, Sherrod 90
Buiter, Willem 90
Bundle Theory 212n.44
Burczak, Theodore 74, 139, 212n.48
Bureau of Labor Statistics 56
Burford, Anne McGill 101
Burlington, VT
  publicly owned enterprises 34–5, 68
  waterfront development 34

Caldwell, Bruce
  The Road to Serfdom: Text and Documents 65
California
  chemical testing in 101
  public banking 20
  transportation investments 106
California Public Employees' Retirement System (CalPERS) 106
Cameron, David 33
capitalism 83, 144
carbon bubble 68, 109, 185n.101
carbon reduction 107
Carbon Tracker Initiative 109
Carney, Mark 109
Carnoy, Martin 132, 136, 190n.6
  Economic Democracy 84
Carson, Rachel
  Silent Spring 100
Catalan independence movement 13
Caves, Douglas 40
Center for Responsive Politics 63
CEOs (Chief Executive Officers)
  salaries and compensations 53–4, 178n.22

216 Index

CGN (China's state owned nuclear company) 14
Chaffetz, Jason 147
Chandler, Alfred, Jr. 206n.182
Chang, Ha-Joon 37, 44, 46, 52, 175n.60, 176n.8
chemical product sector
  chemical testing 101
  environmental impact 100–1
  impact on public health 100
  political-economic power of 101–2
  regulations 101
  revenue 100
Chernobyl disaster 102
China National Petroleum Corporation 154n.7
Choksi, Armeane 52, 176n.6
Christensen, Laurits 40
Christopherson, Susan 122
Chrysler 33, 49, 176n.5
Ciccariello-Maher, George 140
Citigroup Inc. 49
Civilian Conservation Corps (CCC) 125
Clarke, Susan 122
coal industry
  decline of 109–10
  idea of nationalization of 68
  prospect of public ownership 110
Cole, G. D. H. 59
Coll, Steve
  Private Empire: Exxon Mobil and American Power 108
commercial ports 26
common wealth trusts 166n.126
communal ownership 138
communism 4, 73
Community Choice Aggregation (CCA) 17–18
competition
  and autonomy 42–50
  four conditions for perfect 45
  impact on efficiency 42–5, 47

Consolidated Rail Corporation (Conrail) 33
Continental Illinois National Bank and Trust Company 91
Cook, Paul 43
cooperative ownership 75–6, 128, 187–8n.16, 210–11n.25
Corbyn, Jeremy 1, 2, 15
Crawford, Susan 119
  Captive Audience 117
Cray, Charlie 115
Cumbers, Andrew 36, 77–8, 79, 134, 135, 147, 188n.27, 209n.8, 210n.15
  Reclaiming Public Ownership 7, 133
Cummine, Angela 166n.126

Dahl, Robert 81, 137, 138, 142, 210–11n.25, 210n.18
  Politics, Economics, and Welfare 5
  A Preface to Economic Democracy 135
Daly, Michael 54
Davidoff, Steven 48, 49
Davis, Alyssa 53
Debs, Eugene 22, 23
decentralization
  components of 134
  concept of 134, 209–10n.13
  vs. decentering 135
  functional 135
  geographical 134–5
  state intervention and 139–40
DeFazio, Peter 64
defense industry
  economic conversion proposals 115–16
  government contracts 114
  public support of 114
  resistance to downsizing 116–17
  subsidies 114
DeMartino, George 5, 139, 211n.35
democracy 61–6, 132–3, 139
democratic economy 148–9
Denver Health 26

Devine, Pat 81, 133, 134, 138, 189n.44, 209n.6
DeVos, Betsy 130
Dodds, Walter 69
Donaghy, Maureen 140
Donahue, John 40
Dow Chemical Company 101
Drew, Deborah J. 196n.65
Drew Quality Group 196n.65
Drutman, Lee 115
Dugher, Michael 33
Duke Energy 62
Dulles Greenway 104, 106

Eaton, George 3
economic democracy 2, 72, 75, 142
economic growth
  limits of 69
economic inequality
  causes of 133
  change of ownership and 54
  compensation structures 53
  inheritance and 57–8
  public ownership and 53–9, 55
  scale of 53–4
  trade unions as check on 55
economic performance
  measurement 171–2n.20
Economic Policy Institute (EPI) 53, 55
EDF (Électricité de France) 13, 14
Edison Electric Institute 62
Edison International 62
Edmond Electric company 52
Edmundson, William 55
education sector
  charter schools 130
  financial support 130–1
  for-profit schools 130–1, 208n.207
  non-profit private schools 131
  privatization debates 129–30
  reforms 130
efficiency
  autonomy and 45–6, 174–5n.53

competition and 40, 42–5
indicators of 39–40
market conditions and 41
natural monopolies 44
ownership type and 41–2
productivity and 41
of public and private enterprises 43–4
studies of 42–3
Eisenhower, Dwight 113
Ekelund, Robert, Jr. 57
electric utility sector
  competition in 191n.9
  private and publicly owned companies 53–4, 62–3
  spending 62–3
Ellerman, David 141–2, 212n.48
Elliot, Larry 165n.125
employer of last resort (ELR) concept 125
employment
  fears about future of 60
  gender inequality 180n.44
  technological impact on 59–60
Endo Pharmaceuticals 98
Energy Future Holdings Corp. 62
Energy Policy Acts 62, 86, 191n.9
energy sector
  climate-related legislation and 107–8, 109–10
  definition 107
  investments in 111
  nationalization plans 110–12
  regulations 64
Engels, Friedrich 58
Enron Corporation scandal 64
Entergy Corp. 62
Entwistle, Tom
  Public Service Efficiency: Reframing the Debate 39
environmental movement 68
Environmental Protection Agency (EPA) 101
EpiPens 97
Epstein, Gerald 89
Estrin, Saul 7

Exelon Corp. 62
Exxon-Mobil 108–9

Farmers' Alliance 22
Farrell, John 87
fascism 1, 82, 145
Federal Aviation Administration (FAA) 26
Federal Communications Commission (FCC) 19
Federal Oil and Gas Corporation 112
financial sector
  bailouts 92–3
  Brown-Kaufman amendment 90
  characteristics of 89
  crisis of 2008–2009 91–2
  democratization of 93
  idea of postal bank 90–1
  ownership forms 78
  public ownership 20, 91, 92–3
  re-regulation proposals 89–90
  temporarily nationalization, idea of 91, 92
  'too-big-to fail' 89
First International (The International Workingmen's Association) 58
Fixing America's Surface Transportation (FAST) Act 183n.84
Flores-Macias, Francisco 37
For the Many Not the Few manifesto 3
fossil fuel industry 68, 109, 110–12
Fourier, Charles 72
Fowke, Ben 54
Franklin National Bank 91, 92
Frase, Peter 60
Freedom of Information Act (FOIA) 63
Freeman, Richard 60, 137
free market 84
Frees, Bob 121
Friedman, Milton 65, 123, 130
  Capitalism and Freedom 65

Friends of Locally Owned Water (FLOW) 18
Fullerton, John 109
Fung, Archon 209n.10

Gade, Mary 101
Gaile, Gary 122
Galbraith, John Kenneth 114
Geddes, Richard 31
General Atomics 62
General Dynamics 114
Germany
  'codetermination' system 136
  green 'utility' company 87
  health care model 195n.52
  municipally owned enterprises 12–13
  publicly owned companies 11, 37, 53
Gholz, Eugene 113
Global Climate Coalition 109
globalization 145–6
GMAC (General Motors Acceptance Corporation) 49
GM (General Motors) 49, 176n.5
Gonzales, Javier 19
government owned corporations (GOCs) 5
Gowan, Peter 138
Graeber, David 139
Greater London Council (GLC) 140
Green Investment Bank 111
Guidelines on Corporate Governance of State-Owned Enterprises 46
Guinan, Joe 72, 146
Gunasekar, Sangeetha 174–5n.53
Gupta, Sanjay 98

Hacker, Jacob 96
Hahnel, Robin 80, 189n.37
Halpin, Helen 96
Hamilton, Alexander
  Report on Manufactures 66
Harbage, Peter 96
Harrison, Ann 41

Hayek, Friedrich 65, 73, 78
healthcare systems
  in Canada 96
  efforts to reform 96
  expenditure 94
  fraudulent practices 94
  insurance industry and 95
  models of 93–4, 96, 195n.52
  single-payer option 96, 97
  in the United States, structure of 94–6
Hirsch, Barry 56
Hirschman, Albert
  Exit, Voice, and Loyalty 43
Hoan, Daniel 24
Hobbs, Cat 5
Hobday, Victor 132
Honoré, A. M. 212n.44
  'Ownership' 141
hospitals
  public ownership 26–7
Hudson, Michael 36, 38
Hughes, Craig 199n. 97

Indiana Toll Road 106
Indonesian privatization program 41
inheritance tax 57, 58–9, 181n.56
innovation 66–7
Institute for Local Self Reliance's (ILSR) community broadband initiative 19
insurance industry 21, 70, 95
International Monetary Fund's report on competitive markets 41
Internet systems
  access to 118, 119–20
  invention of 67
  municipal broadband network 19
  public ownership of 18–19, 119

Japan Post Bank 11
Jefferson, Thomas 66
Jensen, Mark 213n.53
Johnson, Bill 53–4
Johnson, Christopher 37

Johnson & Johnson 98
Johnson, Kenneth 121
Johnson, Simon 90
Jones, Leroy 65
Jones, Owen 169n.153
Judd, Richard William 23

Kansas City Southern company 54
Kashkari, Neel 92
Kass, Stephen 110
Kaufman, Ted 90
Kay, John 42
Kelly, Marjorie
  The Divine Right of Capital 142
  Owning Our Future 142
Kelton, Stephanie 125
Kennedy, Edward 111
Ketlaphela Pharmaceuticals 99
Keynes, John Maynard 60, 181n.63
Khan, Sadiq 15
Kirkpatrick, Colin 37, 43
Knights of Labor 22
Kole, Stacey 37
Kruse, Douglas 137
Kurlantzick, Joshua 3
Kuttner, Robert
  American Prospect 86

Labour Energy Forum (UK) 14, 87
Labour Party (UK) 1, 3, 15, 61, 67–8, 85, 116
Labra, Armando 176n.6
Lange, Oskar 73, 74, 186n.3
Laseter, Timothy 126
LaVecchia, Olivia 128
Lawson, Alex 98
Layne, Aubrey 103
Lazzarini, Sergio 6, 152n.19
leisure occupation, problem of 181n.63
Le Pen, Marine 145
Lewis, H. Gregg 55
Limits to Growth (report) 69
Lindblom, Charles
  Politics, Economics, and Welfare 5

Lippmann, Walter 24
Liquor Control Board of Ontario (LCBO) 28
Lockheed Martin 114
Long-Bailey, Rebecca 3
Longman, Philip 32
Lundgren, Bo 91
Lunn, George 24

McDonnell, John 3, 15, 67–8, 134
McGovern, George 112, 116
McKibben, Bill 108
McKinsey Global Institute 59
Macron, Emmanuel 145
majority-owned companies 12, 155–6n.19, 156n.20
Malleson, Tom 75–6, 187n.16
Manchin, Joe 97
Mandel, Ernest 79–80
manufacturing sector
  contribution to economy 120, 121
  cost of production 124
  decline of 120–1
  economic development agencies 122–3, 124
  investment strategy 123–4
  job statistics 120, 204n.165
  network model 124
  profitability 121
  public ownership 122, 124–5
  size of companies 121–2, 124
  subsidies 122
market failure 51–2, 85
market socialism
  vs. centrally-planned model 76
  concept of 73–4
  critique of 72–3, 74, 79–80, 189n.35
  means of production 73–4
  ownership forms 73–4, 76
  planning 74
  roots of 73
  variants of 74–5
Markusen, Ann 116
Martinez, Susana 27

Marx, Karl 4, 212n.48
  The Communist Manifesto 58, 84
Massachusetts Bay Transportation Authority (MBTA) 104, 105
Massachusetts Department of Transportation (MassDOT) 104
Maurer, Marvin 209n.3
May, Theresa 148
Mazzucato, Mariana 66–7, 99
  The Entrepreneurial State 67
Meade, James 54–5, 59, 166n.126, 181n.59
Meadows, Dennis 69
Meadows, Donella 69
Means, Gardiner
  The Modern Corporation and Private Property 142, 213n.53
means of production 4, 65, 73–4, 76, 80, 133, 137, 141, 152n.14, 188n.22, 189n.39, 209n.5, 209n.10
Meek, James 13
Meer, Hendriekje van der 40
Megginson, William 38, 39, 40, 44, 65, 184n.87
Meidner Plan 138
Mélenchon, Jean-Luc 145
Melman, Seymour 115, 116
Metropolitan Transportation Authority (MTA) 105
Michigan
  contamination of waterways 101
  infrastructure upgrade 34
Miller, David 137
Miller, Matthew 110
Mill, John Stuart 57
Mises, Ludwig von 65, 186n.3
Mishel, Lawrence 53
Mitchell, Christopher 19
Mitchell, Stacy 126, 127, 128–9
  Big Box Swindle 126
Modern Monetary Theory (MMT) 125
Monbiot, George
  Heat 108

Mondragón cooperative network 143
Montoya, Detra 125
Montreal Protocol (1987) 100
Moore, Stanley
  Marx Versus Markets 84
Moorman, Charles 178n.22
More, Thomas
  Utopia 72
Morris, David 120
Muhlenkamp, Holger 39, 44
Mulherin, J. Harold 37
multiunit business enterprises 206n.182
municipal ownership 12–13, 19–20, 23–4, 34
municipal socialism 22–3, 24
Murphy, Phil 20
Musacchio, Aldo 6, 37, 152n.19

Nader, Ralph 31
National Grange Movement 22
nationalization 48–50, 141, 146–7
natural monopolies 44–5, 52
Naylor, Thomas H. 123
Nebraska
  Enabling Act 88
  public utility services 16, 34, 85, 87, 88
negative externalities 52
Nelson, Robert R. 25
Netter, Jeffry 38, 39, 40, 44
New Deal 30
New Public Management (NPM) 45
Newsom, Gavin 20
NextEra Energy 62
Next System Project 190n.47
North American Free Trade Agreement (NAFTA) 145
North American Industry Classification System 84
North Dakota Mill 21, 128
North Dakota Mill and Elevator Association 128

Northwest Bancshares, Inc., 54
Norway
  publicly owned companies 12
  sovereign wealth funds 165n.125
Nove, Alec 79, 138, 188n.22
  The Economics of Feasible Socialism 76

Obama, Barack 30, 67, 183n.84, 185n.97
Obamacare *see* Affordable Care Act
Obama's Clean Power Plan 110
oil and gas industry
  in China 154n.7
  nationalization plan 110–11
  public ownership 153–4n.7
  in Russia 153n.7
Oliver, Michael 37
Ollman, Bertell 79
Organisation for Economic Co-operation and Development (OECD)
  guidelines on SOEs management 46–7
  studies of publicly ownership 10–11, 37
Owen, Robert 72
ownership
  analysis of concept of 4–5, 212n.44
  control of modern corporation and 213n.53
  management and 142
  models of 5, 76
  in relation to property rights 141, 142
  sectional private 209n.6
  transfer of 79

Pai, Ajit 120
Paine, Thomas 57
Pannekoek, Anton 7, 137
Parenti, Michael 114
Parker, David 37, 42, 43, 44
participatory economics 80, 140–1

Passenger Rail Reform and Investment Act (2015) 64
Patman, Wright 32
Peabody Energy 109, 110
Pearson, J. Michael 98
Peng, Mike 51, 65
pension plans 56–7
People's Party (the 'Populists') 22
Permanent University Fund 29
PG&E Corp. 62
pharmaceutical industry
   focus on profit 97–8
   fraudulent practices 97
   government support of 98–9
   national strategic importance of 98
   non-profit companies 196n.65
   opioid epidemic and 98
   publicly funded research 99
   publicly ownership 99–100
   public opinion polls about 97
   revenue 99
   in South Africa 99
Pickard, Victor 118
Piketty, Thomas 53, 54, 58–9, 177n.16
   Capital in the Twenty-First Century 53
Pluralist Commonwealth 77
Polanyi, Karl 146
   The Great Transformation 84
'Polanyi moment' 146
political-economic systems 4, 5
Polman, Paul 69
Port Authority of New York and New Jersey 26, 183n.80
POSCO 176n.8
Posen, Adam 92
Postal Accountability and Enhancement Act 31
PPL Corporation 54
PricewaterhouseCoopers 12, 51
private companies
   definition 6–7
   effectiveness of 174n.48
   environmental issues and 69–70
   government interventions in 48–9
   lack of transparency 63, 64
   responsibility to shareholders 69
   short-term mindset 69
private ownership
   and democracy 61–6
   and innovation 66–8
   vs. public ownership 65–6
   social return 52
privatization 2, 43, 173n.39–40
productivity 57, 61
profitability 39–40
Progressive movement 22
property rights 141, 142, 212n.48
Prybla, Jan 152n.14
publicly owned enterprises
   in alternative political-economic models 47
   in banking industry 11
   community representation 138
   compensation for workers 56
   competition 174n.44
   definition 5
   economic and social role of 46
   efficiency of 174–5n.53, 174n.48
   financial advantage of 47–8
   in hospitality industry 25
   in international airlines 11
   local participation 132–3
   management structure 45–6, 143–4
   minimal size of 190n.7
   in oil industry 10–11
   organizational principles 175n.60
   statistics 10–11
   in telecommunication industry 11
   during times of crisis 48
   transparency of 63–4
   tripartite supervision model 138–9
   worker self-management 137–8, 139
public markets 25

public ownership
  advantages of 51, 52, 70, 132, 135
  alternative political-economic models and 44–5, 50, 72
  and automation 59–61
  capacity for adaptation and redeployment 133–4
  in capitalist formation, role of 176n.6
  challenge of deployment of 9, 148
  common view of 170n.4
  competition and 42–5
  contemporary experience of 4
  corporatization of 48
  critique of 36, 65–6
  decentralisation of 134–5, 148, 149
  definition of 5–6
  democracy and 65, 132, 209n.8
  democratization of 138, 142–3
  development of framework of 83
  dismissal of role of state in 211–12n.37
  economic viability of 15
  effectiveness of different forms of 79
  efficiency debate 8, 36, 38–41, 42–5, 170–1n.7
  environmental issues and 68–71
  focus on long-term benefits 70
  historical context 2, 4–5
  industries with 8–9, 190n.6
  innovation and 66–8
  of land 24–5, 29, 147, 167n.130
  of marijuana shops 28–9
  Marxist vision of 84
  models of 5–6
  motivations for pursuing 52
  in natural monopoly sectors 44–5, 52
  objectives for 78
  in OECD countries 10
  politics and 65
  vs. private ownership 65–6
  question of restructuring 142
  revenue 52–3
  right-wing populism and 148
  scholarly literature on 3–4, 36–8, 133
  shortcomings of 134
  social issues and 48
  state intervention 46–7
  theoretical perspectives 7–8
  transition of large enterprises to 124–5
  in transportation sector 102–3
  types of 78
  in the United Kingdom 3
  as wealth redistribution instrument 53, 55, 57, 133
  worker participation 135, 138
public ownership in the United States
  of airports 25–6
  of alcohol distribution facilities 27–8
  in banking industry 19–21, 29–30
  of commercial ports 26
  in electric utility sector 16–18, 62
  of high-speed internet systems 18–19
  of hospitals and clinics 26–7
  of investment funds 29
  local initiatives with 16, 23–4, 34–5
  of lotteries 28
  and pension and union funds 34
  popular support for 147
  of postal service 31
  prevalence of 16
  of railroads 31–3
  revenue from 27–8, 52
  of sales of recreational marijuana 28–9
  of schools and universities 27, 35
  of Social Security Administration 29
  structure and management of 33–4
  of Veteran's Administration 29
  of water systems 18, 34

Index

Public Ownership League of
    America 24
Public Ownership Party 23
public-private partnerships (PPPs)
    103–4, 198n.83
public-public partnerships 34
public services 12, 78
public transportation systems
    development projects 24–5
    ownership forms 24, 78, 104–5
Public Utilities Commission (PUC)
    17
Public Utility Holding Company
    Act (PUHCA) 62, 63, 86,
    191n.11
Purdue Pharma 98

'Quantitative Easing' program 111
quasi-firms 135

Rabinovich, Elliot 126
railroads
    in Canada 40
    freight companies 104
    infrastructure 32, 33, 104
    inter-city 105–6
    in Nigeria 43
    ownership 104–5, 169n.153
    passenger service 104, 105–6
Ramírez Rojas, Kléber 140
Randers, Jorgen 69
Raymond, Lee 108
Reagan, Ronald 36
Reed, Debra 54
Reich, Robert 95
Reinert, Erik 66
re-municipalization 12–13, 156n.22
Resnick, Philip 136, 137
retail sector
    chain giants 126–7
    consolidation in 125–6
    global distribution network 126
    public ownership in 128–9
Reuss, Henry 92
Rifkin, Jeremy 119
Romagna, Emilia 124

Roosevelt, Franklin Delano 30
Roosevelt, Theodore
    'New Nationalism' speech 58
Rosenfeld, Jake 55
Rutgers, Mark 40

Sacristan, Emilio 176n.6
Saint Simon, Henri de 58, 72
Sanders, Bernie 34, 90, 91
Sapolsky, Harvey 113
Sarbanes-Oxley Act (2002) 64
Sarkar, Jayati 175n.53
Savings Banks Financial Group 11
Schumacher, E. F. 124–5, 133, 134,
    135, 141, 190n.7
    Small Is Beautiful 85
Schweickart, David 75, 137, 142,
    213n.56
Scott, Gregory M. 107
self-employment 188n.27
self-governing enterprises 135–6,
    210n.18
self-management 135–7
Selucký, Radoslav 138
Selznik, Philip 208n.3
    TVA and the Grassroots 133
Sempra Energy 54
Senate Caucus on International
    Narcotics Control 98
Shankar, Venkatesh 125
Shapiro, Carl 65, 174n.53
Shearer, Derek 84, 132, 136, 190n.6
Shell USA 109
Shirley, Mary M. 42, 44, 51
Shkreli, Martin 97
Shuster, Bill 64
Simons, H. C. 123
Smith, Adam
    The Wealth of Nations 189n.46
Smith, John Robert 32
Smyth, Joe 108
socialism, popular view of 186n.1
socialist movement 22–3
Socialist Party 22, 23, 24
social ownership 7, 80–2, 133, 136,
    138, 148, 189n.44, 209n.5

social property enterprises (EPS) 138
Social Security Administration 56
Social Security Works 98
Solow, Robert 57
Southern Co. 62
sovereign wealth funds 6, 7, 29, 52, 106, 107, 152n.19, 165n.125, 166n.126
Soviet Union
    economic reforms 73
    environmental disasters in 102
    search for alternative to central planning 186n.2
Starmer, Elanor 128
state capitalism 83, 152n.19
State Life Fund 21-2
state owned enterprises (SOEs)
    advantages 51-2, 184n.87
    definition 5
    effects of autonomy on 175n.53
    governance and efficiency 175n.57
    natural monopoly and 44
    problems of 171n.10
    reform of 46-7
    regulations 47
state ownership of capital wealth 181n.59
state's role in economy 48-9, 67-8
Stave, Bruce 23
Stevens, Larry 52
Stevenson, Adlai, III 111, 112

taxation 58-9, 213n.56
Tcherneva, Pavlina 125
technology
    benefits 61
    impact on employment 60
telecommunications and information technology sector
    abusive practices 117-18
    accessible infrastructure 119-20
    contribution to market failures 118
    leading private companies 117
    monopoly submarkets 117
    'net neutrality' debates 120
    privatization 43
    public ownership proposals 119
    restructure of 119
    wireless carriers 117
Teles, Nuno 93
Telia 6
Tennessee Valley Authority (TVA) 8, 30, 38, 54, 132-3, 147, 208-9n.3
Texaco 109
Texas Permanent School Fund 29
Thatcher, Margaret 1, 36, 37
'There Is No Alternative (TINA)' 42
Thomas, Alan 181n.59
Thompson, Carl 22, 24
Thompson, Derek 60
Thompson, D. J. 42
Thompson, Noel 55
Toxic Substances Control Act (1976) 101
trade unions *see* unions
Transatlantic Trade and Investment Partnership (TTIP) 145
Transnational Institute (TNI) 12, 156n.22
Trans-Pacific Partnership (TPP) 145
transparency 63-4
transportation sector
    air transportation 102
    components of 102
    foreign investments 106-7
    infrastructure ownership 105-6
    local transit systems 104-5
    natural monopolies 102
    public-private partnerships 103-4, 106
    roads 103-4
    service ownership 104, 105-6
    see also railroads
Trump, Donald
    economic policy 64, 145-6, 148
    election of 1, 64, 145
    health care policy 194n.49

Tulkens, Henry 46
Turing Pharmaceuticals 97
Turner, Graham 69

Uber 60
unions 34, 55–6, 143
United Kingdom
　East Coast Mainline 33
　electricity sector 13–14, 15
　foreign ownership 14
　nuclear projects 14
　privatization 13
　productivity growth 38
　publicly owned companies 15, 33
　public opinion on public ownership 3
　wind power 14
United States
　agriculture sector 127–9
　chemical product sector 100–2
　climate action plans 16
　decline of small towns 121, 122
　defense sector 113–17
　education system 129–31
　electric utility sector 53–4, 62–3, 191n.9
　employment data 57
　energy sector 107–13
　financial sector 19–20, 89–93
　fossil fuel corporations 107–9
　'Gilded Age' of economy 22
　healthcare 93–7
　income inequality 53
　manufacturing sector 120–5
　municipalization efforts 17
　nationalization schemes 146
　opposition to privatization 18, 85, 147
　pension plans 56–7
　pharmaceutical industry 97–100
　privately owned water systems 18
　productivity growth 38
　public ownership in 16–35, 47, 84–5, 147
　response to financial crisis 49–50
　retail sector 125–7
　telecommunications and information technology sector 117–20
　threat to democracy 145–6
　transportation sector 102–7
United States Postal Service (USPS) 31, 147
US Export-Import Bank 30
utility sector
　deregulation efforts 86–7
　independent grid management 88
　as natural monopoly 85–6
　ownership models 78, 87–8
　services provided by 85
　wind power 87

Valeant Pharmaceuticals 98
Vancouver Hilton Hotel & Convention Center 25
Van Lear, Thomas 23
Vattenfall 14
Verhoest, Koen 45
Vickers, John 42
Viktorsson, Mio Tastas 138
Vilsack, Tom 30
Vining, Aidan 43, 44
Virginia
　alcohol distribution 27
　public-private partnerships 103–4, 198n.83
Vogelsang, Ingo 51, 53
Volkow, Nora 98

Wagner, William 54
Wainwright, Hilary 140
Walker, Douglas 57
Wallsten, Scott 43, 173n.39
Wal-Mart 126, 127
Walsh, Patrick 42, 44, 51
Warner, Mildred 37
Warren, Elizabeth 89
Washington Metropolitan Transit Authority (WMATA) 105
wealth
　accumulation and redistribution of 57, 59

Weaver, Sam 64
Weidenbaum, Murray 213n.53
Weiss, Jonathan
  Public Schools and Economic Development 27
We Own It! group 5
Wesson, Herb 20
Western, Bruce 55
Western Petroleum Association 109
Wicker, Roger 32
Wilcox, Nathan 108
Wiles, Peter 5
Willig, Robert 65, 174n.53
Willimon, William H. 123
Willner, Johan 36, 42, 44
Wolff, Richard 137, 142
Wolf, Martin 67
worker participation 135, 136, 139, 211n.33
Worker Self Directed Enterprises (WSDEs) 137
Works Progress Administration (WPA) 125
World Bank reports 52, 134
Wray, L. Randall 125
Wright, Erik Olin 209n.10
Wright, M. A. 112
Wu, Tim 118

Xcel Energy 16–17, 54

Yarrow, George 42
Yglesias, Matthew 104
Yugoslavia
  constitutional clause on means of production 189n.39
  experiment with self-management 7, 135, 210n.19
  property rights 80–1

Zamagni, Vera 124
Zhang, Yin-Fang 37, 43
Zovanyi, Gabor 70